Do you know who said—
"Butter wouldn't melt in her mouth."
"I'm from Missouri; you must show me."
"Advice to persons about to marry—Don't."
"Public office is the last refuge of the incompetent."

These are all familiar quotations which everyone has heard time and again. Yet for how many can you name the author?

BEST QUOTATIONS FOR ALL OCCASIONS gives these and thousands of other quotations and their sources. For your convenience the quotations are listed alphabetically by subject and by author within the subject heading. There is also a handy selective authors' index. You'll find here a quotation to fit your every need—whether you are making a speech, writing a paper, or proving a point in an argument.

Books published by The Ballantine Publishing Group are available at quantity discounts on bulk purchases for premium, educational, fund-raising, and special sales use. For details, please call 1-800-733-3000.

NEW AND REVISED EDITION

Best Quotations
for
All Occasions

Arranged and Edited by
Lewis C. Henry

FAWCETT PREMIER ● NEW YORK

A Fawcett Premier Book
Published by Ballantine Books
Copyright © MCMXLV by Doubleday & Company, Inc.

ISBN 0-449-30037-4

This edition published by arrangement with Doubleday &
Company, Inc.

Manufactured in the United States of America

First Fawcett Crest Edition: November 1955
First Ballantine Books Edition: September 1986

50 49 48 47 46 45 44 43 42

Contents

v

Contents / vii

Introduction

The purpose of this book is to bring within the reach of all a selection of useful quotations in prose and poetry from the greatest writers, ancient and modern. First, it serves as a reference work. A book of this kind is almost as necessary as a dictionary or an encyclopedia. Speakers and writers, among others, will draw upon it for an apt definition or a telling phrase. This book also deserves to be read for its own sake. Arranged as it is by subjects, the reader can explore any idea that interests him, and browse through the book as fancy dictates. For under each subject heading are collected the utterances of the world's greatest thinkers and writers, giving the reader stimulating and sometimes opposing views.

The subject headings and the authors quoted under each heading are arranged in alphabetical order, so that the reader can quickly locate the particular quotation needed for any special occasion. There is also a selective authors' index.

In the use of this book we need to point out that topics that fall naturally under group headings are frequently to be found under the group heading rather than under the individual heading. Thus entries referring to various flowers, such as rose, lily, and so forth, will be found under the group heading, Flowers. In the case of Birds the same practice is followed for the most part, but there are separate entries for a few birds, such as lark, nightingale, and swan.

Here then is a work which may be described as a distillation of the best that has been said and written on the most important subjects—from the earliest times to our own day—thus making it a comprehensive and up-to-date book for frequent reference and leisurely reading.

L.C.H.

Ability

Behind an able man there are always other able men.
—CHINESE PROVERB

As we advance in life, we learn the limits of our abilities.
—FROUDE, *Short Studies on Great Subjects*

We judge ourselves by what we feel capable of doing, while others judge us by what we have already done.
—LONGFELLOW

Ability is of little account without opportunity.
—NAPOLEON

They are able because they think they are able.
—VERGIL, *Aeneid*

Absence

Absence makes the heart grow fonder.
—THOMAS HAYNES BAYLY, *Isle of Beauty*

Absent in body, but present in spirit.
—I CORINTHIANS. V. 3

Achilles absent, was Achilles still.
>—HOMER, *Iliad*

Let no one be willing to speak ill of the absent.
>—PROPERTIUS, *Elegiae*

Acquaintance

A wise man knows everything; a shrewd one, everybody.
>—ANONYMOUS

Sudden acquaintance brings repentance.
>—THOMAS FULLER

If a man is worth knowing at all, he is worth knowing well.
>—ALEXANDER SMITH,
>*Dreamthorp*

Acting

The most difficult character in comedy is that of the fool, and he must be no simpleton that plays that part.
>—CERVANTES

When an actor has money, he doesn't send letters but telegrams.
>—ANTON CHEKHOV

The drama's laws, the drama's patrons give.
For we that live to please, must please to live.
>—SAMUEL JOHNSON,
>*Prologue*

The play's the thing.
>—SHAKESPEARE, *Hamlet*.
>Act II. Sc. 2

Action

Let us do or die.

>   —BURNS, *Bruce to His Men
>   at Bannockburn*

Did nothing in particular
And did it very well.

>   —W. S. GILBERT, *Lord
>   Mountararat*

He started to sing as he tackled the thing
     That couldn't be done, and he did it.

>   —EDGAR A. GUEST, *It
>   Couldn't Be Done*

Do well and right, and let the world sink.

>   —HERBERT, *Country
>   Parson*

Trust no future, howe'er pleasant!
     Let the dead past bury its dead!
Act,—act in the living Present!
     Heart within and God o'erhead.

>   —LONGFELLOW, *Psalm of
>   Life*

Let us then be up and doing,
     With a heart for any fate;
Still achieving, still pursuing,
     Learn to labor and to wait.

>   —LONGFELLOW, *Psalm of
>   Life*

Every man feels instinctively that all the beautiful sentiments in the world weigh less than a single lovely action.
>   —LOWELL

He nothing common did, or mean,
Upon that memorable scene.
> —MARVELL, *Horatian
> Ode.* Upon Cromwell's
> Return from Ireland

Go, and do thou likewise.
> —LUKE X. 37

So much to do; so little done.
> —CECIL RHODES, *Last
> Words*

Get good counsel before you begin: and when you have
decided, act promptly.
> —SALLUST, *Catilina*

He that is overcautious will accomplish little.
> —SCHILLER, *Wilhelm Tell*

What's done can't be undone.
> —SHAKESPEARE, *Macbeth*.
> Act. V. Sc. 1

Heaven ne'er helps the men who will not act.
> —SOPHOCLES, *Fragment*

Theirs not to make reply,
Theirs not to reason why,
Theirs but to do and die.
> —TENNYSON, *Charge of the
> Light Brigade*

Out of the strain of the doing,
Into the peace of the done.
> —JULIA WOODRUFF, *Gone*

Adam and Eve

Adam and Eve had many advantages, but the principal one was that they escaped teething.

—S. L. CLEMENS (MARK
   TWAIN), *Pudd'nhead
   Wilson*

Whilst Adam slept, Eve from his side arose;
Strange his first sleep would be his last repose.

—ANONYMOUS

When Adam dolve, and Eve span,
Who was then the gentleman?

—JOHN BALL, *Wat Tyler's
   Rebellion*

When Eve upon the first of men
  The apple pressed with specious cant,
Oh! what a thousand pities then
  That Adam was not adamant.

—HOOD, *Adam and Eve*

Adam ate the apple, and our teeth still ache.

—HUNGARIAN PROVERB

In Adam's fall—
We sinned all.

—NEW ENGLAND PRIMER

Admiration

Admiration is a very short-lived passion, that immediately decays upon growing familiar with its object.

—ADDISON, *The Spectator*

Our polite recognition of another's resemblance to ourselves.

—BIERCE, *The Devil's Dictionary*

Distance is a great promoter of admiration!
—DIDEROT

We always love those who admire us, and we do not always love those whom we admire.
—LA ROCHEFOUCAULD

For fools admire, but men of sense approve.
—POPE, *Essay on Criticism*

Adversity

Adversity introduces a man to himself.
—ANONYMOUS

God brings men into deep waters, not to drown them, but to cleanse them.

—AUGHEY

Constant success shows us but one side of the world; adversity brings out the reverse of the picture.
—COLTON

Prosperity is a great teacher; adversity is a greater. Possession pampers the mind; privation trains and strengthens it.

—HAZLITT

Sweet are the uses of adversity;
Which, like the toad, ugly and venomous,
Wears yet a precious jewel in his head.
—SHAKESPEARE, *As You Like It*. Act II. Sc. 1

There is no education like adversity.
—DISRAELI

Advertising

When business is good it pays to advertise; when business is bad you've got to advertise.
—ANONYMOUS

You can tell the ideals of a nation by its advertisements.
—DOUGLAS, *South Wind*

Advertisements contain the only truth to be relied on in a newspaper.
—JEFFERSON, *Letter to Nathaniel Macon*

Advice

Never give advice in a crowd.
—ARAB PROVERB

Never give advice unless asked.
—GERMAN PROVERB

Whatever advice you give, be short.
—HORACE, *Ars Poetica*

Old men are fond of giving good advice, to console themselves for being no longer in a position to give bad examples.
—LA ROCHEFOUCAULD

We give advice, but we do not inspire conduct.
—LA ROCHEFOUCAULD

Good counsel has no price.
>—MAZZINI

Never advise anyone to go to war or to marry.
>—SPANISH PROVERB

Many receive advice, only the wise profit by it.
>—SYRUS

Admonish your friends privately, but praise them openly.
>—SYRUS

Affliction

The eternal stars shine out as soon as it is dark enough.
>—CARLYLE

Whom the Lord loveth he chasteneth.
>—HEBREWS. XII. 6

Be still, sad heart, and cease repining,
Behind the clouds the sun is shining;
Thy fate is the common fate of all,
Into each life some rain must fall,—
Some days must be dark and dreary.
>—LONGFELLOW

Age

It is always in season for old men to learn.
>—AESCHYLUS, *Age*

Youth is a blunder; Manhood a struggle; Old Age a regret.
>—DISRAELI, *Coningsby*

To know how to grow old is the master work of wisdom, and one of the most difficult chapters in the great art of living.

—AMIEL

Old wood best to burn, old wine to drink, old friends to trust, and old authors to read.

—Quoted by BACON,
Apothegm

At 20 years of age the will reigns, at 30 the wit; at 40 the judgment.

—FRANKLIN, *Poor Richard's Almanac*

If wrinkles must be written upon our brows, let them not be written upon the heart. The spirit should not grow old.

—JAMES A. GARFIELD

The riders in a race do not stop short when they reach the goal. There is a little finishing canter before coming to a standstill. There is time to hear the kind voice of friends and to say to one's self: "The work is done."

—HOLMES II, Speech on
his 90th birthday

Study until twenty-five, investigation until forty, profession until sixty, at which age I would have him retired on a double allowance.

—WILLIAM OSLER

In youth the days are short and the years are long; in old age the years are short and the days long.

—PANIN

The days of our years are threescore years and ten; and
if by reason of strength they be fourscore years, yet is
their strength labour and sorrow; for it is soon cut off,
and we fly away.

—PSALMS. XC. 10

The first forty years of life give us the text; the next
thirty supply the commentary on it.

—SCHOPENHAUER

Age cannot wither her, nor custom stale
Her infinite variety.

—SHAKESPEARE, *Antony
and Cleopatra*. Act II.
Sc. 2

An old man is twice a child.

—SHAKESPEARE, *Hamlet*.
Act II. Sc. 2

The old believe everything: the middle-aged suspect
everything: the young know everything.

—WILDE

Agriculture

Earth is here so kind, that just tickle her with a hoe and
she laughs with a harvest.

—JERROLD, *A Land of
Plenty*

A field becomes exhausted by constant tillage.

—OVID

Praise a large domain, cultivate a small estate.

—VERGIL, *Georgics*

Blessed be agriculture! If one does not have too much of it.

>—CHARLES DUDLEY
>WARNER, *My Summer
>in a Garden*

When tillage begins, other arts follow. The farmers, therefore, are the founders of human civilization.

>—DANIEL WEBSTER,
>*Remarks on
>Agriculture*

Ambition

When you are aspiring to the highest place, it is honorable to reach the second or even the third rank.

>—CICERO, *De Oratore*

Hitch your wagon to a star.

>—EMERSON, *Society and
>Solitude*

Most people would succeed in small things if they were not troubled with great ambitions.

>—LONGFELLOW, *Driftwood*

Better to reign in hell than serve in heaven.

>—MILTON, *Paradise Lost*

When that the poor have cried, Caesar hath wept:
Ambition should be made of sterner stuff:
Yet Brutus says he was ambitious;
And Brutus is an honourable man.

>—SHAKESPEARE, *Julius
>Caesar.* Act. IV. Sc. 3

If you wish to reach the highest, begin at the lowest.

>—SYRUS, *Maxims*

Ambition destroys its possessor.
—THE TALMUD, *Yoma*

Ambition has but one reward for all:
A little power, a little transient fame,
A grave to rest in, and a fading name!
—WILLIAM WINTER, *The
Queen's Domain*

America

O beautiful for patriot dream
      That sees beyond the years
Thine alabaster cities gleam
      Undimmed by human tears!
America! America!
      God shed his grace on thee,
And crown thy good with brotherhood
      From sea to shining sea!
—KATHARINE LEE BATES,
America the Beautiful

I pledge allegiance to the flag of the United States and to the
Republic for which it stands, one nation, indivis-
ible, with liberty and justice for all.
—JAMES B. UPHAM AND
FRANCIS BELLANY,
Pledge to the Flag

America is a country of young men.
—EMERSON

Hail, Columbia! happy land!
Hail, ye heroes! heavenborn band!
Who fought and bled in Freedom's cause.
—JOSEPH HOPKINSON, *Hail,
Columbia*

America is a tune. It must be sung together.
> —GERALD STANLEY LEE,
> *Crowds*

Thou, too, sail on, O Ship of State!
Sail on, O Union, strong and great!
Humanity with all its fears,
With all the hopes of future years,
Is hanging breathless on thy fate!
> —LONGFELLOW, *Building of
> the Ship*

Only those Americans who are willing to die for their country are fit to live.
> —DOUGLAS MACARTHUR

I was born an American; I live an American; I shall die an American.
> —DANIEL WEBSTER

Some Americans need hyphens in their names, because only part of them has come over; but when the whole man has come over, heart and thought and all, the hyphen drops of its own weight out of his name.
> —WOODROW WILSON

This generation of Americans has a rendezvous with destiny.
> —F. D. ROOSEVELT,
> Speech, 1936

America is God's crucible, the great Melting-Pot where all the races of Europe are melting and reforming! . . . The Real American has not yet arived. He is only in the crucible, I tell you—he will be the fusion of all races, the common superman.
> —ISRAEL ZANGWILL

Ancestry

A degenerate nobleman, or one that is proud of his birth, is like a turnip. There is nothing good of him but that which is underground.
> —BUTLER, *Characters*

My father was a creole, his father a Negro, and his father a monkey; my family, it seems, begins where yours left off.
> —DUMAS, on being asked
> "Who was your father?"

There is no king who has not had a slave among his ancestors, and no slave who has not had a king among his.
> —HELEN KELLER, *Story of
> My Life*

Noble ancestry makes a poor dish at table.
> —ITALIAN PROVERB

People who take no pride in the noble achievements of remote ancestors will never achieve anything worthy to be remembered with pride by remote descendants.
> —MACAULAY

Whoever serves his country well has no need of ancestors.
> —VOLTAIRE

Anger

Men often make up in wrath what they want in reason.
> —W. R. ALGER

Anger makes dull men witty, but it keeps them poor.
> —FRANCIS BACON

An angry man opens his mouth and shuts up his eyes.
— CATO

Never answer a letter while you are angry.
— CHINESE PROVERB

When angry, count four; when very angry, swear.
— SAMUEL L. CLEMENS
(MARK TWAIN),
Pudd'nhead Wilson

Heav'n has no rage, like love to hatred turn'd,
Nor Hell a fury, like a woman scorn'd.
— CONGREVE

Beware the fury of a patient man.
— DRYDEN, *Absalom and Achitophel*

Anger is momentary madness, so control your passion or it will control you.
— HORACE, *Epistles*

Anger blows out the lamp of the mind. In the examination of a great and important question, every one should be serene, slow-pulsed, and calm.
— INGERSOLL

He that is slow to anger is better than the mighty; and he that ruleth his spirit than he that taketh a city.
— PROVERBS. XVI. 32

Animals

Animals are such agreeable friends; they ask no questions, pass no criticisms.
— GEORGE ELIOT

If't were not for my cat and dog, I think I could not live.
—EBENEZER ELLIOTT

A mule has neither pride of ancestry nor hope of posterity.
—INGERSOLL

Men show their superiority inside; animals, outside.
—RUSSIAN PROVERB

Apology

No sensible person ever made an apology.
—EMERSON

Apology is only egotism wrong side out.
—HOLMES

Appearance

O wad some power the giftie gie us
To see oursel's as ithers see us!
—BURNS, *To a Louse*

All that glisters is not gold.
—CERVANTES, *Don Quixote*

Polished brass will pass upon more people than rough gold.
—CHESTERFIELD

Handsome is that handsome does.
—FIELDING, *Tom Jones*

Things are seldom what they seem,
Skim milk masquerades as cream.
—W. S. GILBERT, *H.M.S. Pinafore*

Men in general judge more from appearances than from reality. All men have eyes, but few have the gift of penetration.

—MACHIAVELLI

Whited sepulchres, which indeed appear beautiful outward, but are within full of dead men's bones.

—MATTHEW. XXIII. 27

She looks as if butter wouldn't melt in her mouth.

—SWIFT, *Polite Conversation*

Appetite

Animals feed, man eats; the man of intellect alone knows how to eat.

—BRILLAT-SAVARIN

All philosophy in two words,—sustain and abstain.

—EPICTETUS

If you are surprised at the number of our maladies, count our cooks.

—SENECA

Applause

The echo of a platitude.

—BIERCE, *The Devil's Dictionary*

Applause is the spur of noble minds, the end and aim of weak ones.

—COLTON, *Lacon*

About the only person we ever heard of that wasn't spoiled
by being lionized was a Jew named Daniel.
——G. D. PRENTICE

Architecture

Old houses mended,
Cost little less than new before they're ended.
——COLLEY CIBBER

Architecture is frozen music.
——GOETHE

Ah, to build, to build! That is the noblest of all the arts.
——LONGFELLOW,
Michelangelo

Argument

Arguments out of a petty mouth are unanswerable.
——ADDISON

Many can argue; not many converse.
——ALCOTT

Wise men argue causes, and fools decide them.
——ANACHARSIS

When Bishop Berkeley said, "there was no matter,"
And proved it——'twas no matter what he said.
——BYRON, *Don Juan*

Neither irony nor sarcasm is argument.
——RUFUS CHOATE

I am bound to furnish my antagonists with arguments,
but not with comprehension.
—DISRAELI

How agree the kettle and the earthen pot together?
—ECCLESIASTES. XIII. 2

Strong and bitter words indicate a weak cause.
—VICTOR HUGO

Insolence is not logic; epithets are the arguments of mal-
ice.
—INGERSOLL

Myself when young did eagerly frequent
Doctor and Saint, and heard great argument
About it and about: but evermore
Came out by the same door where in I went.
—OMAR KHAYYÁM,
Rubaiyat

Never argue at the dinner table, for the one who is not
hungry always gets the best of the argument.
—WHATELY

When people agree with me I always feel that I must be
wrong.
—WILDE, *The Critic as an
Artist*

Art

Art for art's sake.
—VICTOR COUSIN

Art, as far as it is able, follows nature, as a pupil imitates his master; thus your art must be, as it were, God's grandchild.

—DANTE, *Inferno*

Great art is as irrational as great music. It is mad with its own loveliness.

—GEORGE JEAN NATHAN,
House of Satan

A picture is a poem without words.

—HORACE

Art hath an enemy called ignorance.

—BEN JONSON

It's clever, but is it art?

—KIPLING, *The Conundrum
of the Workshops*

Art is not an end in itself, but a means of addressing humanity.

—M. P. MOUSSORGSKY

Art is a kind of illness.

—GIACOMO PUCCINI

Art is indeed not the bread but the wine of life.

—JEAN PAUL RICHTER

Art is difficult, transient is her reward.

—SCHILLER

The artist does not see things as they are, but as he is.

—ALFRED TONNELLE

Associate

When a dove begins to associate with crows its feathers remain white but its heart grows black.
—GERMAN PROVERB

If you always live with those who are lame, you will yourself learn to limp.
—LATIN PROVERB

He that walketh with wise men shall be wise.
—PROVERBS. XIII. 20

Atheism

I am an atheist, thank God!
—ANONYMOUS

I don't believe in God because I don't believe in Mother Goose.
—CLARENCE DARROW

The fool hath said in his heart, There is no God.
—PSALMS. CIV. 1

That the universe was formed by a fortuitous concourse of atoms, I will no more believe than that the accidental jumbling of the alphabet would fall into a most ingenious treatise of philosophy.
—SWIFT

By night an atheist half believes in God.
—YOUNG, *Night Thoughts*

Audacity

Audacity, more audacity, always audacity.
—DANTON, during French
Revolution

Fortune favors the audacious.
—ERASMUS

Authority

Every great advance in natural knowledge has involved
the absolute rejection of authority.
—HUXLEY, *Lay Sermons*

All authority belongs to the people.
—JEFFERSON

The highest duty is to respect authority.
—POPE LEO XIII

Authorship

He who writes prose builds his temple to Fame in rubble;
he who writes verses builds it in granite.
—BULWER-LYTTON

The pen is the tongue of the mind.
—CERVANTES, *Don
Quixote*

The author who speaks about his own books is almost
as bad as a mother who talks about her own children.
—DISRAELI

An incurable itch for scribbling takes possession of many,
and grows inveterate in their insane breasts.

> —JUVENAL, *Satires*

You do not publish your own verses, Laelius; you criticise
mine. Pray cease to criticise mine, or else publish your
own.

> —MARTIAL

The ink of the scholar is more sacred than the blood of
the martyr.

> —MOHAMMED, *Tribute to
> Reason*

Autumn

The melancholy days have come, the saddest of the year,
Of wailing winds, and naked woods, and meadows brown
    and sear.

> —BRYANT, *The Death of the
> Flowers*

The year's in the wane;
    There is nothing adoring;
The night has no eve,
    And the day has no morning;
Cold winter gives warning!

> —HOOD, *Autumn*

O, it sets my heart a clickin' like the tickin' of a clock,
When the frost is on the punkin and the fodder's in the
    shock.

> —JAMES WHITCOMB RILEY,
> *When the Frost Is on
> the Punkin*

Aviation

What can you conceive more silly and extravagant than
to suppose a man racking his brains, and studying night
and day how to fly?

> —WILLIAM LAW, *A Serious
> Call to a Devout and
> Holy Life* (1728)

The birds can fly,
An' why can't I?

> —TROWBRIDGE, *Darius
> Green and His Flying
> Machine* (1869)

He rode upon a cherub, and did fly: yea, he did fly upon
the wings of the wind.

> —PSALMS. XVIII. 10

Babyhood

Here we have baby. It is composed of a bald head and a
pair of lungs.

> —EUGENE FIELD, *The
> Tribune Primer*

Where did you come from, baby dear?
Out of the Everywhere into here.

> —GEORGE MACDONALD,
> Song in *At the Back of
> the North Wind*

Rock-a-bye baby on the tree top,
When the wind blows the cradle will rock,
When the bough bends the cradle will fall,
Down comes the baby, cradle and all.

> —OLD NURSERY RHYME

Out of the mouth of babes and sucklings hast thou
ordained strength.

—PSALMS. VIII. 2

Hush, my dear, lie still and slumber,
    Holy angels guard thy bed!
Heavenly blessings without number
    Gently falling on thy head.

—ISAAC WATTS, *A Cradle
Hymn*

Sweetest li'l feller, everybody knows;
Dunno what to call him, but he's mighty lak' a rose;
Lookin' at his mammy wid eyes so shiny blue
Mek' you think that Heav'n is comin' clost ter you.

—FRANK L. STANTON,
Mighty Lak' a Rose

Bachelor

A bachelor is one who enjoys the chase but does not eat
the game.

—ANONYMOUS

A bachelor is a souvenir of some woman who found a
better one at the last minute.

—ANONYMOUS

The best work, and of greatest merit for the public, has
proceeded from the unmarried or childless men.

—BACON, *Essays*

A single man has not nearly the value he would have in
a state of union. He is an incomplete animal. He resem-
bles the odd half of a pair of scissors.

—FRANKLIN

By persistently remaining single a man converts himself into a permanent public temptation.

—WILDE, *The Importance of Being Earnest*

Bank

A banker is a man who lends you an umbrella when the weather is fair, and takes it away from you when it rains.

—ANONYMOUS

Banking establishments are more dangerous than standing armies

—JEFFERSON, Letter to Gerry

Bargain

It takes two to make a bargain.

—ENGLISH PROVERB

It's a bad bargain where nobody gains.

—ENGLISH PROVERB

The best of a bad bargain.

—PEPYS, *Diary*

Beauty

There is no cosmetic for beauty like happiness.

—LADY BLESSINGTON

That which is striking and beautiful is not always good, but that which is good is always beautiful.

—NINON DE L'ENCLOS

Beauty is eternity gazing at itself in a mirror.
—KAHLIL GIBRAN

A thing of beauty is a joy forever.
—KEATS, *Endymion*

Beauty is truth, truth beauty.
—KEATS, *Ode on a Grecian Urn*

She walks in beauty like the night
Of cloudless climes and starry skies;
And all that's best of dark and bright
Meet in her aspect and her eyes:
Thus mellowed to that tender light
Which heaven to gaudy day denies.
—BYRON, *She Walks in Beauty*

Beauty is the first present Nature gives to women, and the first it takes away.
—MÉRÉ

Beauty is power; a smile is its sword.
—CHARLES READE

Remember that the most beautiful things in the world are the most useless; peacocks and lilies, for instance.
—RUSKIN

Bed

In bed we laugh, in bed we cry;
And born in bed, in bed we die;
The near approach a bed may show
Of human bliss to human woe.
—ISAAC DE BENSERADE

As you make your bed you must lie in it.
—ENGLISH PROVERB

The bed has become a place of luxury to me! I would not exchange it for all the thrones in the world.
—NAPOLEON

Bee

The bee is more honored than other animals, not because she labors, but because she labors for others.
—ST. CHRYSOSTOM

The bee that hath honey in her mouth hath a sting in her tail.
—LYLY, *Euphues*

How doth the little busy bee
  Improve each shining hour,
And gather honey all the day
  From every opening flower.
—ISAAC WATTS, *Against Idleness*

Begging

Beggars must be no choosers.
—BEAUMONT AND FLETCHER, *Scornful Lady*

Set a beggar on horseback, and he will ride a gallop.
—BURTON, *Anatomy of Melancholy*

Better a living beggar than a buried emperor.
—LA FONTAINE

Borrowing is not much better than begging.
—LESSING, *Nathan the
Wise*

Beginning

Well begun is half done.
—HORACE

He that climbs a ladder must begin at the first round.
—SCOTT, *Kenilworth*

It is the beginning of the end.
—TALLEYRAND

The first step, my son, which one makes in the world,
is the one on which depends the rest of our days.
—VOLTAIRE

Belief

Men willingly believe what they wish.
—JULIUS CAESAR

Believe only half of what you see and nothing that you
hear.
—DINAH MULOCK CRAIK

A man must not swallow more beliefs than he can digest.
—HAVELOCK ELLIS, *The
Dance of Life*

He that believeth not shall be damned.
>   —MARK. XVI. 16

Nothing is so firmly believed as what we least know.
>   —MONTAIGNE

She deceiving, I believing; What need lovers wish for more?
>   —SIR CHARLES SEDLEY

Bells

Curfew must not ring tonight.
>   —ROSA H. THORPE

Those evening bells! those evening bells!
How many a tale their music tells!
>   —MOORE, *Those Evening
>   Bells*

Ring out the old, ring in the new,
Ring, happy bells, across the snow.
>   —TENNYSON, *In Memoriam*

Bible

I call the Book of Job, apart from all theories about it, one of the grandest things ever written with pen.
>   —CARLYLE

The Bible is a window in this prison-world, through which we may look into eternity.
>   —TIMOTHY DWIGHT

The inspiration of the Bible depends upon the ignorance of the gentleman who reads it.
—INGERSOLL, Speech, 1881

The English Bible—a book which, if everything else in our language should perish, would alone suffice to show the whole extent of its beauty and power.
—MACAULAY

Biography

Biography is the only true history.
—CARLYLE

One anecdote of a man is worth a volume of biography.
—CHANNING

Lives of great men all remind us
    We can make our lives sublime,
And, departing, leave behind us
    Footprints on the sands of time.
—LONGFELLOW, A *Psalm
of Life*

To be ignorant of the lives of the most celebrated men of antiquity is to continue in a state of childhood all our days.
—PLUTARCH

Every great man nowadays has his disciples, and it is always Judas who writes the biography.
—WILDE, *The Critic as
Artist*

Birds

A bird in the hand is worth two in the bush.
> —CERVANTES, *Don
> Quixote*

O thrush, your song is passing sweet,
But never a song that you have sung
Is half so sweet as thrushes sang
When my dear love and I were young.
> —WILLIAM MORRIS, *Other
> Days*

Birds of a feather will flock together.
> —MINSHEU

And the Raven, never flitting,
    Still is sitting, still is sitting
On the pallid bust of Pallas
    Just above my chamber door;
    And his eyes have all the seeming
    Of a demon's that is dreaming,
And the lamplight o'er him streaming
    Throws his shadow on the floor,
And my soul from out that shadow,
    That lies floating on the floor,
    Shall be lifted—nevermore.
> —POE, *The Raven*

Birth

Born on Monday, fair in the face;
Born on Tuesday, full of God's grace;
Born on Wednesday, sour and sad;
Born on Thursday, merry and glad;
Born on Friday, worthily given;

Born on Saturday, work hard for your living;
Born on Sunday, you will never know want.
—ANONYMOUS

Man alone at the very moment of his birth, cast naked
upon the naked earth, does she abandon to cries and
lamentations.

—PLINY THE ELDER,
Natural History

Birthday

JANUARY

By her who in this month is born,
No gems save *Garnets* should be worn;
They will insure her constancy,
True friendship and fidelity.

FEBRUARY

The February born will find
Sincerity and peace of mind;
Freedom from passion and from care,
If they the *Pearl* (*also green amethyst*) will wear.

MARCH

Who in this world of ours their eyes
In March first open shall be wise;
In days of peril firm and brave,
And wear a *Bloodstone* to their grave.

APRIL

She who from April dates her years,
Diamonds should wear, lest bitter tears
For vain repentance flow; this stone,
Emblem of innocence is known.

MAY

Who first beholds the light of day
In Spring's sweet flowery month of May
And wears an *Emerald* all her life,
Shall be a loved and happy wife.

JUNE

Who comes with Summer to this earth
And owes to June her day of birth,
With ring of *Agate* on her hand,
Can health, wealth, and long life command.

JULY

The glowing *ruby* should adorn
Those who in warm July are born,
Then will they be exempt and free
From love's doubt and anxiety.

AUGUST

Wear a *Sardonyx* or for thee
No conjugal felicity.
The August-born without this stone
'Tis said must live unloved and lone.

SEPTEMBER

A maiden born when Autumn leaves
Are rustling in September's breeze,
A *Sapphire* on her brow should bind,
'Twill cure diseases of the mind.

OCTOBER

October's child is born for woe,
And life's vicissitudes must know;
But lay an *Opal* on her breast,
And hope will lull those woes to rest.

NOVEMBER

Who first comes to this world below
With drear November's fog and snow
Should prize the *Topaz'* amber hue—
Emblem of friends and lovers true.

DECEMBER

If cold December gave you birth,
The month of snow and ice and mirth,
Place on your hand a *Turquoise* blue,
Success will bless whate'er you do.

—ANONYMOUS

Blessing

God bless me and my son John,
Me and my wife, him and his wife,
Us four, and no more.

—ANONYMOUS

Blessings never come in pairs; misfortunes never come alone.

—CHINESE PROVERB

God bless us every one.

—DICKENS, *Christmas Carol*

Blindness

In the country of the blind the one-eyed man is king.

—ERASMUS

If the blind lead the blind, both shall fall into the ditch.

—MATTHEW. XV. 14

There's none so blind as they that won't see.
> —SWIFT, *Polite
> Conversation*

Blood

Whoso sheddeth man's blood, by man shall his blood be shed.
> —GENESIS. IX. 6

Blood is thicker than water.
> —Attributed to
> COMMODORE
> TATTNAL

The blood of the martyrs is the seed of the church.
> —TERTULLIAN

The old blood is bold blood, the wide world round.
> —BYRON WEBBER, *Hands
> Across the Sea*

Body

A healthy body is a guest-chamber for the soul; a sick body is a prison.
> —BACON, *The Advancement
> of Learning*

Your body is the temple of the Holy Ghost.
> —I CORINTHIANS. VI. 19

No knowledge can be more satisfactory to a man than that of his own frame, its parts, their functions and actions.
> —JEFFERSON, Letter to
> Thomas Cooper

We are bound to our bodies like an oyster to its shell.
—PLATO, *Phaedrus*

If any thing is sacred, the human body is sacred.
—WHITMAN, *I Sing the
Body Electric*

Books

Some books are to be tasted, others to be swallowed, and
some few to be chewed and digested.
—BACON, *Of Studies*

Laws die, Books never.
—BULWER-LYTTON,
Richelieu

A book is the only immortality.
—RUFUS CHOATE

Beware of the man of one book.
—ISAAC D'ISRAELI,
*Curiosities of
Literature*

Of making many books there is no end; and much study
is a weariness of the flesh.
—ECCLESIASTES. XII. 12

My desire is ... that mine adversary had written a book.
—JOB. XXXI. 35

Except a living man there is nothing more wonderful
than a book! a message to us from ... human souls we
never saw ... And yet these arouse us, terrify us, teach
us, comfort us, open their hearts to us as brothers.
—KINGSLEY

The writings of the wise are the only riches our posterity cannot squander.
—LANDOR

There is no such thing as a moral or an immoral book. Books are well written or badly written. That is all.
—WILDE, *The Picture of Dorian Gray*

A good book is the precious life-blood of a master-spirit, embalmed and treasured up on purpose to a life beyond life.
—MILTON, *Areopagitica*

As good almost kill a man as kill a good book: who kills a man kills a reasonable creature, God's image; but he who destroys a good book kills reason itself, kills the image of God, as it were, in the eye.
—MILTON, *Areopagitica*

A best-seller is the gilded tomb of a mediocre talent.
—LOGAN P. SMITH, *Afterthoughts*

All the known world, excepting only savage nations, is governed by books.
—VOLTAIRE

Camerado, this is no book. Who touches this, touches a man.
—WHITMAN, *So Long*

Bores

Bore: a person who talks when you wish him to listen
—BIERCE, *The Devil's Dictionary*

Society is now one polished horde,
Formed of two mighty tribes, the *Bores* and *Bored*.
—BYRON, *Don Juan*

He says a thousand pleasant things,—
  But never says "Adieu"
—J. G. SAXE, *My Familiar*

Borrowing

Debt is a bottomless sea.
—CARLYLE

Borrowing from Peter to pay Paul.
—CICERO

The borrower is servant to the lender.
—PROVERBS. XXII. 7

Neither a borrower nor a lender be:
For loan oft loses both itself and friend,
And borrowing dulls the edge of husbandry.
—SHAKESPEARE, *Hamlet*,
Act I. Sc. 3

Who goeth a borrowing
Goeth a sorrowing.
—TUSSER

Boston

And this is good old Boston,
The home of the bean and the cod,
Where the Lowells talk to the Cabots,
And the Cabots talk only to God.
—J. C. BOSSIDY, *On the
Aristocracy of Harvard*

Then here's to the City of Boston,
The town of the cries and the groans,
Where the Cabots can't see the Kabotschniks,
And the Lowells won't speak to the Cohns.
                    —FRANKLIN P. ADAMS,
                              Revised

Boy

One boy is more trouble than a dozen girls.
                    —ENGLISH PROVERB

Boys will be boys.

                    —ENGLISH PROVERB

A boy is, of all wild beasts, the most difficult to manage.
                    —PLATO

Bravery

How sleep the brave, who sink to rest,
By all their country's wishes blest!
                    —ANONYMOUS

Bravery is a cheap and vulgar quality, of which the bright-
est instances are frequently found in the lowest savages.
                    —CHATFIELD

True bravery is shown by performing without witness
what one might be capable of doing before all the world.
                    —LA ROCHEFOUCAULD

None but the brave deserves the fair.
                    —DRYDEN

Physical bravery is an animal instinct; moral bravery is a much higher and truer courage.

—WENDELL PHILLIPS

Bread

Man doth not live by bread only.

—DEUTERONOMY. VIII. 4

Cast thy bread upon the waters: for thou shalt find it after many days.

—ECCLESIASTES. XI. 1

Bread is the staff of life.

—ENGLISH SAYING

I know on which side my bread is buttered.

—HEYWOOD, *Proverbs*

Better is half a loaf than no bread.

—HEYWOOD, *Proverbs*

What man is there of you, whom if his son ask bread, will he give him a stone?

—MATTHEW. VII. 9

Jesus said unto them, I am the bread of life: he that cometh to me shall never hunger; and he that believeth on me shall never thirst.

—JOHN. VI. 35

Give us this day our daily bread.

—MATTHEW. VI. 2

Oh, God! that bread should be so dear,
And flesh and blood so cheap!
>   —HOOD, *The Song of the*
>   *Shirt*

I won't quarrel with my bread and butter.
>   —SWIFT, *Polite*
>   *Conversation*

Brevity

Let thy speech be short, comprehending much in few words.
>   —ECCLESIASTICUS. XXXII. 8

The more you say, the less people remember. The fewer the words, the greater the profit.
>   —FÉNELON

The fewer the words, the better prayer.
>   —LUTHER

The wisdom of nations lies in their proverbs, which are brief and pithy.
>   —WILLIAM PENN

God helps the brave.
>   —SCHILLER, *Wilhelm Tell*

Brevity is the soul of wit.
>   —SHAKESPEARE, *Hamlet*.
>   Act II. Sc. 2

Bribery

Every man has his price.

—SIR ROBERT WALPOLE

The universe would not be rich enough to buy the vote of an honest man.

—ST. GREGORY

Few men have virtue to withstand the highest bidder.

—WASHINGTON, *Moral
Maxims*

Brotherhood

Am I my brother's keeper?

—GENESIS. IV. 9

A new commandment I give unto you, That ye love one another; as I have loved you, that ye also love one another.

—JOHN. XIII. 34

The crest and crowning of all good, Life's final star, is Brotherhood.

—EDWIN MARKHAM,
Brotherhood

When man to man shall be a friend and brother.

—GERALD MASSEY

Building

Old houses mended
Cost little less than new before they're ended.

—COLLEY CIBBER

Never build after you are five and forty; have five years'
income in hand before you lay a brick; and always calculate
the expense at double the estimate.
—KETT

Business

Christmas is over and Business is Business.
—F. P. A.

Nation of shopkeepers.
—Attributed to SAMUEL
ADAMS

Anybody can cut prices, but it takes brains to produce a better article.
—P. D. ARMOUR

Business is religion, and religion is business. The man who
does not make a business of his religion has a religious life of
no force, and the man who does not make a religion of his
business has a business life of no character.
—MALTBIE BABCOCK

The nature of business is swindling.
—AUGUST BEBEL

There are two times in a man's life when he should not spec-
ulate: when he can't afford it, and when he can.
—SAMUEL L. CLEMENS
(MARK TWAIN)

They (corporations) cannot commit treason, nor be out-
lawed, nor excommunicated, for they have no souls.
—COKE, *The Case of
Sutton's Hospital*

The business of America is business.
— CALVIN COOLIDGE

Business is like oil. It won't mix with anything but business.
— J. GRAHAM

Whose merchants are princes.
— ISAIAH. XXII. 8

Wist ye not that I must be about my Father's business?
— LUKE. II. 49

We demand that big business give people a square deal; in return we must insist that when anyone engaged in big business honestly endeavors to do right, he shall himself be given a square deal.
— THEODORE ROOSEVELT

That which is everybody's business, is nobody's business.
— IZAAK WALTON, *Compleat Angler*

Call on a business man at business times only, and on business, transact your business and go about your business, in order to give him time to finish his business.
— WELLINGTON

The way to stop financial "joy-riding" is to arrest the chauffeur, not the automobile.
— WOODROW WILSON

It is not the crook in modern business that we fear, but the honest man who does not know what he is doing.
— OWEN D. YOUNG

Calumny

Cutting honest throats by whispers.
—SCOTT

Calumniate, calumniate; there will always be something which sticks.
—BEAUMARCHAIS, *Barber of Seville*

Calumny is a vice of curious constitution; trying to kill it keeps it alive; leave it to itself and it will die a natural death.
—THOMAS PAINE

To persevere in one's duty and to be silent is the best answer to calumny.
—WASHINGTON
—LONGFELLOW, *Hyperion*

Capital and Labor

Capital is a result of labor, and is used by labor to assist it in further production. Labor is the active and initial force, and labor is therefore the employer of capital.
—HENRY GEORGE, *Progress and Poverty*

Labor is prior to, and independent of, capital. Capital is only the fruit of labor, and could never have existed if labor had not first existed. Labor is the superior of capital, and deserves much the higher consideration.
—LINCOLN, *Message to Congress*, 1861

Capital is dead labor that, vampirelike, lives only by sucking living labor, and lives the more, the more labor it suck.
—KARL MARX, *Capital*

Each needs the other: capital cannot do without labor, nor labor without capital.

—POPE LEO XIII

Care

To carry care to bed is to sleep with a pack on your back.

—HALIBURTON

The night shall be filled with music
    And the cares that infest the day
Shall fold their tents like the Arabs,
    And as silently steal away.

—LONGFELLOW, *The Day Is
Done*

Old Care has a mortgage on every estate,
And that's what you pay for the wealth that you get.

—J. G. SAXE, *Gifts of the
Gods*

Providence has given us hope and sleep as a compensation for the many cares of life.

—VOLTAIRE

Carelessness

For want of a nail the shoe was lost; for want of a shoe the horse was lost; and for want of a horse the rider was lost; being overtaken and slain by the enemy, all for want of care about a horseshoe nail.

—FRANKLIN, *Poor Richard's
Almanac*

Carelessness does more harm than a want of knowledge.

—FRANKLIN

The wife of a careless man is almost a widow.
—HUNGARIAN PROVERB

Cats

Ding, dong, bell,
Pussy's in the well;
Who put her in?
Little Tommy Green.
Who pulled her out?
Little Johnny Stout.

—ANONYMOUS

When the cat's away the mice will play.
—ENGLISH PROVERB

It has been the providence of nature to give this creature nine
lives instead of one.
—PILPAY, *Fable*

There is not room to swing a cat.
—SMOLLETT, *Humphrey Clinker*

A cat may look at a king.

—JOHN HEYWOOD, *Proverbs*

Cause

There is one basic cause of all effects.
— GIORDANO BRUNO

In war events of importance are the result of trivial causes.
—JULIUS CAESAR

Christian Science explains all cause and effect as mental, not physical.

—MARY BAKER EDDY,
Science and Health

God befriend us, as our cause is just!

—SHAKESPEARE, *Henry IV.*
Pt. I. Act V. Sc. 1

Everything in nature is a cause from which there flows some effect.

—SPINOZA

The first springs of great events, like those of great rivers, are often mean and little.

—SWIFT

Caution

If your lips would keep from slips
    five things observe with care:
To whom you speak, of whom you speak,
    And how, and when, and where.

—ANONYMOUS

Hasten slowly.

—AUGUSTUS CAESAR

A wise man does not trust all his eggs to one basket.

—CERVANTES, *Don Quixote*

When you go to buy use your eyes, not your ears.

—CZECH PROVERB

Be slow of tongue and quick of eye.

—CERVANTES

The cautious seldom err.
—CONFUCIUS

Among mortals second thoughts are wisest.
—EURIPIDES

Little boats should keep near shore.
—FRANKLIN

Caution is the eldest child of wisdom.
—VICTOR HUGO

Drink nothing without seeing it, sign nothing without reading it.
—SPANISH PROVERB

It is a good thing to learn caution by the misfortunes of others.
—SYRUS

Censorship

I am mortified to be told that, in the United States of America, the sale of a book can become a subject of inquiry, and of criminal inquiry too.
—JEFFERSON

If there had been a censorship of the press in Rome we should have had today neither Horace nor Juvenal, nor the philosophical writings of Cicero.
—VOLTAIRE

Every burned book enlightens the world.
—EMERSON, *Compensation*

Change

Never swap horses crossing a stream.
—AMERICAN PROVERB

Earth changes, but thy soul and God stand sure.
—BROWNING, *Rabbi Ben
Ezra*

    I am not now
That which I have been.

—BYRON, *Childe Harold*

There is a certain relief in change, even though it be from bad to worse; as I have found in travelling in a stagecoach, that it is often a comfort to shift one's position and be bruised in a new place.

—IRVING, *Tales of a Traveller*

Can the Ethiopian change his skin, or the leopard his spots?
—JEREMIAH. XIII. 23

The world goes up and the world goes down,
    And the sunshine follows the rain;
And yesterday's sneer and yesterday's frown
    Can never come over again.

—KINGSLEY, *Songs*

All things must change
To something new, to something strange.
—LONGFELLOW

Revolutions are not made; they come.
—WENDELL PHILLIPS

The old order changeth, yielding place to new.
—TENNYSON, *The Passing of
Arthur*

Everything changes but change.

—ZANGWILL

Character

When wealth is lost, nothing is lost;
When health is lost, something is lost;
When character is lost, all is lost!

—ANONYMOUS

Every one is as God made him, and often a great deal worse.

—CERVANTES, *Don Quixote*

The great hope of society is individual character.

—CHANNING

You must look into people as well as at them.

—CHESTERFIELD

Human improvement is from within outward.

—FROUDE

Talent is nurtured in solitude; character is formed in the stormy billows of the world.

—GOETHE, *Torquato Tasso*

O Douglas, O Douglas!
Tender and true.

—SIR RICHARD HOLLAND,
The Duke of the Howlat

Only what we have wrought into our character during life can we take away with us.

—HUMBOLDT

Every man has three characters—that which he exhibits,
that which he has, and that which he thinks he has.
—ALPHONSE KARR

Not in the clamor of the crowded street,
Not in the shouts and plaudits of the throng,
But in ourselves, are triumph and defeat.
—LONGFELLOW, *The Poets*

Who knows nothing base,
Fears nothing known.
—OWEN MEREDITH, A
Great Man

In men whom men condemn as ill
I find so much of goodness still,
In men whom men pronounce divine
I find so much of sin and blot
I do not dare to draw a line
Between the two, where God has not.
—JOAQUIN MILLER, *Byron*

Oh, East is East and West is West, and never the twain
shall meet
Till earth and sky stand presently at God's great judgment seat;
But there is neither East nor West, border nor breed nor
birth
When two strong men stand face to face, tho' they come
from the ends of the earth!
—KIPLING, *Ballad of East
and West*

In this world a man must either be anvil or hammer.
—LONGFELLOW, *Hyperion*

Charity

It is more blessed to give than to receive.
—ACTS. XX. 35

Charity is the perfection and ornament of religion.
—ADDISON

Every charitable act is a stepping stone toward heaven.
—HENRY WARD BEECHER

My poor are my best patients. God pays for them.
—BOERHAAVE

Though I have all faith, so that I could remove mountains, and have not charity, I am nothing.
—I CORINTHIANS. XIII. 2

And now abideth faith, hope, charity, these three; but the greatest of these is charity.
—I CORINTHIANS. XIII. 13

What we frankly give, forever is our own.
—GEORGE GRANVILLE

As the purse is emptied the heart is filled.
—VICTOR HUGO

That charity which longs to publish itself, ceases to be charity.
—HUTTON

He who waits to do a great deal of good at once, will never do anything.
—SAMUEL JOHNSON

I was an hungred, and ye gave me meat; I was thirsty, and ye gave me drink; I was a stranger, and ye took me in.

—MATTHEW. XXV. 35

Organized charity, scrimped and iced,
In the name of the cautious, statistical Christ.

—JOHN BOYLE O'REILLY,
In Bohemia

Charity shall cover the multitude of sins.

—I PETER. IV. 8

Our charity begins at home, And mostly ends where it begins.

—HORACE SMITH, *Horace
in London*

Cheerfulness

I exhort you to be of good cheer.

—ACTS. XXVII. 22

He who sings frightens away his ills.

—CERVANTES

The creed of the true saint is to make the best of life, and make the most of it.

—CHAPIN

A cheerful look makes a dish a feast

—HERBERT, *Jacula
Prudentum*

Cheer up, the worst is yet to come.

—PHILANDER JOHNSON

Let us be of good cheer, remembering that the misfortunes hardest to bear are those which never happen.
—LOWELL

A good laugh is sunshine in a house.
—THACKERAY

Childhood

Do ye hear the children weeping, O my brothers?
—E. B. BROWNING, *The Cry of the Children*

When I was a child, I spake as a child, I understood as a child, I thought as a child; but when I became a man, I put away childish things.
—I CORINTHIANS. XIII. 11

A little curly-headed, good-for-nothing,
And mischief-making monkey from his birth.
—BYRON, *Don Juan*

Better to be driven out from among men than to be disliked of children.
—R. H. DANA, *The Idle Man*

Children should be seen and not heard.
—ENGLISH PROVERB

Spare the rod and spoil the child.
—ENGLISH PROVERB

Teach your child to hold his tongue,
He'll learn fast enough to speak.
—FRANKLIN, *Poor Richard's Maxims*

There was a little girl,
And she had a little curl,
Right in the middle of her forehead;
When she was good she was very, very good,
When she was bad she was horrid.
——LONGFELLOW

Suffer the little children to come unto me, and forbid
them not; for of such is the kingdom of God.
——MARK. X. 14

A wise son maketh a glad father.
——PROVERBS. X. 1

It is a wise child that knows his own father.
——HOMER, *Odyssey*

Rachel weeping for her children, and would not be comforted, because they are not.
——MATTHEW. II. 18

The childhood shows the man,
As morning shows the day.
——MILTON, *Paradise
Regained*

The children in Holland take pleasure in making
What the children in England take pleasure in breaking.
——OLD NURSERY RHYME

The wildest colts make the best horses.
——PLUTARCH, *Life of
Themistocles*

Train up a child in the way he should go; and when he
is old he will not depart from it.
——PROVERBS. XXII. 6

How dear to this heart are the scenes of my childhood,
When fond recollection presents them to view.
—SAMUEL WOODWORTH,
The Old Oaken Bucket

I think that saving a little child
    And bringing him to his own,
Is a derned sight better business
    Than loafing around the throne.
—JOHN HAY, *Little Breeches*

It is a wise father that knows his own child.
—SHAKESPEARE, *Merchant
of Venice*. Act. II. Sc. 2

It is very nice to think
    The world is full of meat and drink
With little children saying grace
    In every Christian kind of place.
—STEVENSON, *Child's
Garden of Verses*

The best way to make children good is to make them
happy.
—WILDE

The child is father of the man.
—WORDSWORTH, *My Heart
Leaps Up*

Choice

I do not choose to run for President in 1928.
—CALVIN COOLIDGE

Betwixt the devil and the deap sea.
                    —ERASMUS, *Adagia*

There's small choice in rotten apples.
                    —SHAKESPEARE, *Taming of
                        the Shrew*. Act. I. Sc. 1

When to elect there is but one,
'Tis Hobson's Choice; take that or none.
                    —THOMAS WARD,
                        England's Reformation

For many are called, but few are chosen.
                    —MATTHEW. XXII. 14

Christ

In every pang that rends the heart
The Man of Sorrows had a part.
                    —MICHAEL BRUCE, *Gospel
                        Sonnets*

The sages and heroes of history are receding from us,
and history contracts the record of their deeds into a
narrower and narrower page. But time has no power over
the name and deeds and words of Jesus Christ.
                    —CHANNING

Jesus Christ the same yesterday, and today, and forever.
                    —HEBREWS. XIII. 8

The foxes have holes, and the birds of the air have nests;
but the Son of man hath not where to lay his head.
                    —MATTHEW. VIII. 20

Jesus ... was made a little lower than the angels.
—HEBREWS. II. 9

All His glory and beauty come from within, and there He delights to dwell, His visits there are frequent, His conversation sweet, His comforts refreshing; and His peace passing all understanding.
—THOMAS À KEMPIS,
Imitation of Christ

Thou hast conquered, O Galilean.
—Attributed to JULIAN THE
APOSTATE

Alexander, Caesar, Charlemagne and I myself have founded empires; but upon what do these creations of our genius depend? Upon force. Jesus alone founded His empire upon love; and to this very day millions would die for Him.
—NAPOLEON

If the life and death of Socrates were those of a sage, the life and death of Jesus were those of a God.
—ROUSSEAU

Christian

A Christian is God Almighty's gentleman.
—J. C. and A. W. HARE,
Guesses at Truth

Onward, Christian soldiers,
Marching as to war,
With the cross of Jesus
Going on before.
—BARING-GOULD

Servant of God, well done!
    Well hast thou fought
The better fight.

—MILTON, *Paradise Lost*

To be like Christ is to be a Christian.
—WILLIAM PENN, Last
words

Whatever makes men good Christians, makes them good citizens.

—DANIEL WEBSTER,
Speech at Plymouth

Christianity

Christianity is completed Judaism, or it is nothing.
—DISRAELI

His Christianity was muscular.
—DISRAELI, *Endymion*

Christianity ruined emperors, but saved peoples.
—ALFRED DE MUSSET

Christianity is a battle, not a dream
—WENDELL PHILLIPS

I desire no other evidence of the truth to Christianity than the Lord's Prayer.

—MME. DE STAËL

Christianity, with its doctrine of humility, of forgiveness, of love, is incompatible with the state, with its haughtiness, its violence, its punishment, its wars.
—TOLSTOY

Christmas

Let's dance and sing and make good cheer,
For Christmas comes but once a year.
> —G. MacFarren (Before
> 1580)

O little town of Bethlehem,
    How still we see thee lie!
Above thy deep and dreamless sleep
    The silent stars go by.
> —Phillips Brooks, *O
> Little Town of
> Bethlehem*

No Santa Claus! Thank God, he lives, and he lives forever. A thousand years from now, Virginia, nay, ten times
ten thousand years from now, he will continue to make
glad the heart of childhood.
> —Francis P. Church, *Is
> There a Santa Claus?*

Holy night, peaceful night,
    Wondrous Star, lend thy light!
With the angels let us sing
    Alleluia to our King,
Jesus the Saviour is here.
> —Translated from Joseph
> Mohr, 1818

I heard the bells on Christmas Day
Their old, familiar carols play,
    And wild and sweet
    The words repeat
Of peace on earth, good-will to men!
> —Longfellow, *Christmas
> Bells*

For unto you is born this day in the city of David, a
Saviour, which is Christ the Lord.

—LUKE. II. 11

God rest ye, little children; let nothing you affright,
For Jesus Christ, your Saviour, was born this happy
     night;
Along the hills of Galilee the white flocks sleeping lay,
When Christ, the Child of Nazareth, was born on Christ-
     mas day.

—DINAH MULOCK CRAIK,
     Christmas Carol

'Twas the night before Christmas, when all through the
     house,
Not a creature was stirring—not even a mouse;
The stockings were hung by the chimney with care,
In hopes that St. Nicholas soon would be there.

—CLEMENT C. MOORE, A
     Visit from St. Nicholas

Hark the herald angels sing,
"Glory to the new-born king."
Peace on earth, and mercy mild,
God and sinners reconciled!

—CHARLES WESLEY,
     Christmas Hymn

Church

Cathedrals,
Luxury liners laden with souls,
Holding to the east their hulls of stone.

—W. H. AUDEN, *On This
     Island*

It was founded upon a rock.
                    —MATTHEW. VII. 25

The nearer the church, the further from God.
                    —BISHOP ANDREWS,
                         Sermon on the
                         Nativity before James I

Whenever God erects a house of prayer
The devil always builds a chapel there;
And 'twill be found, upon examination,
The latter has the largest congregation.
                    —DANIEL DEFOE, *True
                         Born Englishman*

Division has done more to hide Christ from the view of
men than all the infidelity that has ever been spoken.
                    — GEORGE MacDONALD

I never weary of great churches. It is my favourite kind
of mountain scenery. Mankind was never so happily
inspired as when it made a cathedral.
                    —STEVENSON, *Inland
                         Voyage*

See the Gospel Church secure,
     And founded on a Rock!
All her promises are sure;
     Her bulwarks who can shock?
Count her every precious shrine;
     Tell, to after-ages tell,
Fortified by power divine,
     The Church can never fail.
                    —CHARLES WESLEY

The itch of disputing is the scab of the churches.
                    —SIR HENRY WOTTON, A
                         *Panegyric to King
                         Charles*

Circumstance

The long arm of coincidence.
　　　　　—HADDEN CHAMBERS,
　　　　　　Captain Swift

Man is not the creature of circumstances,
Circumstances are the creatures of men.
　　　　　—DISRAELI, *Vivian Grey*

Circumstances alter cases.
　　　　　—HALIBURTON, *The Old
　　　　　　Judge*

The happy combination of fortuitous circumstances.
　　　　　—SCOTT

The circumstances of others seem good to us, while ours
seem good to others.
　　　　　—SYRUS, *Maxims*

Citizen

I am a citizen, not of Athens or Greece, but of the world.
　　　　　—Attributed to SOCRATES

Paul said, I am a man which am a Jew of Tarsus, a city
in Cilicia, a citizen of no mean city.
　　　　　—ACTS. XXI. 39

City

This poor little one-horse town.
　　　　　—S. L. CLEMENS (MARK
　　　　　　TWAIN), *The
　　　　　　Undertaker's Story*

If you would know and not be known, live in a city.
— COLTON

God made the country, and man made the town.
— COWPER, *The Task*

Cities force growth, and make men talkative and entertaining, but they make them artificial.
— EMERSON

In the busy haunts of men.
— FELICIA D. HEMANS,
*Tale of the Secret
Tribunal*

Far from gay cities, and the way of men.
— HOMER, *Odyssey*

Ye are the light of the world. A city that is set on a hill cannot be hid.
— MATTHEW. V. 14

The people are the city.
— SHAKESPEARE,
Coriolanus, Act III.
Sc. 1

Civilization

A sufficient measure of civilization is the influence of good women.
— EMERSON

We think our civilization near its meridian, but we are yet only at the cock-crowing and the morning star.
— EMERSON, *Politics*

The path of civilization is paved with tin cans.
—ELBERT HUBBARD

Nations, like individuals, live and die; but civilization cannot die.
—MAZZINI

Civilization is a movement and not a condition, a voyage and not a harbor.
—ARNOLD TOYNBEE,
    Civilization On Trial

Cleanliness

All will come out in the washing.
—CERVANTES, *Don Quixote*

He that toucheth pitch shall be defiled therewith.
—ECCLESIASTES. XIII. 1

Wash you, make you clean.
—ISAIAH. I. 16

God loveth the clean.
—THE KORAN

If dirt was trumps, what hands you would hold!
—LAMB, *Lamb's Suppers*

Certainly this is a duty, not a sin. "Cleanliness is indeed next to godliness."
—JOHN WESLEY

Clergyman

If you would lift me you must be on a higher ground.
—EMERSON

Politics and the pulpit are terms that have little agreement.
—BURKE

As a career, the business of an orthodox preacher is about as successful as that of a celluloid dog chasing an asbestos cat through Hell.
—ELBERT HUBBARD

The life of a conscientious clergyman is not easy. I have always considered a clergyman as the father of a larger family than he is able to maintain. I would rather have chancery suits upon my hands than the cure of souls.
—SAMUEL JOHNSON

The defects of a preacher are soon spied.
—LUTHER

Cleverness

Cleverness is serviceable for everything, sufficient for nothing.
—AMIEL, *Journal*

Cleverness is not wisdom.
—EURIPIDES

Be good, sweet maid, and let who will be clever.
—KINGSLEY, *A Farewell*

Clothes

The clothes make the man.
> —LATIN PROVERB

Whenas in silks my Julia goes,
Then, then, methinks, how sweetly flows
The liquefaction of her clothes!
> —HERRICK, *Hesperides*

Costly thy habit as thy purse can buy,
But not express'd in fancy; rich, not gaudy;
For the apparel oft proclaims the man.
> —SHAKESPEARE, *Hamlet*.
> Act I. Sc. 3

The soul of this man is his clothes.
> —SHAKESPEARE, *All's Well
> that Ends Well*. Act II.
> Sc. 5

She wears her clothes as if they were thrown on her with
a pitchfork.
> —SWIFT, *Polite
> Conversation*

Color

Colors speak all languages.
> —ADDISON, *The Spectator*

Blue is true,
Yellow's jealous,
Green's forsaken,
Red's brazen,
White is love,
And black is death.
> —ANONYMOUS

Commerce

More pernicious nonsense was never devised by man than treaties of commerce.

—DISRAELI

Commerce links all mankind in one common brotherhood of mutual dependence and interests.

—JAMES A. GARFIELD

Commerce is the equalizer of the wealth of nations.

—GLADSTONE

Whatever has a tendency to promote the civil intercourse of nations by an exchange of benefits is a subject as worthy of philosophy as of politics.

—THOMAS PAINE

Common Sense

Common sense is very uncommon.

—HORACE GREELEY

Common sense is in spite of, not the result of, education.

—VICTOR HUGO

Common sense is instinct, and enough of it is genius.

—H. W. SHAW

Communism

From each according to his ability, to each according to his needs.

—Attributed to LOUIS
BLANC

What is a Communist? One who hath yearnings
For equal division of unequal earnings,
Idler or bungler, or both, he is willing,
To fork out his copper and pocket your shilling.
—EBENEZER ELLIOTT

The Communist is a Socialist in a violent hurry.
—G. W. GOUGH, *The
Economic
Consequences of
Socialism*

The theory of Communism may be summed up in one
sentence: Abolish all private property.
—KARL MARX AND
FRIEDRICH ENGELS,
*The Communist
Manifesto*

Communism is the exploitation of the strong by the weak.
In communism, inequality springs from placing medioc-
rity on a level with excellence.
—PROUDHON

Companionship

Tell me thy company and I will tell thee what thou art.
—CERVANTES, *Don
Quixote*

Two's a company, three's a crowd.
—ENGLISH PROVERB

We are in the same boat
—POPE CLEMENT I, to the
Church of Corinth

The right hands of fellowship.
—GALATIANS. II. 9

Comparison

Comparisons are odious.
—ARCHBISHOP BOIARDO,
Orlando Innamorato

Some say, compared to Bononcini,
That Mynheer Handel's but a ninny;
Others aver, that he to Handel
Is scarcely fit to hold a candle:
Strange all this difference should be,
'Twixt Tweedle-dum and Tweedle-dee!
—JOHN BYROM

The bee and the serpent often sip from the selfsame
flower.
—METASTASIO, *Morte
d'Abele*

Compensation

Cast thy bread upon the waters; for thou shalt find it
after many days.
—ECCLESIASTES. XI. 1

If the poor man cannot always get meat, the rich man
cannot always digest it.
—HENRY GILES

'Tis always morning somewhere in the world.
—RICHARD HENGEST
HORNE, *Orion*

Nothing is pure and entire of a piece. All advantages are attended with disadvantages. A universal compensation prevails in all conditions of being and existence.
—HUME

The prickly thorn often bears soft roses.
—OVID

Complaining

Those who complain most are most to be complained of.
—MATTHEW HENRY

The usual fortune of complaint is to excite contempt more than pity.
—SAMUEL JOHNSON

Complaint is the largest tribute Heaven receives.
—SWIFT

Compliment

Compliments are only lies in court clothes.
—ANONYMOUS

When two people compliment each other with the choice of anything, each of them generally gets that which he likes least.
—POPE

Compliments and flattery oftenest excite my contempt by the pretension they imply; for who is he that assumes to flatter me? To compliment often implies an assumption of superiority in the complimenter. It is, in fact, a subtle detraction.
—THOREAU

Compromise

All government—indeed, every human benefit and enjoyment, every virtue and every prudent act—is founded on compromise and barter.

—EDMUND BURKE, Speech
on Conciliation

Compromise makes a good umbrella, but a poor roof; it is a temporary expedient, often wise in party politics, almost sure to be unwise in statesmanship.

—LOWELL

Better bend than break.

—SCOTTISH PROVERB

Conceit

No man was ever so much deceived by another as by himself.

—GREVILLE

The art of making much show with little substance.

—MACAULAY

Seest thou a man wise in his own conceit? There is more hope of a fool than of him.

—PROVERBS. XXVI. 12

Conduct

Be swift to hear, slow to speak, slow to wrath.

—JAMES. I. 19

The integrity of men is to be measured by their conduct, not by their professions.

—JUNIUS

Confession

Open confession is good for the soul.

—SCOTTISH PROVERB

To confess a fault freely is the next thing to being innocent of it.

—SYRUS

Confidence

The confidence which we have in ourselves gives birth to much of that which we have in others.

—LA ROCHEFOUCAULD

Society is built upon trust.

—SOUTH

Be courteous to all, but intimate with few; and let those few be well tried before you give them your confidence.

—WASHINGTON, Letter, 1783

Congress

Every man in it is a great man, an orator, a critic, a statesman; and therefore every man upon every question must show his oratory, his criticism, and his political abilities.

—JOHN ADAMS, Letter to his wife

Fleas can be taught nearly anything that a Congressman can.

> —S. L. CLEMENS (MARK
> TWAIN), *What Is
> Man?*

Some statesmen go to Congress and some go to jail. It is the same thing, after all.

> —EUGENE FIELD, *Tribune
> Primer*

Conquest

How grand is victory, but how dear!

> —BOUFFLERS

He who surpasses or subdues mankind must look down on the hate of those below.

> —BYRON

I came, I saw, I conquered.

> —JULIUS CAESAR

To rejoice in conquest is to rejoice in murder.

> —LAO-TSZE

Self-conquest is the greatest of victories.

> —PLATO

Conscience

Nor ear can hear nor tongue can tell
The tortures of that inward hell!

> —BYRON

The only incorruptible thing about us.
—FIELDING

Liberty of conscience (when people have consciences) is
rightly considered the most indispensable of liberties.
—HADDON CHAMBERS

There is no pillow so soft as a clear conscience.
—FRENCH PROVERB

A still, small voice.
—I KINGS. XIX. 12

Conscience is a sacred sanctuary where God alone may
enter as judge.
—LAMENNAIS

I am more afraid of my own heart than of the pope and
all his cardinals. I have within me the great pope, self.
—LUTHER

Thus conscience does make cowards of us all;
And thus the native hue of resolution
Is sicklied o'er with the pale cast of thought;
And enterprises of great pith and moment,
With this regard, their currents turn awry,
And lose the name of action.
—SHAKESPEARE, Hamlet.
Act III. Sc. 1

The soft whispers of the God in man.
—YOUNG

Conservatism

A statesman who is enamored of existing evils, as distinquished from the Liberal, who wishes to replace them with others.

—BIERCE, *The Devil's Dictionary*

We are reformers in spring and summer; in autumn and winter we stand by the old; reformers in the morning, conservers at night. Reform is affirmative, conservatism negative; conservatism goes for comfort, reform for truth.

—EMERSON

A conservative is a man who will not look at the new moon, out of respect for that "ancient institution," the old one.

—DOUGLAS JERROLD

What is conservatism? Is it not adherence to the old and tried, against the new and untried?

—LINCOLN, 1860

Consistency

A foolish consistency is the hobgoblin of little minds, adored by little statesmen and philosophers and divines.

—EMERSON, *Self-Reliance*

Inconsistency is the only thing in which men are consistent.

—HORACE SMITH, *Tin Trumpet*

Shoemaker, stick to your last.

—PLINY

Constitution

What's the Constitution among friends?
>   —Attributed to
>   CONGRESSMAN
>   TIMOTHY CAMPBELL,
>   of New York

Constitutions should consist only of general provisions; the reason is that they must necessarily be permanent, and that they cannot calculate for the possible change of things.
>   —ALEXANDER HAMILTON

We are under a Constitution, but the Constitution is what the judges say it is.
>   —CHARLES EVANS
>   HUGHES, Speech

In questions of power let no more be heard of confidence in man, but bind him down from mischief by the chains of the constitution.
>   —JEFFERSON, *Kentucky*
>   *Resolutions*

A good constitution is infinitely better than the best despot.
>   —MACAULAY

Contentment

Enjoy your own life without comparing it with that of another.
>   —CONDORCET

I earn that I eat, get that I wear, owe no man hate, envy
no man's happiness; glad of other men's good, content
with my harm.
>—SHAKESPEARE, *As You*
Like it. Act III. Sc. 2

He is well paid that is well satisfied.
>—SHAKESPEARE, *Henry VI*.
Pt. III. Act III. Sc. 1

It is not for man to rest in absolute contentment.
>—SOUTHEY

Controversy

No great advance has ever been made in science, politics,
or religion, without controversy.
>—LYMAN BEECHER

If a cause be good, the most violent attack of its enemies
will not injure it so much as an injudicious defense of it
by its friends.
>—COLTON

Conversation

Debate is masculine; conversation is feminine.
>—ALCOTT

Never hold any one by the button or the hand in order
to be heard out; for if people are unwilling to hear you,
you had better hold your tongue than them.
>—CHESTERFIELD

Conversation enriches the understanding, but solitude is the school of genius.

— GIBBON

Silence is one great art of conversation.

—HAZLITT

Conceit causes more conversation than wit.

—LA ROCHEFOUCAULD

The less men think; the more they talk.

—MONTESQUIEU

Cooking

The discovery of a new dish does more for human happiness than the discovery of a new star.

—BRILLAT-SAVARIN

We may live without friends; we may live without books;
But civilized man cannot live without cooks.

—BULWER-LYTTON

Too many cooks spoil the broth.

—ENGLISH PROVERB

God sends meat, and the Devil sends cooks.

—JOHN TAYLOR, *Works*

Corruption

The more corrupt the state, the more laws.

—TACITUS

Just for a handful of silver he left us,
    Just for a ribbon to stick in his coat.
                    —BROWNING, *The Lost
                    Leader*

If the chief party, whether it be the people, or the army,
or the nobility, which you think most useful and of most
consequence to you for the conservation of your dignity,
be corrupt, you must follow their humor and indulge
them, and in that case honesty and virtue are pernicious.
                    —MACHIAVELLI, *The Prince*

Country Life

I consider it the best part of an education to have been
born and brought up in the country.
                    —ALCOTT

The town is man's world, but this (country life) is of
God.
                    —COWPER, *The Task*

Courage

Often the test of courage is not to die but to live.
                    —ALFIERI, *Orestes*

A man of courage is also full of faith.
                    —CICERO

When moral courage feels that it is in the right, there is
no personal daring of which it is incapable.
                    —LEIGH HUNT

Watch ye, stand fast in the faith, quit you like men, be strong.
—I CORINTHIANS. XVI. 13

Fortune and Love befriend the bold.
—OVID

Women and men of retiring timidity are cowardly only in dangers which affect themselves, but the first to rescue when others are endangered.
—JEAN PAUL RICHTER

Hail, Caesar, those who are about to die salute thee.
—SUETONIUS.

Courtesy

The small courtesies sweeten life; the greater ennoble it.
—BOVEE

A moral, sensible, and well-bred man
Will not affront me, and no other can.
—COWPER

Life is not so short but that there is always time enough for courtesy.
—EMERSON, *Social Aims*

Cowardice

One who in a perilous emergency thinks with his legs.
—BIERCE, *The Devil's Dictionary*

He who fights and runs away
May live to fight another day.
But he who is in battle slain,
Can never rise to fight again.

—GOLDSMITH

A cowardly act! What do I care about that? You may be
sure that I should never fear to commit one if it were to
my advantage.

—NAPOLEON

A cowardly cur barks more fiercely than it bites.

—QUINTUS CURTIUS
RUFUS

All men would be cowards if they durst.

—EARL OF ROCHESTER

Cows

I never saw a Purple Cow,
    I never hope to see one:
But I can tell you, anyhow
    I'd rather see than be one.

—GELETT BURGESS, *The
Purple Cow*

There was an old man who said, "How
Shall I flee from this horrible cow?
I will sit on this stile, and continue to smile,
Which may soften the heart of that cow."

—EDWARD LEAR, *The Book
of Nonsense*

Creation

In the beginning God created the Heaven and the earth.
And the earth was without form, and void; and darkness
was upon the face of the deep. And the Spirit of God
moved upon the face of the waters. And God said, Let
there be light; and there was light.
—GENESIS I. 1–3

Nature they say, doth dote,
And cannot make a man
Save on some worn-out plan,
Repeating us by rote.

—LOWELL, Ode at Harvard
Commemoration

All are but parts of one stupendous whole,
Whose body Nature is, and God the soul.
—POPE

It is easier to suppose that the universe has existed from
all eternity than to conceive a Being beyond its limits
capable of creating it.
—SHELLEY, *Queen Mab*

The world embarrasses me, and I cannot dream
That this watch exists and has no watchmaker.
—VOLTAIRE

Credit

In God we trust; all others must pay cash.
—AMERICAN SAYING

He that hath lost his credit is dead to the world.
—HERBERT, *Outlandish
Proverbs*, 1639

No man's credit is as good as his money.
—E. W. HOWE, *Sinner*
Sermons

Ah, take the cash, and let the credit go.
—OMAR KHAYYÁM,
Rubaiyat

Credulity

Better be too credulous than too skeptical
—CHINESE PROVERB

Let us believe neither half of the good people tell us of
ourselves, nor half the evil they say of others.
—J. PETTIT-SENN

I wish I was as sure of anything as Macaulay is of everything.
—WILLIAM WINDHAM

Crime

Society prepares the crime; the criminal commits it.
—BUCKLE

Many commit the same crimes with a very different result.
One bears a cross for his crime; another a crown.
—JUVENAL, *Satires*

One crime is everything; two nothing.
—MME. DELUZY

Whoever profits by the crime is guilty of it.
—FRENCH PROVERB

It is not the thief who is hanged, but one who was caught stealing.

— CZECH PROVERB

We enact many laws that manufacture criminals, and then a few that punish them.

— TUCKER, *Instead of a Book*

Yet each man kills the thing he loves,
　　By each let this be heard,
Some do it with a bitter look,
　　Some with a flattering word,
The coward does it with a kiss,
　　The brave man with a sword.

— WILDE, *Ballad of Reading Gaol*

Criticism

Said the pot to the kettle, "Get away, blackface."

— CERVANTES, *Don Quixote*

Critics are the men who have failed in literature and art.

— DISRAELI

As a bankrupt thief turns thief-taker in despair, so an unsuccessful author turns critic.

— SHELLEY, *Fragments of Adonais*

What a blessed thing it is that nature, when she invented, manufactured and patented her authors, contrived to make critics out of the chips that were left!

— HOLMES

Even the lion has to defend himself against flies.

— GERMAN PROVERB

I had rather be hissed for a good verse than applauded for a bad one.
—VICTOR HUGO

Of all the cants which are canted in this canting world—though the cant of hypocrites may be the worst—the cant of criticism is the most tormenting.
—LAURENCE STERNE,
Tristram Shandy

Cruelty

Man's inhumanity to man
Makes countless thousands mourn!
—BURNS, *Man Was Made
to Mourn*

It is not linen you're wearing out,
But human creatures' lives.
—HOOD, *Song of the Shirt*

All cruelty springs from weakness.
—SENECA

I must be cruel, only to be kind.
—SHAKESPEARE, *Hamlet*.
Act III. Sc. 4

Culture

Culture, with us, ends in headache.
—EMERSON, *Experience*

Reading makes a full man, conference a ready man, and writing an exact man.
—BACON

Culture is what your butcher would have if he were a surgeon.

—MARY PETTIBONE
POOLE, *A Glass Eye
at the Keyhole*

Curiosity

Curiosity killed the cat.

—AMERICAN PROVERB

Ask me no questions, and I'll tell you no fibs.

—GOLDSMITH, *She Stoops
to Conquer*

Curiosity is one of the permanent and certain characteristics of a vigorous intellect.

—SAMUEL JOHNSON

Custom

Other times, other customs.

—ITALIAN PROVERB

Ancient custom has the force of law.

—LEGAL MAXIM

Custom is the law of fools.

—VANBRUGH

Cynicism

A cynic is a man who knows the price of everything, and the value of nothing.

—WILDE, *Lady
Windermere's Fan*

The cynic is one who never sees a good quality in a man, and never fails to see a bad one. He is the human owl, vigilant in darkness and blind to light, mousing for vermin, and never seeing noble game. The cynic puts all human actions into two classes—openly bad and secretly bad.

—HENRY WARD BEECHER

Dancing

On with the dance! Let joy be unconfin'd;
No sleep till morn, when Youth and Pleasure meet.
—BYRON, *Childe Harold*

No man in his senses will dance.
—CICERO

Come and trip it as ye go,
On the light fantastic toe.

—MILTON, *L'Allegro*

They who love dancing too much seem to have more brains in their feet than in their head.
—TERENCE

Danger

We triumph without glory when we conquer without danger.
—CORNEILLE, *The Cid*

Danger for danger's sake is senseless.
—LEIGH HUNT

The pitcher that goes too often to the well is broken at last.
—ENGLISH PROVERB

A timid person is frightened before a danger, a coward
during the time, and a courageous person afterwards.
—JEAN PAUL RICHTER

Daring

Who dares nothing, need hope for nothing.
—SCHILLER, *Don Carlos*

No one reaches a high position without daring.
—SYRUS

Darkness

Darkness which may be felt.
—EXODUS. X. 21

It is always darkest just before the day dawneth.
—THOMAS FULLER

Daughters

My son is my son till he have got him a wife,
But my daughter's my daughter all the days of her life.
—THOMAS FULLER

If thy daughter marry well, thou hast found a son; if not,
thou hast lost a daughter.
—QUARLES

Day

Think that day lost whose (low) descending sun
Views from thy hand no noble action done.
>   —JACOB BOBART, Krieg's
>   Album in British
>   Museum

For mem'ry has painted this perfect day.
>   With colors that never fade,
And we find at the end of a perfect day,
>   The soul of a friend we've made
>   —CARRIE JACOBS BOND, A
>   Perfect Day

What a day may bring a day may take away.
>   —THOMAS FULLER

Monday for wealth,
Tuesday for health,
Wednesday the best day of all:
Thursday for crosses,
Friday for losses,
Saturday no luck at all.
>   —OLD ENGLISH RHYME

Boast not thyself of tomorrow; for thous knowest not
what a day may bring forth.
>   —PROVERBS. XXVII. 1

One glance of Thine creates a day.
>   —ISAAC WATTS

Death

Call no man happy till he is dead.
>   —AESCHYLUS, Agamemnon

Though this may be play to you,
'Tis death to us.

—AESOP, *Fables*

Earth to earth, ashes to ashes, dust to dust, in sure and
certain hope of the resurrection.

—BOOK OF COMMON
PRAYER

In the midst of life we are in death.

—BOOK OF COMMON
PRAYER

Man that is born of a woman hath but a short time to
live, and is full of misery. He cometh up, and is cut
down, like a flower; he fleeth as it were a shadow, and
never continueth in one stay.

—BOOK OF COMMON
PRAYER

Death, so called, is a thing which makes men weep,
And yet a third of life is pass'd in sleep.

—BYRON, *Don Juan*

O death, where is thy sting?
O grave, where is thy victory?

—I CORINTHIANS. XV. 55

Why fear death? It is the most beautiful adventure in
life.

—CHARLES FROHMAN

Now I am about to take my last voyage, a great leap in
the dark.

—THOMAS HOBBES

Is death the last sleep? No, it is the last final awakening.

—SCOTT

The Lord gave, and the Lord hath taken away; blessed
be the name of the Lord.

—JOB. I. 21

We begin to die as soon as we are born, and the end is
linked to the beginning.

—MANILIUS

There is no death! the stars go down
     To rise upon some other shore,
And bright in Heaven's jeweled crown,
     They shine for ever more.

—JOHN L. MCCREERY

Strange—is it not?—that of the myriads who
Before us passed the door of Darkness through,
Not one returns to tell us of the road
Which to discover we must travel too.

—OMAR KHAYYÁM,
     Rubaiyat

I am dying, Egypt, dying.

—SHAKESPEARE, *Antony
     and Cleopatra.* Act IV.
     Sc. 15

Yet a little sleep, a little slumber, a little folding of the
hands to sleep.

—PROVERBS. VI. 10

I am going to seek a great perhaps; draw the curtain, the
farce is played.

—Attributed to RABELAIS

I have a rendezvous with Death
At some disputed barricade.

—ALAN SEEGER

Till tired, he sleeps, and life's poor play is o'er.
—POPE, *Essay on Man*

To die:—to sleep:
No more; and, by a sleep to say we end
The heart-ache and the thousand natural shocks
That flesh is heir to, 'tis a consummation
Devoutly to be wished.
—SHAKESPEARE, *Hamlet*.
Act III. Sc. 1

Nothing in his life
Became him like the leaving it.
—SHAKESPEARE, *Macbeth*.
Act I. Sc. 4

Death lies on her, like an untimely frost
Upon the sweetest flower of all the field.
—SHAKESPEARE, *Romeo
and Juliet*. Act IV. Sc. 5

First our pleasures die—and then
Our hopes, and then our fears—and when
These are dead, the debt is due,
Dust claims dust—and we die too.
—SHELLEY, *Death*

God's finger touched him, and he slept.
—TENNYSON, *In Memoriam*

Sunset and evening star,
        And one clear call for me!
And may there be no moaning of the bar
        When I put out to sea.
—TENNYSON, *Crossing the
Bar*

Nothing can happen more beautiful than death.
>   —WALT WHITMAN,
>   *Starting from*
>   *Paumanok*

For he who lives more lives than one
>   More deaths than one must die.
>   —WILDE, *Ballad of Reading*
>   *Gaol*

Debt

A church debt is the devil's salary.
>   —HENRY WARD BEECHER

Wilt thou seal up the avenues of ill?
Pay every debt as if God wrote the bill!
>   —EMERSON

If you want the time to pass quickly, just give your note
for 90 days.
>   —R. B. THOMAS, *Farmer's*
>   *Almanack*

Owe no man anything.
>   —ROMANS. XII. 8

He that dies pays all debts.
>   —SHAKESPEARE, *Tempest.*
>   Act III. Sc. 2

A national debt, if it is not excessive, will be to us a
national blessing.
>   —HAMILTON

Debt is the worst poverty.
>   —M. G. LICHTWER

Deception

A delusion, a mockery, and a snare.
> —LORD DENMAN

We are never deceived; we deceive ourselves.
> —GOETHE

Which I wish to remark—
    And my language is plain,—
That for ways that are dark
    And for tricks that are vain,
The heathen Chinese is peculiar.
> —BRET HARTE, *Plain
> Language from
> Truthful James*

Hateful to me as are the gates of hell,
Is he who, hiding one thing in his heart,
Utters another.
> —HOMER, *Iliad*

You can fool some of the people all of the time, and all
of the people some of the time, but you cannot fool all
of the people all the time.
> —LINCOLN

It is double pleasure to deceive the deceiver.
> —LA FONTAINE

"Will you walk into my parlour?"
    Said the spider to a fly:
"'Tis the prettiest little parlour
    That ever you did spy."
> —MARY HOWITT, *The
> Spider and the Fly*

One is easily fooled by that which one loves.
> —MOLIÈRE, *Tartuffe*

Deeds

We have left undone those things which we ought to have done; and we have done those things which we ought not to have done.

—BOOK OF COMMON
PRAYER

Little deeds of kindness, little words of love,
Make our earth an Eden like the heaven above.
—JULIA F. CARNEY, *Little
Things*

Whatever is worth doing at all is worth doing well.
—CHESTERFIELD

Give me the ready hand rather than the ready tongue.
—GARIBALDI

Noble deeds that are concealed are most esteemed.
—PASCAL

Heaven ne'er helps the man who will not help himself.
—SOPHOCLES

Defeat

It is defeat that turns bone to flint; it is defeat that turns gristle to muscle; it is defeat that makes men invincible.
—HENRY WARD BEECHER,
Royal Truths

What is defeat? Nothing but education, nothing but the first step to something better.
—WENDELL PHILLIPS

Defeat should never be a source of discouragement but rather a fresh stimulus.

—SOUTH

Democracy

It would be folly to argue that the people cannot make political mistakes. They can and do make grave mistakes. They know it, they pay the penalty, but compared with the mistakes which have been made by every kind of autocracy they are unimportant.

—CALVIN COOLIDGE

Democracy is based upon the conviction that there are extraordinary possibilities in ordinary people.

—HARRY EMERSON
FOSDICK, *Democracy*

The world must be made safe for democracy.

—WOODROW WILSON, War
Address to Congress,
1917

Democracy is the government of the people, by the people, for the people.

—LINCOLN

Democracy means not "I am as good as you are," but "You are as good as I am."

—THEODORE PARKER

All the ills of democracy can be cured by more democracy.

—ALFRED E. SMITH,
Speech, 1933

I believe in Democracy because it releases the energies of every human being.

—WOODROW WILSON

While democracy must have its organization and controls, its vital breath is individual liberty.

> —CHARLES EVANS
> HUGHES, Speech,
> 1939

Demagogues

Demagogues and agitators are very unpleasant, but they are incidents to a free and constitutional country, and you must put up with these inconveniences or do without many important advantages.

> —DISRAELI, Speech

In every age the vilest specimens of human nature are to be found among demagogues.

> —MACAULAY, History of
> England

Every one that was in distress, and every one that was in debt, and every one that was discontented, gathered themselves unto him; and he became a captain over them.

> —I SAMUEL. XXII. 2

A wise fellow who is also worthless always charms the rabble.

> —EURIPIDES

Dependence

People may live as much retired from the world as they please; but sooner or later, before they are aware, they will find themselves debtor or creditor to somebody.

> —GOETHE

He who imagines he can do without the world deceives himself much; but he who fancies the world cannot do without him is still more mistaken.

> —LA ROCHEFOUCAULD

Desire

It is easier to suppress the first desire than to satisfy all that follow it.

—FRANKLIN

There are two tragedies in life. One is not to get your heart's desire. The other is to get it.

— GEORGE BERNARD
SHAW, *Man and
Superman*

Our desires always increase with our possessions. The knowledge that something remains yet unenjoyed impairs our enjoyment of the good before us.

—SAMUEL JOHNSON

He who desires naught will always be free.

—E. R. LEFEBVRE
LABOULAYE

Ah love! could you and I with Him conspire
To grasp this sorry scheme of things entire,
Would not we shatter it to bits—and then
Re-mold it nearer to the heart's desire!

—OMAR KHAYYÁM,
Rubaiyat

Despair

All hope abandon, ye who enter here.

—DANTE, *Inferno*

Despair is the conclusion of fools.

—DISRAELI

Despair doubles our strength.

—ENGLISH PROVERB

Despotism

It is the old practice of despots to use a part of the people to keep the rest in order.

—JEFFERSON

Despotism can no more exist in a nation until the liberty of the press be destroyed than the night can happen before the sun is set.

—COLTON

I will believe in the right of one man to govern a nation despotically when I find a man born unto the world with boots and spurs, and a nation with saddles on their backs.

—ALGERNON SIDNEY

Destiny

We are but as the instrument of Heaven.
Our work is not design, but destiny.

—OWEN MEREDITH,
Clytemnestra

Every man meets his Waterloo at last.

—WENDELL PHILLIPS

There is a divinity that shapes our ends,
Rough-hew them how we will.

—SHAKESPEARE, *Hamlet*.
Act V. Sc. 2

Devil

Here is the devil-and-all to pay.

—CERVANTES, *Don
Quixote*

Resist the Devil, and he will flee from you.
                    —JAMES. IV. 7

The devil was sick, the devil a monk would be;
The devil was well, the devil a monk was he.
                    —ANONYMOUS

How art thou fallen from heaven,
O Lucifer, son of the morning!
                    —ISAIAH. XIV. 12

Get thee behind me, Satan.
                    —MARK. VIII. 33

The Devil and me, we don't agree;
I hate him; and he hates me.
                    —SALVATION ARMY HYMN

He will give the devil his due.
                    —SHAKESPEARE, *Henry IV.*
                        Pt. I. Act I. Sc. 2

The prince of darkness is a gentleman.
                    —SHAKESPEARE, *King Lear.*
                        Act III. Sc. 4

The devil can cite Scripture for his purpose.
                    —SHAKESPEARE, *Merchant*
                        of Venice. Act I. Sc. 3

Dew

'Tis of the tears which stars weep, sweet with joy.
                    —BAILEY, *Festus*

Every dew-drop and raindrop had a whole heaven within
it.
                    —LONGFELLOW, *Hyperion*

Difficulty

The best way out of a difficulty is through it.
—ANONYMOUS

The three things most difficult are—to keep a secret, to forget an injury, and to make good use of leisure.
—CHILO

Many things difficult to design prove easy to performance.
—SAMUEL JOHNSON

Diplomacy

A diplomat is a man who remembers a lady's birthday but forgets her age.
—ANONYMOUS

When a diplomat says yes he means perhaps; when he says perhaps he means no; when he says no he is no diplomat.
—ANONYMOUS

I have discovered the art of deceiving diplomats. I speak the truth, and they never believe me.
—DI CAVOUR

Diplomacy is to do and say
The nastiest thing in the nicest way.
—ISAAC GOLDBERG, *The Reflex*

Disappointment

Disappointment is the nurse of wisdom.
—SIR BOYLE ROCHE

The best-laid schemes o' mice an' men,
    Gang aft a-gley,
And leave us nought but grief and pain,
    For promised joy.
           —BURNS, *To a Mouse*

Disappointments are to the soul what a thunder-storm is to the air.
           —SCHILLER

Discontent

Men would be angels;
Angels would be gods.
           —POPE

Now is the Winter of our discontent.
           —SHAKESPEARE, *Richard III*. Act 3. Sc. 1

I was *born* to other things.
           —TENNYSON, *In Memoriam*

Discontent is the first step in the progress of a man or a nation.
           —WILDE, *Woman of No Importance*

Discretion

Discretion in speech is more than eloquence.
           —BACON

A sound discretion is not so much indicated by never making a mistake as by never repeating it.
           —BOVEE

Great ability without discretion comes almost invariably to a tragic end.

—GAMBETTA

Let your own discretion be your tutor; suit the action to the word, the word to the action.

—SHAKESPEARE, *Hamlet.*
Act III. Sc. 2

The better part of valour is discretion.

—SHAKESPEARE, *Henry IV.*
Pt. I. Act V. Sc. 4

Disease

Disease is the retribution of outraged Nature.

—HOSEA BALLOU

Disease is an experience of so-called mortal mind. It is fear made manifest on the body.

—MARY BAKER EDDY,
Science and Health

Desperate diseases require desperate remedies.

—ENGLISH PROVERB

Some remedies are worse than the disease.

—SYRUS

Disgrace

Whatever disgrace we may have deserved, it is almost always in our power to re-establish our character.

—PLAUTUS

No one can disgrace us but ourselves.

—J. G. HOLLAND

Distrust

Doubt the man who swears to his devotion.
—MME. LOUISE COLET

Women distrust men too much in general, and too little in particular.
—COMMERSON

What loneliness is more lonely than distrust?
—GEORGE ELIOT,
Middlemarch

Doctrine

Doctrine is nothing but the skin of truth set up and stuffed.
—HENRY WARD BEECHER

How absurd to try to make two men think alike on matters of religion, when I cannot make two timepieces agree!
—CHARLES V

In religion as in politics it so happens that we have less charity for those who believe half our creed, than for those who deny the whole of it.
—COLTON

You can and you can't,
You will and you won't;
You'll be damn'd if you do,
You'll be damn'd if you don't.
—LORENZO DOW,
(Definition of
Calvinism)

"Orthodoxy, my Lord," said Bishop Warburton, in a whisper,—"orthodoxy is my doxy,—heterodoxy is another man's doxy."

—JOSEPH PRIESTLEY,
Memoirs

Dogs

Do not disturb the sleeping dog.
—ALESSANDRO ALLEGRI

Every dog is entitled to one bite.
—ANONYMOUS

Who loves me will love my dog also.
—ST. BERNARD OF
CLAIRVAUX

You're only a dog, old fellow; a dog, and you've had your
day;
But never a friend of all my friends has been truer than
you alway.

—JULIAN S. CUTLER, *Roger
and I*

I agree with Agassiz that dogs possess something very
like a conscience.

—DARWIN, *The Descent of
Man*

Oh, the saddest of sights in a world of sin
Is a little lost pup with his tail tucked in!
—ARTHUR GUITERMAN,
Little Lost Pup

A living dog is better than a dead lion.
—ECCLESIASTES. IX. 4

Fox-terriers are born with about four times as much original sin in them as other dogs.

> —JEROME K. JEROME,
> *Three Men in a Boat*

The more one comes to know men, the more one comes to admire the dog.

> —JOUSSENEL

The dogs eat of the crumbs which fall from their masters' table.

> —MATTHEW. XV. 27

The cowardly dog barks more violently than it bites.

> —QUINTUS CURTIUS
> RUFUS

Every dog must have his day.

> —SWIFT

Gentlemen of the Jury: The one, absolute, unselfish friend that man can have in this selfish world, the one that never deserts him, the one that never proves ungrateful or treacherous, is his dog.

> —SENATOR GEORGE
> GRAHAM VEST,
> *Eulogy on the Dog*

Doubt

Galileo called doubt the father of invention; it is certainly the pioneer.

> —BOVEE

Of that there is no manner of doubt—
No probable, possible shadow of doubt—
No possible doubt whatever.

> —W. S. GILBERT, *The*
> *Gondoliers*

We know accurately only when we know little; with knowledge doubt increases.
— GOETHE

When in doubt, win the trick.
—HOYLE

I respect faith, but doubt is what gets you an education.
—WILSON MIZNER

And he that doubteth is damned if he eat.
—ROMANS. XIV. 23

To be, or not to be, that is the question:
Whether 'tis nobler in the mind to suffer
The slings and arrows of outrageous fortune;
Or to take arms against a sea of troubles,
And by opposing end them?
—SHAKESPEARE, *Hamlet*.
Act III. Sc. 1

Our doubts are traitors
And make us lose the good we oft might win
By fearing to attempt.
—SHAKESPEARE, *Measure for Measure*. Act I. Sc. 5

There lives more faith in honest doubt,
Believe me, than in half the creeds
—TENNYSON, *In Memoriam*

I'm from Missouri; you must show me.
—COLONEL WILLARD D. VANDIVER

Dreams

If there were dreams to sell,
Merry and sad to tell,
And the crier rung his bell,
    What would you buy?

—T. L. BEDDOES, *Dream-
Pedlary*

I dreamt that I dwelt in marble halls,
With vassals and serfs at my side.

—ALFRED BUNN, *Bohemian
Girl*: Song

Abou Ben Adhem (may his tribe increase!)
Awoke one night from a deep dream of peace.

—LEIGH HUNT, *Abou Ben
Adhem*

For dhrames always go by conthraries, my dear.

—SAMUEL LOVER

    We are such stuff
As dreams are made on, and our little life
Is rounded with a sleep.

—SHAKESPEARE, *The
Tempest*. Act IV. Sc. 1

Your old men shall dream dreams, your young men shall
see visions.

—JOEL. II. 28

There's a long, long trail a-winding
Into the land of my dreams,
Where the nightingales are singing
And the white moon beams;
There's a long, long night of waiting
Until my dreams all come true,

Till the day when I'll be going down that
Long, long trail with you.
—STODDARD KING, *There's
a Long, Long Trail*

Dress

When you're all dressed up and no place to go.
—BENJAMIN HAPGOOD
BURT

If a woman were about to proceed to her execution, she
would demand a little time to perfect her toilet.
—CHAMFORT

Eat to please thyself, but dress to please others.
—FRANKLIN

Drinking

Drunkenness is temporary suicide: the happiness that it
brings is merely negative, a momentary cessation of
unhappiness.
—BERTRAND RUSSELL, *The
Conquest of Happiness*

There was an old hen
And she had a wooden leg,
And every damned morning
She laid another egg;
She was the best damned chicken
On the whole damned farm—
And another little drink
Wouldn't do us any harm.
—AMERICAN FOLKSONG

It's a long time between drinks.
—ANONYMOUS

He is a drunkard who takes more than three glasses, though he be not drunk.
—EPICTETUS

Drink today, and drown all sorrow;
You shall perhaps not do it tomorrow.
—JOHN FLETCHER, *The Bloody Brother*

Woe unto them that rise up early in the morning, that they may follow strong drink; that continue until night, till wine inflame them.
—ISAIAH. V. 11

The habit of using ardent spirits by men in office has occasioned more injury to the public, and more trouble to me, than all other causes. Were I to commence my administration again, the first question I would ask respecting a candidate for office would be, Does he use ardent spirits?
—JEFFERSON

I would appeal to Philip, she said, but to Philip sober.
—VALERIUS MAXIMUS

Drink! for you know not whence you came, nor why:
Drink! for you know not why you go, nor where.
—OMAR KHAYYÁM, *Rubaiyat*

All excess is ill, but drunkeness is of the worst sort. It spoils health, dismounts the mind, and unmans men. It reveals secrets, is quarrelsome, lascivious, impudent, dangerous and bad.
—WILLIAM PENN

There St. John mingles with my friendly bowl
The feat of reason and the flow of soul.
>—POPE, *Second Book of*
Horace

Water is the only drink for a wise man.
>—THOREAU, *Walden*

Duty

To do my duty in that state of life unto which it shall
please God to call me.
>—BOOK OF COMMON
PRAYER

It is thy duty oftentimes to do what thou wouldst not;
thy duty, too, to leave undone that thou wouldst do.
>—THOMAS Á KEMPIS

So nigh is grandeur to our dust,
>So near is God to man.
When Duty whispers low,
>*Thou must*,
The youth replies, *I can*.
>—EMERSON, *Voluntaries*

No personal consideration should stand in the way of
performing a public duty.
>—ULYSSES S. GRANT

Let us have faith that right makes might, and in that faith
let us, to the end, dare to do our duty as we understand
it.
>—LINCOLN

England expects every man to do his duty.
>—NELSON

Theirs not to make reply,
Theirs not to reason why,
Theirs but to do and die.

—TENNYSON, *The Charge
of the Light Brigade*

Not once or twice in our rough island story,
The path of duty was the way to glory.

—TENNYSON, *Ode on the
Death of the Duke of
Wellington*

Early Rising

Early to bed and early to rise,
Makes a man healthy, wealthy and wise.

—FRANKLIN, *Poor Richard's
Almanac*

Easter

Tomb, thou shalt not hold Him longer;
Death is strong, but Life is stronger;
Stronger than the dark, the light;
Stronger than the wrong, the right;
Faith and Hope triumphant say
Christ will rise on Easter Day.

—PHILLIPS BROOKS, *An
Easter Carol*

Come, ye saints, look here and wonder,
See the place where Jesus lay;
He has borne our sins away;
Joyful tiding,
Yes, the Lord has risen today.

—THOMAS KELLY

Hallelujah! Hallelujah!
On the third morning He arose,
Bright with victory o'er his foes.
      Sing we lauding,
And applauding,
         Hallelujah!

—From the Latin of the
12th Century

"Christ the Lord is risen today,"
Sons of men and angels say.
Raise your joys and triumphs high;
Sing, ye heavens, and earth reply.
                    —CHARLES WESLEY

In the bonds of Death He lay
      Who for our offense was slain;
But the Lord is risen today,
      Christ hath brought us life again,
Wherefore let us all rejoice,
      Singing loud, with cheerful voice,
Hallelujah!

                    —LUTHER

Eating

Eat, drink, and be merry, for tomorrow ye diet.
                    —WILLIAM GILMORE
                    BEYMER

Tell me what you eat, and I will tell you what you are.
                    —BRILLAT-SAVARIN,
                    Physiologie du Gout

Better halfe a loafe than no bread.
                    —CAMDEN, *Remaines*

The proof of the pudding is in the eating.
—CERVANTES, *Don
Quixote*

Thou shouldst eat to live; not live to eat.
—CICERO

The nearer the bone, the sweeter the meat.
—ENGLISH PROVERB

I want every peasant to have a chicken in his pot on Sundays.

—HENRY IV of France

When I demanded of my friend what viands he preferred,
He quoth: "A large cold bottle, and a small hot bird!"
—EUGENE FIELD, *The
Bottle and the Bird*

Let us eat and drink; for tomorrow we shall die.
—ISAIAH, XXII. 13

For a man seldom thinks with more earnestness of anything than he does of his dinner.
—SAMUEL JOHNSON

Man shall not live by bread alone
—MATTHEW. IV. 4

The way to a man's heart is through his stomach.
—MRS. SARAH PAYSON
PARTON, *Willis Parton*

Better is a dinner of herbs where love is, than a stalled ox and hatred therewith.
—PROVERBS. XV. 17

He hath eaten me out of house and home.

—SHAKESPEARE, *Henry IV.*
Pt. II. Act II. Sc. 1

They say fingers were made before forks, and hands before knives.

—SWIFT, *Polite
Conversation*

Bread is the staff of life.

—SWIFT, *Tale of a Tub*

Economy

Buy not what you want, but what you have need of; what you do not want is dear at a farthing.

—CATO, *The Censor*

He who will not economize will have to agonize.

—CONFUCIUS

After order and liberty, economy is one of the highest essentials of a free government. . . . Economy is always a guarantee of peace.

—CALVIN COOLIDGE,
Speech, 1923

Beware of little expenses; a small leak will sink a great ship.

—FRANKLIN

No man is rich whose expenditure exceeds his means; and no one is poor whose incomings exceed his outgoings.

—HALIBURTON

Have more than thou showest,
Speak less than thou knowest.

—SHAKESPEARE, *King Lear.*
Act I. Sc. 4

Education

Schoolhouses are the republican line of fortifications.
—HORACE MANN

Education commences at the mother's knee, and every word spoken within the hearsay of little children tends towards the formation of character.
—HOSEA BALLOU

Education makes a people easy to lead, but difficult to drive; easy to govern, but impossible to enslave.
—Attributed to LORD
BROUGHAM

What greater or better gift can we offer the republic than to teach and instruct our youth?
—CICERO

Training is everything. The peach was once a bitter almond; cauliflower is nothing but cabbage with a college education.
—SAMUEL L. CLEMENS
(MARK TWAIN)

The things taught in schools and colleges are not an education, but the means of education.
—EMERSON, *Journal*, 1831

'Tis education forms the common mind;
Just as the twig is bent the tree's inclined.
—POPE, *Moral Essays*

There is nothing so stupid as an educated man, if you get off the thing that he was educated in.
—WILL ROGERS

Education is the process of driving a set of prejudices down your throat.

—MARTIN H. FISCHER

If a man empties his purse into his head, no one can take it from him.

—FRANKLIN

Education is an admirable thing, but it is well to remember from time to time that nothing that is worth knowing can be taught.

—WILDE, *The Critic as Artist*

Efficiency

He did nothing in particular,
And did it very well.

—W. S. GILBERT, *Iolanthe*

The best carpenters make the fewest chips.

—GERMAN PROVERB

Egotism

The reason why lovers are never wary of one another is this—they are always talking of themselves.

—LA ROCHEFOUCAULD

Do you wish men to speak well of you? Then never speak well of yourself.

—PASCAL

Nothing is more to me than myself.

—STIRNER, *The Ego and His Own*

Eloquence

Eloquence is the poetry of prose.
—BRYANT

The manner of your speaking is full as important as the matter, as more people have ears to be tickled than understandings to judge.
—CHESTERFIELD

Noise proves nothing. Often a hen who has merely laid an egg cackles as if she laid an asteroid.
—SAMUEL L. CLEMENS
(MARK TWAIN)

Thoughts that breathe and words that burn.
—GRAY

True eloquence consists in saying all that is necessary, and nothing but what is necessary.
—LA ROUCHEFOUCAULD

Enemy

They love him most for the enemies that he has made.
—GENERAL E. S. BRAGG,
Nominating Speech
for Cleveland, 1884

Man is his own worst enemy.
—CICERO

He who has a thousand friends has not a friend to spare,
And he who has one enemy will meet him everywhere.
—EMERSON, *Translations*

None but yourself who are your greatest foe.
—LONGFELLOW

If thine enemy hunger, feed him; if he thirst, give him drink.

—ROMANS. XII. 20

My prayer to God is a very short one "Oh Lord, make my enemies ridiculous!" God has granted it.

—VOLTAIRE

A man cannot be too careful in the choice of his enemies.

—WILDE, *Picture of Dorian Gray*

England

If I should die, think only this of me:
    That there's some corner of a foreign field
That is forever England.

—RUPERT BROOKE, *The Soldier*

Oh, to be in England,
Now that April's there.

—BROWNING, *Home Thoughts from Abroad*

In England there are sixty different religions, and only one sauce.

—MARQUIS CARACCIOLI

I have nothing to offer but blood, toil, tears and sweat.

—WINSTON CHURCHILL, Speech, May 28, 1940

Be England what she will,
With all her faults, she is my country still.

—CHARLES CHURCHILL, *The Farewell*

We shall go on to the end, we shall fight in France, we shall fight on the seas and oceans, we shall fight with growing confidence and growing strength in the air, we shall defend our Island whatever the cost may be, we shall fight on the landing grounds, we shall fight in the fields and in the streets, we shall fight in the hills; we shall never surrender, and even if, which I do not for a moment believe, this Island or a large part of it were subjugated and starving, then our Empire beyond the seas, armed and guarded by the British Fleet, would carry on the struggle, until, in God's good time, the New World, with all its power and might steps forth to the rescue and the liberation of the old.

—WINSTON CHURCHILL,
Speech, June 4, 1940

Let us therefore brace ourselves to our duties, and so bear ourselves that, if the British Empire and its Commonwealth last for a thousand years, men will still say, "This was their finest hour."

—WINSTON CHURCHILL,
Speech, June 18, 1940

Never in the field of human conflict was so much owed by so many to so few.

—WINSTON CHURCHILL,
1941, referring to
England's debt to its
Royal Air Force

O, it's a snug little island!
A right little, tight little island!

—THOMAS DIBDIN, The
Snug Little Island

The English nation is never so great as in adversity.

—DISRAELI, Speech, 1857

We are indeed a nation of shopkeepers.

> —DISRAELI, *The Young
> Duke*

For he might have been a Rooshian
A French or Turk or Proosian,
Or perhaps Itali-an.
But in spite of all temptations
To belong to other nations,
He remains an Englishman.

> —W. S. GILBERT, *H.M.S.
> Pinafore*

What have I done for you,
    England, my England?
What is there I would not do,
    England, my own?

> —W. E. HENLEY, *England,
> My England*

Froth at the top, dregs at bottom, but the middle excellent.

> —VOLTAIRE, *Description of
> the English Nation*

The royal throne of kings, this scepter'd isle,
This earth of majesty, this seat of Mars,
This other Eden, demi-paradise,
This fortress built by nature for herself
Against infection and the hand of war;
This happy breed of men, this little world,
This precious stone set in the silver sea.

> —SHAKESPEARE, *Richard II.*
> Act II. Sc. I

There is nothing so bad or so good that you will not find
Englishmen doing it; but you will never find an Englishman in the wrong. He does everything on principle. He

fights you on patriotic principles; he robs you on business principles; he enslaves you on imperial principles.
— GEORGE BERNARD
SHAW, *The Man of
Destiny*

When Britain first at Heaven's command,
Arose from out the azure main,
This was the charter of the land,
And Guardian angels sung this strain;
   "Rule Britannia! rule the waves;
   Britons never will be slaves."
— JAMES THOMSON,
Masque of Alfred

An Englishman thinks he is moral when he is only uncomfortable.
— GEORGE BERNARD SHAW

Enthusiasm

Nothing is so contagious as enthusiasm; it moves stones, it charms brutes. Enthusiasm is the genius of sincerity and truth accomplishes no victories without it.
— BULWER-LYTTON

Nothing great was ever achieved without enthusiasm.
— EMERSON, *On Circles*

The world belongs to the Enthusiast who keeps cool.
— WILLIAM McFEE,
Casuals of the Sea

The sense of this word among the Greeks affords the noblest definition of it: enthusiasm signifies God in us.
— MME. DE STAËL

Envy

As a moth gnaws a garment, so doth envy consume a man.

—St. Chrysostom

Thou shalt not covet thy neighbor's house, thou shalt not covet they neighbor's wife, nor his manservant, nor his maidservant, nor his ox, nor his ass, nor anything that is thy neighbor's.

—Exodus. XX. 17

The hen of our neighbor appears to us a goose, says the Oriental proverb.

—Mme. Deluzy

It is better to be envied than pitied.

—Herodotus

It is the practice of the multitude to bark at eminent men, as little dogs do at strangers.

—Seneca, *Of a Happy Life*

Epitaph

A tomb now suffices him for whom the whole world was not sufficient.

—Epitaph on Alexander the Great

O man! whosoever thou art, and whensoever thou comest, for come I know thou wilt, I am Cyrus, founder of the Persian empire. Envy me not the little earth that covers my body.

—Epitaph of Cyrus

Life is a jest, and all things show it,
I thought so once, but now I know it.
—GAY, *My Own Epitaph*

Here lies one whose name was writ in water.
—Engraved on Keats's
tombstone

If you would see his monument look around.
—Inscription on the tomb of
Sir Christopher Wren
in St. Paul's, London

Requiescat in pace.
May he rest in peace.
—Order of the Mass

Excuse my dust.

—DOROTHY PARKER, Her
Own Epitaph

Under the wide and starry sky,
Dig the grave and let me lie;
Glad did I live and gladly die,
And I laid me down with a will.
This be the verse you grave for me:
"Here he lies, where he longed to be;
Home is the sailor, home from the sea,
And the hunter home from the hill."
—STEVENSON, Engraved on
his tombstone

The poet's fate is here in emblem shown,
He asked for bread, and he received a stone.
—SAMUEL WESLEY, On
Butler's Monument in
Westminster Abbey

Equality

For the colonel's lady an' Judy O'Grady
Are sisters under their skins.
> —KIPLING, *Barrack Room
> Ballads*

Fourscore and seven years ago, our fathers brought forth
on this continent a new nation, conceived in liberty, and
dedicated to the proposition that all men are created equal.
> —LINCOLN, *Gettysburg
> Address*

Your levellers wish to level down as far as themselves,
but they cannot bear levelling up to themselves.
> —SAMUEL JOHNSON,
> *Boswell's Life of
> Johnson*

Men are made by nature unequal. It is vain, therefore,
to treat them as if they were equal.
> —FROUDE, *Party Politics*

We hold these truths to be self-evident: that all men are
created equal; that they are endowed by their Creator
with inalienable rights; that among these are life, liberty
and the pursuit of happiness.
> —JEFFERSON

Error

To stumble twice against the same stone is a proverbial
disgrace.
> —CICERO

To err is human, to forgive divine.
> —POPE, *An Essay on
> Criticism*

The cautious seldom err.
>—CONFUCIUS

An error gracefully acknowledged is a victory won.
>—CAROLINE L.
>GASCOIGNE

When every one is in the wrong, every one is in the right.
>—LA CHAUSSÉE

The man who makes no mistakes does not usually make anything.
>—EDWARD J. PHELPS,
>Speech at Mansion
>House

Error will slip through a crack, while truth will stick in a doorway.
>—H. W. SHAW

Evening

The curfew tolls the knell of parting day,
The lowing herd winds slowly o'er the lea,
The ploughman homeward plods his weary way,
    And leaves the world to darkness and to me.
>—GRAY, *Elegy in a*
>*Country Churchyard*

One by one the flowers close,
Lily and dewy rose
Shutting their tender petals from the moon.
>—CHRISTINA G. ROSSETTI,
>*Twilight Calm*

Day hath put on his jacket, and around
His burning bosom buttoned it with stars.
>—HOLMES, *Evening*

Events

Coming events cast their shadows before.
—CAMPBELL

Events of great consequence often spring from trifling circumstances.
—LIVY

Evidence

One eye-witness is of more weight than ten hearsays.
—PLAUTUS

Facts are stubborn things.
—SMOLLETT

Some circumstantial evidence is very strong, as when you find a trout in the milk.
—THOREAU

Evil

Evil events from evil causes spring.
—ARISTOPHANES

Evil and good are God's right hand and left.
—BAILEY, *Prelude to Festus*

Touch not; taste not; handle not.
—COLOSSIANS. II. 21

Evil communications corrupt good manners.
—I CORINTHIANS. XV. 33

Woe unto them that call evil good, and good evil.
—ISAIAH. V. 20

Of two evils choose the least.
—ERASMUS

What is evil?—Whatever springs from weakness.
—NIETZSCHE, *The*
Antichrist

Never throw mud. You may miss your mark; but you must have dirty hands.
—JOSEPH PARKER

Be not overcome of evil, but overcome evil with good.
—ROMANS. XII. 21

Evil often triumphs, but never conquers.
—JOSEPH ROUX

The evil that men do lives after them;
The good is oft interred with their bones.
—SHAKESPEARE, *Julius*
Caesar Act III. Sc.2

As sure as God is good, so surely there is no such thing as necessary evil.
—SOUTHEY

Evolution

There is no more reason to believe that man descended from some inferior animal than there is to believe that a stately mansion has descended from a small cottage.
—W. J. BRYAN, 1925

Some call it Evolution,
And others call it God.

—W. H. CARRUTH, *Each in*
His Own Tongue

When you were a tadpole and I was a fish in the Palaozoic
      time
And side by side in the sluggish tide, we sprawled in the
ooze and slime.

—LANGDON SMITH,
Evolution

Example

Lives of great men all remind us
      We can make our lives sublime,
And, departing, leave behind us
      Footprints on the sands of time.

—LONGFELLOW, A *Psalm
of Life*

None preaches better than the ant, and she says nothing.
—FRANKLIN

Example is more efficacious than precept.
—SAMUEL JOHNSON

Children have more need of models than of critics.
—JOUBERT

Excellence

Excellent things are rare.
—PLATO, *The Republic*

If a man has good corn, or wood, or boards, or pigs to
sell, or can make better chairs or knives, crucibles, or
church organs, than anybody else, you will find a broad,
hardbeaten road to his house, though it be in the woods.
—EMERSON, *Journal*, 1855

Excuse

An excuse is worse and more terrible than a lie; for an excuse is a lie guarded.

—POPE

And oftentimes, excusing of a fault
Doth make the fault the worse by the excuse,—
As patches, set upon a little breach,
Discredit more in hiding of the fault
Than did the fault before it was so patched.

—SHAKESPEARE, *King John.*
Act IV. Sc. 2

Expectation

Everything comes if a man will only wait.

—DISRAELI, *Tancred*

Blessed are those that nought expect,
For they shall not be disappointed.

—WALCOT, *Ode to Pitt*

I have known him (Micawber) come home to supper with a flood of tears, and a declaration that nothing was now left but a jail; and go to bed making a calculation of the expense of putting bow-windows to the house, "in case anything turned up," which was his favorite expression.

—DICKENS, *David
Copperfield*

Experience

Experience is the best of schoolmasters, only the school-fees are heavy.

—CARLYLE, *Miscellaneous
Essays*

A burnt child dreads the fire.
>—ENGLISH PROVERB

Experience is the extract of suffering.
>—ARTHUR HELPS

I have but one lamp by which my feet are guided, and that is the lamp of experience.
>—PATRICK HENRY

One thorn of experience is worth a whole wilderness of warning.
>—LOWELL, *Among My Books*

Experience is the name men give to their follies or their sorrows.
>—ALFRED DE MUSSET

Men are wise in proportion, not to their experience, but to their capacity for experience.
>—GEORGE BERNARD SHAW, *Maxims for Revolutionists*

Is there anyone so wise as to learn by the experience of others?
>—VOLTAIRE

Expert

An expert is one who knows more and more about less and less.
>—NICHOLAS MURRAY BUTLER

The shoemaker makes a good shoe because he makes nothing else.

—EMERSON, *Letters and Social Aims*

Eye

A gray eye is a sly eye,
    And roguish is a brown one;
Turn full upon me thy eye,—
    Ah, how its wavelets drown one!

A blue eye is a true eye;
    Mysterious is a dark one,
Which flashes like a sparksun!
    A black eye is the best one.

—W. R. ALGER, *Oriental Poetry*

Among the blind the one-eyed man is king.
—ANONYMOUS

The mind has a thousand eyes,
    And the heart but one;
Yet the light of a whole life dies
    When love is done.

—F. W. BOURDILLON, *Light*

The love light in her eye.
—HARTLEY COLERIDGE

In the twinkling of an eye.
—I CORINTHIANS. XV. 52.

He kept him as the apple of his eye.
—DEUTERONOMY. XXXII. 10

The eyes believe themselves; the ears believe other people.
>—GERMAN PROVERB

Drink to me only with thine eyes,
And I will pledge with mine.
>—BEN JONSON

Face

He had a face like a benediction.
>—CERVANTES

Was this the face that launch'd a thousand ships,
And burnt the topless towers of Ilium?
Sweet Helen, make me immortal with a kiss.—
Her lips suck forth my soul; see, where it flies!—
>—MARLOWE, *Dr. Faustus*

A cheerful face is nearly as good for an invalid as healthy weather.
>—FRANKLIN

The worst of faces still is human.
>—LAVATER

"What is your fortune, my pretty maid?"
"My face is my fortune, sir," she said.
>—NURSERY RHYME

Lift thou up the light of thy countenance upon us.
>—PSALMS. IV. 6

A countenance more in sorrow than in anger.
>—SHAKESPEARE, *Hamlet.*
Act I. Sc. 2

God has given you one face, and you make yourselves
another.

—SHAKESPEARE, *Hamlet*.
Act III. Sc. 1

Facts

I grow daily to honor facts more and more, and theory
less and less.

—CARLYLE

There are no eternal facts, as there are no absolute truths.

—NIETZSCHE, *Human, All-
too-Human*

Every fact that is learned becomes a key to other facts.

—E. I. YOUMANS

Facts are stubborn things.

—SMOLLETT

Failure

In the lexicon of youth, which
Fate reserves for a bright manhood, there is no such word
As—*fail*!

—BULWER-LYTTON,
Richelieu

But to him who tries and fails and dies,
I give great honor and glory and tears.

—JOAQUIN MILLER, *For
Those Who Fail*

How are the mighty fallen!

—II SAMUEL. I. 25

Here's to the men who lose!
    What though their work be e'er so nobly plann'd
And watched with zealous care;
    No glorious halo crowns their efforts grand—
Contempt is Failure's share!

> —G. L. SCARBOROUGH, *To the Vanquished*

Failure is more frequently from want of energy than want of capital.

> —DANIEL WEBSTER

Fairies

Nothing can be truer than fairy wisdom. It is as true as sunbeams.

> —DOUGLAS JERROLD

When the first baby laughed for the first time, the laugh broke into a million pieces, and they all went skipping about. That was the beginning of fairies.

> —BARRIE, *Peter Pan*

Fairies, black, grey, green, and white,
You moonshine revellers, and shades of night.

> —SHAKESPEARE, *Merry Wives of Windsor.* Act V. Sc. 5

Fair Play

Thou shouldst not decide until thou hast heard what both have to say.

> —ARISTOPHANES, *The Wasps*

All is fair in love and war.
>—ENGLISH PROVERB

What is sauce for the goose is sauce for the gander.
>—ENGLISH PROVERB

Faith

Faith is the continuation of reason.
>—WILLIAM ADAMS

Faith is to believe what we do not see; and the reward of this faith is to see what we believe.
>—ST. AUGUSTINE

We walk by faith, not by sight.
>—II CORINTHIANS. V. 7

An outward and visible sign of an inward and spiritual grace.
>—BOOK OF COMMON
>PRAYER

All I have seen teaches me to trust the Creator for all I have not seen.
>—EMERSON

Faith is the substance of things hoped for, the evidence of things not seen.
>—HEBREWS, XI. 1

Let us have faith that right makes might; and in that faith, let us, to the end, dare to do our duty as we understand it.
>—LINCOLN

Here I stand. I can do no otherwise. God help me. Amen.
>—LUTHER at Diet of Worms

There lives more faith in honest doubt,
Believe me, than in half the creeds.
—TENNYSON

I have fought a good fight, I have finished my course, I have kept the faith.
—II TIMOTHY. IV. 7

Faith is the force of life.
—TOLSTOY

I can believe anything, provided it is incredible.
—WILDE, *The Picture of Dorian Gray*

Falsehood

There is no such thing as white lies; a lie is as black as a coalpit, and twice as foul.
—HENRY WARD BEECHER

Round numbers are always false.
—SAMUEL JOHNSON

False in one thing, false in everything
—Law Maxim

Falsehoods not only disagree with truths, but usually quarrel among themselves.
—DANIEL WEBSTER

Fame

I awoke one morning and found myself famous.
—BYRON, From Moore's *Life of Byron*

To many fame comes too late.
—CAMOENS

If you would not be forgotten as soon as you are dead, either write things worth reading or do things worth writing.
—FRANKLIN

Men think highly of those who rise rapidly in the world; whereas nothing rises quicker than dust, straw, and feathers.
—HARE

Fame is the perfume of heroic deeds.
—SOCRATES

Fame is but the breath of the people, and that often unwholesome.
—ROUSSEAU

No true and permanent Fame can be founded except in labors which promote the happiness of mankind.
—CHARLES SUMNER, *Fame and Glory*

What a heavy burden is a name that has become too famous.
—VOLTAIRE

In fame's temple there is always a niche to be found for rich dunces, importunate scoundrels, or successful butchers of the human race.
—ZIMMERMANN

Familiarity

Familiarity breeds contempt.
—ANONYMOUS

Though familiarity may not breed contempt, it takes off the edge of admiration.

—HAZLITT

The living together for three long, rainy days in the country has done more to dispel love than all the perfidies in love that have ever been committed.

—ARTHUR HELPS

Familiarity is a magician that is cruel to beauty, but kind to ugliness.

—OUIDA

Family

The happiest moments of my life have been the few which I have passed at home in the bosom of my family.

—JEFFERSON

There is little less trouble in governing a private family than a whole kingdom.

—MONTAIGNE

None but a mule denies his family.

—MOROCCAN PROVERB

The family is more sacred than the state.

—POPE PIUS XI

Farewell

Fare thee well! and if for ever,
Still for ever, fare thee well.

—BYRON, *Fare Thee Well*

Sweets to the sweet; farewell!
> —SHAKESPEARE, *Hamlet.*
> Act V. Sc. 1

Farming

A farmer is always going to be rich next year.
> —PHILEMON

Farming is a most senseless pursuit, a mere laboring in a circle. You sow that you may reap, and then you reap that you may sow. Nothing ever comes of it.
> —STOBAEUS

Some people tell us that there ain't no Hell,
But they never farmed, so how can they tell?
> —ANONYMOUS

Those who labor in the earth are the chosen people of God, if He ever had a chosen people, whose breasts He has made His peculiar deposit for substantial and genuine virtue.
> —JEFFERSON, *Notes on Virginia*

The farmer works the soil,
The agriculturist works the farmer.
> —EUGENE F. WARE, *The Kansas Bandit*

Let us never forget that the cultivation of the earth is the most important labor of man. When tillage begins, other arts follow. The farmers, therefore, are the founders of civilization.
> —DANIEL WEBSTER

Fashion

The fashion of this world passeth away.
—I CORINTHIANS. VII. 31

A fashionable woman is always in love—with herself.
—LA ROCHEFOUCAULD

I see that the fashion wears out more apparel than the man.
—SHAKESPEARE, *Much Ado About Nothing*. Act III. Sc. 3

Fashion is a form of ugliness so intolerable that we have to alter it every six months.
—WILDE

Fate

The bow is bent, the arrow flies,
The winged shaft of fate.
—IRA ALDRIDGE, *On William Tell*

He has gone to the demnition bow-wows.
—DICKENS, *Nicholas Nickleby*

'Tis Fate that flings the dice,
    And as she flings
Of kings makes peasants,
    And of peasants kings.
—DRYDEN

Thou must (in commanding and winning, or serving and losing, suffering or triumphing) be either anvil or hammer.

—GOETHE

We make our fortunes and we call them fate.
—DISRAELI

Though men determine, the gods do dispose: and oft times many things fall out between the cup and the lip.
—ROBERT GREENE

The Moving Finger writes; and having writ,
Moves on; nor all your Piety nor Wit
Shall lure it back to cancel half a Line,
Nor all your Tears wash out a Word of it.
—OMAR KAYYÁM, *Rubaiyat*

The die is cast.

—SUETONIUS, —
*Exclamation of Caesar
as he crossed the
Rubicon.*

Father

The fathers have eaten sour grapes, and the children's teeth are set on edge.
—JEREMIAH. XXXI. 29

Call no man your father upon the earth: for one is your Father, which is in heaven.
—MATTHEW. XXIII. 9

It is a wise father that knows his own child.
—SHAKESPEARE, *The
Merchant of Venice.*
Act II. Sc. 2

A father is a banker provided by nature.
—FRENCH PROVERB

The child is father of the man.
—WORDSWORTH

Fault

There is so much good in the worst of us,
And so much bad in the best of us,
That it ill behooves any of us
To find fault with the rest of us.
—ANONYMOUS

The greatest of faults, I should say, is to be conscious of none.

—CARLYLE, *Heroes and Hero-Worship*

The defects of great men are the consolation of the dunces.
—ISAAC D'ISRAELI

We keep on deceiving ourselves in regard to our faults, until we at last come to look upon them as virtues.
—HEINE

Fear

Freedom from fear and injustice and oppression will be ours only in the measure that men who value such freedom are ready to sustain its possession—to defend it against every thrust from within or without.
—DWIGHT D.
EISENHOWER,
Crusade in Europe

Fear always springs from ignorance.
> —EMERSON, *The American
> Scholar*

The only thing we have to fear is fear itself.
> —F. D. ROOSEVELT,
> Inaugural Address,
> 1933

The fear of the Lord is the beginning of knowledge.
> —PROVERBS. I. 7

Festivities

Why should we break up
>Our snug and pleasant party?
Time was made for slaves,
>But never for us so hearty.
>> —JOHN B. BUCKSTONE,
>> *Billy Taylor*

Let us have wine and woman, mirth and laughter.
Sermons and soda-water the day after.
> —BYRON, *Don Juan*

Then I commended mirth, because a man hath no better
thing under the sun, than to eat, and to drink, and to be
merry.
> —ECCLESIASTES. VIII. 15

The feast of reason, and the flow of soul.
> —POPE, *Book of Horace*

Feast, and your halls are crowded;
Fast, and the world goes by.
> —ELLA WHEELER WILCOX,
> *Solitude*

Fire

Your own property is concerned when your neighbor's house is on fire.

—HORACE

The burnt child dreads the fire.

—BEN JONSON, *The Devil Is an Ass*

There can no great smoke arise, but there must be some fire.

—LYLY

All the fat's in the fire.

—MARSTON, *What You Will*

Fish

As lacking in privacy as a goldfish.

—ANONYMOUS

She is neither fish, nor flesh, nor good red herring.

—HEYWOOD, *Proverbs*

Master, I marvel how the fishes live in the sea.
Why, as men do a-land: the great ones eat up the little ones.

—PERICLES

We have here other fish to fry.

—RABELAIS, *Works*

Fishing

When the wind is in the East,
Then the fishes bite the least;
When the wind is in the West,
Then the fishes bite the best;
When the wind is in the North,
Then the fishes do come forth;
When the wind is in the South,
It blows the bait in the fish's mouth.
— ANONYMOUS

There are as good fish in the sea as ever came out of it.
— ENGLISH PROVERB

To fish in troubled waters.
— MATTHEW HENRY,
Commentaries. Psalm
LX

You must lose a fly to catch a trout.
— HERBERT, *Jacula
Prudentum*

A fishing-rod was a stick with a hook at one end and a fool at the other.
— SAMUEL JOHNSON

Angling may be said to be so like the mathematics that it can never be fully learnt.
— IZAAK WALTON, *The
Compleat Angler*

We may say of angling as Dr. Boteler said of strawberries: "Doubtless God could have made a better berry, but doubtless God never did"; and so, (if I might be judge,)

God never did make a more calm, quiet, innocent recreation than angling.

> —IZAAK WALTON, *The*
> *Compleat Angler*

Angling is an innocent cruelty.
> —GEORGE PARKER

Flag

If any one attempts to haul down the American flag, shoot him on the spot.

> —JOHN A. DIX, *Speeches*
> *and Addresses*

When Freedom from her mountain height
    Unfurled her standard to the air,
She tore the azure robe of night,
    And set the stars of glory there.
> —JOSEPH RODMAN DRAKE,
> *The American Flag*

Cheers for the sailors that fought on the wave for it,
Cheers for the soldiers that always were brave for it,
Tears for the men that went down to the grave for it,
Here comes the Flag!
> —ARTHUR MACY, *The Flag*

The flag of our Union forever!
> —GEORGE P. MORRIS, *The*
> *Flag of Our Union*

Oh! say can you see by the dawn's early light
What so proudly we hail'd at the twilight's last gleaming,
Whose broad stripes and bright stars, thro' the perilous
    fight,

O'er the ramparts we watch'd, were so gallantly stream-
    ing;
And the rocket's red glare, the bombs bursting in air,
Gave proof thro' the night that our flag was still there!

CHORUS

Oh! say, does that star-spangled banner yet wave,
O'er the land of the free and the home of the brave.
                        —FRANCIS SCOTT KEY, *The
                        Star-Spangled Banner*

I pledge allegiance to the flag of the United States and
to the republic for which it stands, one nation, indivisible,
with liberty and justice for all.
                        —*The Pledge of Allegiance
                        to the Flag*

Yes, we'll rally round the flag, boys, we'll rally once
    again,
        Shouting the battle-cry of Freedom,
We will rally from the hillside, we'll gather from the
    plain,
        Shouting the battle-cry of Freedom.
                        —GEORGE F. ROOT, *Battle
                        Cry of Freedom*

Your flag and my flag,
        And how it flies today
In your land and my land
        And half a world away!
Rose-red and blood-reed
        The stripes forever gleam;
Snow-white and soul-white—
        The good forefathers' dream;
Sky-blue and true-blue, with stars to gleam aright—
        The gloried guidon of the day, a shelter through
        the night.
                        —WILBUR D. NESBIT, *Your
                        Flag and My Flag*

"Shoot, if you must, this old gray head,
But spare your country's flag," she said.
—WHITTIER, *Barbara
Fritchie*

Flattery

Imitation is the sincerest (form) of flattery.
—COLTON, *Lacon*

Men are like stone jugs—you may lug them where you
like by the ears.
—SAMUEL JOHNSON

A man that flattereth his neighbor spreadeth a net for
his feet.
—PROVERBS. XXIX. 5

O, that men's ears should be
To counsel deaf, but not to flattery!
—SHAKESPEARE, *Timon of
Athens*. Act I. Sc. 2

Their throat is an open sepulchre; they flatter with their
tongue.
—PSALMS. V. 9

It is easy to flatter; it is harder to praise.
—JEAN PAUL RICHTER

Flea

Great fleas have little fleas upon their backs to bite 'em,
And little fleas have lesser fleas, and so ad infinitum.
And the great fleas themselves, in turn, have greater fleas
to go on;

While these again have greater still, and greater still, and
    so on.

—AUGUSTUS DE MORGAN,
    A Budget of Paradoxes

I do honour the very flea of his dog.

—BEN JONSON, *Every Man
    in His Humour*

Flirtation

Flirtation, attention without intention.

—MAX O'RELL, *John Bull
    and His Island*

Men seldom make passes
At girls who wear glasses.

—DOROTHY PARKER

It is the same in love as in war; a fortress that parleys is
half taken.

—MARGUERITE DE VALOIS

Flowers

Flowers may beckon towards us, but they speak toward
heaven and God.

—HENRY WARD BEECHER

Flowers are words
Which even a babe may understand.

—BISHOP COXE, *The
    Singing of Birds*

But ne'er the rose without the thorn.

—HERRICK, *The Rose*

I remember, I remember
    The roses, red and white,
The violets, and the lily-cups,
    Those flowers made of light!
The lilacs, where the robin built,
    And where my brother set
The laburnum on his birthday,—
    The tree is living yet.

            —HOOD, *I Remember, I*
                  Remember

And I will make thee beds of roses,
And a thousand fragrant posies.

            —MARLOWE, *The*
                Passionate Shepherd to
                His Love

Consider the lilies of the field, how they grow; they toil
not, neither do they spin.

            —MATTHEW. VI. 28

Flowers of all hue, and without thorn the rose.

            —MILTON, *Paradise Lost*

In Flanders' fields the poppies blow
    Between the crosses, row on row,
That mark our place, and in the sky,
    The larks, still bravely singing, fly
Scarce heard among the guns below.

            —JOHN MCCRAE, *In*
                Flanders' Fields

'Tis the last rose of summer.
Left blooming alone.

            —MOORE, *Last Rose of*
                Summer

Where flowers degenerate man cannot live.
            —NAPOLEON

"Of what are you afraid, my child?" inquired the kindly
teacher.
"Oh, sir! the flowers, they are wild," replied the timid
creature.

—PETER NEWELL, *Wild
Flowers.*

If of thy mortal goods thou art bereft,
And from thy slender store two loaves alone to thee are
left,
Sell one, and with the dole
Buy hyacinths to feed thy soul.

—SADI, *Gulistan*

Say it with flowers.

—PATRICK F. O'KEEFE,
Slogan for the Society
of American Florists

I sometimes think that never blows so red
The Rose as where some buried Caesar bled;
That every Hyacinth the Garden wears
Dropt in her Lap from some once lovely Head.

—OMAR KHAYYÁM,
Rubaiyat

One thing is certain and the rest is lies;
The Flower that once has blown for ever dies.

—OMAR KHAYYÁM,
Rubaiyat

When lilacs last in the dooryard bloom'd,
And the great star early droop'd in the western sky the
night,
I mourn'd—and yet shall mourn with ever-returning
spring.

—WALT WHITMAN

Let us crown ourselves with rosebuds before they be
  withered.
> —WISDOM OF SOLOMON.
> II. 8

Fly

It is easier to catch flies with honey than with vinegar.
> —ENGLISH PROVERB

A fly sat on the chariot wheel
And said "What a dust I raise."
> —LA FONTAINE

Baby bye
Here's a fly,
Let us watch him, you and I.
  How he crawls
  Up the walls
  Yet he never falls.

> —THEODORE TILTON,
> *Baby Bye*

Folly

The folly of one man is the fortune of another.
> —BACON, *Of Fortune*

He who lives without committing any folly is not so wise
as he thinks.
> —LA ROCHEFOUCAULD

Answer a fool according to his folly.
> —PROVERBS. XXVI. 5

To swallow gudgeons ere they're catch'd
And count their chickens ere they're hatch'd.
— BUTLER, *Hudibras*

To stumble twice against the same stone, is a proverbial disgrace.
— CICERO, *Epistles*

Fools

A fool always finds one still more foolish to admire him.
— BOILEAU

You men think old men are fools; but old men know young men are the fools.
— GEORGE CHAPMAN, *All Fools*

Hain't we got all the fools in town on our side? And ain't that a big enough majority in any town?
— S. L. CLEMENS (MARK TWAIN), *Huckleberry Finn*

A fool and his money are soon parted.
— ENGLISH PROVERB

The fool hath said in his heart, There is no God.
— PSALMS. XIV. 1

A learned fool is more foolish than an ignorant fool.
— MOLIÈRE

For fools rush in where angels fear to tread.
— POPE, *Essay on Criticism*

Even a fool, when he holdeth his peace, is counted wise.
— PROVERBS. XVII. 28

The right to be a cussed fool
 Is safe from all devices human,
It's common (ez a gin'l rule)
 To every critter born of woman.
     —LOWELL, *The Biglow*
       Papers

It is in the half fools and the half wise that the greatest
danger lies.
     —GOETHE

If you wish to avoid seeing a fool you must first break
your looking-glass.
     —RABELAIS

The fool doth think he is wise, but the wise man knows
himself to be a fool.
     —SHAKESPEARE, *As You*
      Like It. Act V. Sc. 1

A fool's bolt is soon shot.
     —SHAKESPEARE, *Henry V.*
      Act III. Sc. 7

Lord, what fools these mortals be!
     —SHAKESPEARE,
      Midsummer Night's
      Dream. Act II. Sc.2

He who thinks himself wise, O heavens! is a great fool.
     —VOLTAIRE

Force

The power that is supported by force alone will have
cause often to tremble.
     —KOSSUTH

Force is all-conquering, but its victories are short-lived.
—LINCOLN

Force and not opinion is the queen of the world; but it is opinion that uses the force.
—PASCAL

Foresight

In life, as in chess, forethought wins.
—CHARLES BUXTON

If a man take no thought about what is distant, he will find sorrow near at hand.
—CONFUCIUS

Forethought we may have, undoubtedly, but not foresight.
—NAPOLEON

Look ere thou leap, see ere thou go.
—TUSSER

Forgetfulness

I am forgotten as a dead man out of mind: I am like a broken vessel.
—PSALMS. XXI. 12

And when he is out of sight, quickly also he is out of mind.
—THOMAS À KEMPIS

God of our fathers, known of old,
    Lord of our far-flung battleline,

Beneath whose awful Hand we hold
    Dominion over palm and pine—
Lord God of Hosts, be with us yet,
    Lest we forget—lest we forget!

The tumult and the shouting dies,
    The captains and the kings depart;
Still stands thine ancient sacrifice,
    A humble and a contrite heart.
Lord God of Hosts, be with us yet,
    Lest we forget—lest we forget.
              —KIPLING, *Recessional*
                     Hymn

The world forgetting, by the world forgot.
              —POPE, *Eloisa to Abélard*

There is no remembrance which time does not obliterate,
nor pain which death does not terminate.
              —CERVANTES

If I forget thee, O Jerusalem, let my right hand forget
her cunning.
              —PSALMS. CXXXVII. 5

Who is the Forgotten Man? He is the clean, quiet, virtuous, domestic citizen, who pays his debts and his taxes
and is never heard of out of his little circle.
              —WILLIAM GRAHAM
                  SUMNER, *The*
                  Forgotten Man

Forgiveness

God pardons like a mother, who kisses the offense into
everlasting forgetfulness.
              —HENRY WARD BEECHER

Good, to forgive;
Best, to forget.

—BROWNING, *La Saisiaz*

It is easier to forgive an enemy than a friend.
—MME. DOROTHEE
DELUZY

His heart was as great as the world, but there was no room in it to hold the memory of a wrong.
—EMERSON, *Letters and
Social Aims*

Bear and forbear.

—EPICTETUS

Forgive us our trespasses, as we forgive them that trespass against us.
—MATTHEW. VI. 12 (The
Lord's Prayer)

To err is human, to forgive, divine.
—POPE, *Essay on Criticism*

Forgive others often, yourself never.
—SYRUS

It is manlike to punish but godlike to forgive.
—PETER VON WINTER

Fortune

Fortune makes him fool, whom she makes her darling.
—BACON

It is fortune, not wisdom, that rules man's life.
—CICERO

Fortune truly helps those who are of good judgment.
—EURIPEDES

The bitter dregs of Fortune's cup to drain.
—HOMER, *Iliad*

Fortunes made in no time are like shirts made in no time;
it's ten to one if they hang long together.
—DOUGLAS JERROLD

Men are seldom blessed with good fortune and good sense
at the same time.
—LIVY

Fortune and Love befriend the bold.
—OVID

Every man is the architect of his own fortune.
—SALLUST

O fortune, fortune! all men call thee fickle.
—SHAKESPEARE, *Romeo
and Juliet*. Act 3. Sc.
5

There is a tide in the affairs of men
Which, taken at the flood, leads on to fortune.
—SHAKESPEARE, *Julius
Caesar*. Act 4. Sc. 3

Fox

A sleeping fox counts hens in his dreams.
—RUSSIAN PROVERB

The little foxes, that spoil the vines.
—SONG OF SOLOMON. IV.
15

Frailty

Frailty, thy name is woman!

—SHAKESPEARE, *Hamlet*.
Act. 1. Sc. 2

An amiable weakness.

—R. B. SHERIDAN, *The
School for Scandal*

France

Forty million Frenchmen can't be wrong.

—ANONYMOUS

France, freed from that monster, Bonaparte, must again
become the most agreeable country on earth. It would
be the second choice of all whose ties of family and fortune give a preference to some other one, and the first
choice of all not under those ties.

—JEFFERSON, 1814

Ye sons of France, awake to glory!
　　Hark! Hark! what myriads bid you rise!
Your children, wives and grandsires hoary,
　　Behold their tears and hear their cries!

—ROUCET DE LISLE, *The
Marseilles Hymn*

France always has plenty men of talent, but it is always
deficient in men of action and high character.

—NAPOLEON

Freedom

The cause of freedom is the cause of God.

—SAMUEL BOWLES

Personal liberty is the paramount essential to human dignity and human happiness.

—BULWER-LYTTON

Hereditary boundsmen! Know ye not
Who would be free themselves must strike the blow?

—BYRON, *Childe Harold*

And Freedom shrieked as Kosciusko fell!

—CAMPBELL, *Pleasures of
Hope*

In a free country there is much clamor, with little suffering; in a despotic state there is little complaint, with much grievance.

—CARNOT

For what avail the plough or sail,
Or land, or life, if freedom fail?

—EMERSON, *Boston*

Ay, call it holy ground,
    The soil where first they trod;
They have left unstained, what there they found,—
    Freedom to worship God.

—FELICIA D. HEMANS,
        *Landing of the Pilgrim
        Fathers*

In the beauty of the lilies Christ was born across the sea,
With a glory in His bosom that transfigures you and me;
As He died to make men holy, let us die to make men free,
    While God is marching on.

—JULIA WARD HOWE,
        *Battle Hymn of the
        Republic*

I am for freedom of religion and against all maneuvers
to bring about a legal ascendancy of one sect over another.
—JEFFERSON, 1799

And ye shall know the truth, and the truth shall make
you free.
—JOHN. VIII. 32

Those who deny freedom to others deserve it not for
themselves and under a just God cannot long retain it.
—LINCOLN

... That this nation, under God, shall have a new birth
of freedom.
—LINCOLN, *Gettysburg
Address*

Since the general civilization of mankind I believe there
are more instances of the abridgement of the freedom of
the people by gradual and silent encroachments of those
in power than by violent and sudden usurpations.
—MADISON

The only freedom which deserves the name is that of
pursuing our own good in our own way, so long as we
do not attempt to deprive others of theirs or impede their
efforts to obtain it.
—JOHN STUART MILL

We must be free or die, who speak the tongue
That Shakespeare spake; the faith and morals hold
Which Milton held.
—WORDSWORTH

No amount of political freedom will satisfy the hungry
masses.
—LENIN, Speech, 1917

I would rather sit on a pumpkin, and have it all to myself, than to be crowded on a velvet cushion.

—THOREAU, *Walden*

Friends

Prosperity makes friends and adversity tries them.

—ANONYMOUS

A friend is one who dislikes the same people that you dislike.

—ANONYMOUS

A true friend is one soul in two bodies.

—ARISTOTLE

Chance makes our parents, but choice makes our friends.

—DELILLE

The best way to keep your friends is to never owe them anything and never lend them anything.

—PAUL DE KOCK

Forsake not an old friend, for the new is not comparable unto him. A new friend is as new wine: when it is old thou shalt drink it with pleasure.

—ECCLESIASTES, IX. 10

The only way to have a friend is to be one.

—EMERSON, *Of Friendship*

Animals are such agreeable friends—they ask no questions, they pass no criticisms.

—GEORGE ELIOT, *Mr. Gilfil's Love-Story*

If you have a friend worth loving,
    Love him. Yes, and let him know
That you love him, ere life's evening
    Tinge his brow with sunset glow.
Why should good words ne'er be said
    Of a friend till he is dead?
                —DANIEL W. HOYT, A
                   Sermon in Rhyme

I desire so to conduct the affairs of this administration
that if at the end, when I come to lay down the reins of
power, I have lost every other friend on earth, I shall at
least have one friend left, and that friend shall be down
inside of me.
                —LINCOLN, Reply to
                    Missouri Committee
                    of Seventy (1864)

Friends are like melons. Shall I tell you why?
To find one good, you must a hundred try.
                —CLAUDE MERMET

A man that hath friends must show himself friendly; and
there is a friend that sticketh closer than a brother.
                —PROVERBS. XVIII. 24

A friend in need is a friend indeed.
                —ENGLISH PROVERB

There are three faithful friends: an old wife, an old dog,
and ready money.
                —FRANKLIN

I am wealthy in my friends.
                —SHAKESPEARE, *Timon of*
                Athens. Act II. Sc. 2

A friend must not be injured, even in jest.

—SYRUS

Reprove your friends in secret, praise them openly.

—SYRUS

God same me from my friends, I can protect myself from my enemies.

—MARSHAL DE VILLARS

Friendship

Should auld acquaintances be forgot,
        And never brought to mind?
Should auld acquaintance be forgot,
        And days o'auld lang syne?

—BURNS, *Auld Lang Syne*

Friendship, peculiar boon of Heaven,
        The noble mind's delight and pride,
To men and angels only given,
        To all the lower world denied.

—SAMUEL JOHNSON,
Friendship

What is thine is mine, and all mine is thine.

—PLAUTUS

Saul and Jonathan were lovely and pleasant in their lives, and in their death they were not divided.

—II SAMUEL. I. 23

Madam, I have been looking for a person who disliked gravy all my life; let us swear eternal friendship.

—SYDNEY SMITH, *Lady
Holland's Memoir*

Be slow to fall into friendship, but when thou art in continue firm and constant.

—SOCRATES

True friendship is a plant of slow growth and must undergo and withstand the shocks of adversity before it is entitled to the appellation.

—WASHINGTON, Letter,
1783

Fruit

By their fruits ye shall know them.

—MATTHEW. VII. 20

The ripest fruit first falls.

—SHAKESPEARE, Richard II.
Act II. Sc. 1

Future

When all else is lost, the future still remains.

—BOVEE

'Tis the sunset of life gives me mystical lore,
And coming events cast their shadows before.

—CAMPBELL, Lochiel's
Warning

I never think of the future. It comes soon enough.

—ALBERT EINSTEIN

I know of no way of judging the future but by the past.

—PATRICK HENRY, Speech,
1775

The present is great with the future
—LEIBNITZ

Trust no Future, howe'er pleasant!
  Let the dead Past bury its dead!
—LONGFELLOW, *A Psalm
of Life*

Go forth to meet the shadowy Future without fear and
with a manly heart.
—LONGFELLOW, *Hyperion*

Take therefore no thought for the morrow; for the morrow shall take thought for the things of itself. Sufficient
unto the day is the evil thereof.
—MATTHEW. VI. 34

There was the Door to which I found no key;
There was the Veil through which I might not see.
—OMAR KHAYYÁM,
Rubaiyat

There was a wise man in the East whose constant prayer
was that he might see today with the eyes of tomorrow.
—ALFRED MERCIER

I believe the future is only the past again, entered through
another gate.
—PINERO, *The Second Mrs.
Tanqueray*

After us the deluge.
—MME. DE POMPADOUR

Till the sun grows cold,
And the stars are old,
And the leaves of the Judgment
Book unfold.

—BAYARD TAYLOR,
Bedouin Song

Gambling

The race is not always to the swift nor the battle to the strong—but that's the way to bet.

—ANONYMOUS

There is but one good throw upon the dice, which is to throw them away.

—CHATFIELD

By gaming we lose both our time and treasure—two things most precious to the life of man.

—FELLTHAM

Man is a gaming animal.

—LAMB

Keep flax from fire, youth from gaming.

—FRANKLIN

It [gaming] is the child of avarice, the brother of iniquity, and the father of mischief.

—WASHINGTON

Gardens

A garden is a lovesome thing—God wot!
Rose plot,
Fringed pool,

Fern grot—
The veriest school
Of peace; and yet the fool
Contends that God is not.—
Not God in gardens! When the sun is cool?
Nay, but I have a sign!
'Tis very sure God walks in mine.

> —THOMAS EDWARD
>   BROWN, *My Garden*

God the first garden made, and the first city Cain.

> —COWLEY, *The Garden*

The Lord God planted a garden eastward in Eden; and there he put the man whom he had formed.

> —GENESIS. II. 3

One is nearer God's heart in a garden
Than anywhere else on earth.

> —DOROTHY FRANCES
>   GURNEY, *God's
>   Garden*

Genius

There is no great genius without a mixture of madness.

> —ARISTOTLE

Genius is only great patience.

> —BUFFON

Genius is one per cent inspiration and ninety-nine per cent perspiration.

> —EDISON

Genius does what it must, and talent does what it can.

> —BULWER-LYTTON

Gift, like genius, I often think only means an infinite capacity for taking pains.
—ELLICE HOPKINS, *Work amongst Working Men*

Genius is a promontory jutting out of the infinite.
—VICTOR HUGO, *William Shakespeare*

Three-fifths of him genius and two-fifths sheer fudge.
—LOWELL, *Fable for Critics*

The lamp of genius burns quicker than the lamp of life.
—SCHILLER

The poet's scrolls will outlive the monuments of stone. The Genius survives; all else is claimed by death.
—SPENSER, *Shepherd's Calendar*

Gentleman

A gentleman is man who can disagree without being disagreeable.
—ANONYMOUS

The gentleman is a Christian product.
—GEORGE H. CALVERT

Once a gentleman, always a gentleman.
—DICKENS, *Little Dorrit*

Propriety of manners and consideration for others are the two main characteristics of a gentleman.
—DISRAELI

To make a fine gentleman, several trades are required, but chiefly a barber.
—GOLDSMITH

Germany

Let us put Germany, so to speak, in the saddle! you will see that she can ride.
—BISMARCK, In Parliament
of Confederation
(1867)

We Germans will never produce another Goethe, but we may produce another Caesar.
—OSWALD SPENGLER,
1925

Gift

It is more blessed to give than to receive.
—ACTS. XX. 35

You give but little when you give of your possessions. It is when you give of yourself that you truly give.
—KAHLIL GIBRAN, The
Prophet

I make presents to the mother, but think of the daughter.
—GOETHE

Give an inch, he'll take an ell.
—HOBBES, Liberty and
Necessity

He gives twice who gives quickly.
—PUBLIUS MIMUS

Or what man is there of you, whom if his son ask bread,
will he give him a stone?
— MATTHEW. VII. 9

Rich gifts wax poor when givers prove unkind.
— SHAKESPEARE, *Hamlet*.
Act III. Sc. 1

I fear the Greeks, even when they bring gifts.
— VERGIL, *Aeneid*

Behold, I do not give lectures or a little charity,
When I give I give myself.
— WALT WHITMAN, *Song of
Myself*

Glory

There is one glory of the sun, and another glory of the
moon, and another glory of the stars: for one star differeth
from another star in glory.
— I CORINTHIANS. XV. 41

The paths of glory lead but to the grave.
— GRAY, *Elegy in a
Country Churchyard*

Mine eyes have seen the coming of the glory of the Lord.
— JULIA WARD HOWE,
*Battle Hymn of the
Republic*

O how quickly passes away the glory of the earth.
— THOMAS À KEMPIS,
Imitation of Christ

One crowded hour of glorious life
  Is worth an age without a name.
                              —SCOTT, *Old Mortality*

God

God helps those who help themselves.
                              —ANONYMOUS

Man proposes, and God disposes.
                              —ARIOSTO, *Orlando
                                 Furioso*

God's in His Heaven—
All's right with the world!
                              —BROWNING, *Pippa Passes*

Fear that man who fears not God.
                              —ABD-EL-KADER

Nearer, my God, to Thee—
    Nearer to Thee—
E'en though it be a cross
    That raiseth me;
Still all my song shall be
    Nearer, my God, to Thee,
Nearer to Thee!
                              —SARAH FLOWER ADAMS

I took a day to search for God,
And found Him not. But as I trod
By rocky ledge, through woods untamed,
Just where one scarlet lily flamed,
I saw His foot print in the sod.
                              —BLISS CARMAN, *Vestigia*

A picket frozen on duty—
    A mother starved for her brood—
Socrates drinking the hemlock,
    And Jesus on the rood;
And millions who, humble and nameless,
    The straight, hard pathway trod—
Some call it Consecration,
    And others call it God.
              —W. H. CARRUTH,
                Evolution

God hath chosen the foolish things of the world to confound the wise; and God hath chosen the weak things of the world to confound the things that are mighty.
              —I CORINTHIANS. I. 27

God moves in a mysterious way
    His wonders to perform;
He plants his footsteps in the sea
    And rides upon the storm.
              —COWPER, *Hymn*

God is incorporeal, divine, supreme, infinite Mind, Spirit, Soul, Principle, Life, Truth, Love.
              —MARY BAKER EDDY,
                Science and Health

An honest God is the noblest work of man.
              —INGERSOLL, *The Gods*

"We trust, Sir, that God is on our side." "It is more important to know that we are on God's side."
              —LINCOLN, Reply to
                deputation during
                Civil War

A mighty fortress is our God,
 A bulwark never failing,
Our helper he amid the flood
 Of mortal ills prevailing.
     —LUTHER

Everyone is in a small way the image of God.
     —MANILIUS

What is it: is man only a blunder of God, or God only
a blunder of man?
     —NIETZSCHE, *The Twilight*
      of the Idols

A God-intoxicated man.
     —NOVALIS (of Spinoza)

He mounts the storm, and walks upon the wind.
     —POPE, *Essay on Man*

The heavens declare the glory of God; and the firmament
showeth his handiwork.
     —PSALMS. XIX. 1

He maketh me to lie down in green pastures; he leadeth
me beside the still warm waters.
     —PSALMS. XXIII. 2

God is our refuge and strength, a very present help in
trouble.
     —PSALMS. XLVI. 1

There is no respect of persons with God.
     —ROMANS. II. 11

If God be for us, who can be against us?
                              —ROMANS. VIII. 31

For the greater glory of God.
                              —Motto of the Society of
                              Jesus

The divine essence itself is love and wisdom.
                              —SWEDENBORG

God, the Great Giver, can open the whole universe to
our gaze in the narrow space of a single lane.
                              —TAGORE

Rock of Ages, cleft for me,
    Let me hide myself in thee.
                              —AUGUSTUS TOPLADY,
                              *Living and Dying
                              Prayer*

God tempers the wind to the shorn lamb.
                              —LAURENCE STERNE

If there were no God, it would be necessary to invent
him.
                              —VOLTAIRE

Gods

The Ethiop gods have Ethiop lips,
    Bronze cheeks, and woolly hair;
The Grecian gods are like the Greeks,
    As keen-eyed, cold and fair.
                              —WALTER BAGEHOT,
                              Ignorance of Man

There's a one-eyed yellow idol to the north of Khat-
    mandu,
There's a little marble cross below the town,
There's a broken-hearted woman tends the grave of Mad
    Carew,
And the yellow god forever gazes down.
                            —J. MILTON HAYES, *The
                              Green Eye of the
                              Yellow God*

Yet verily these issues lie on the lap of the gods.
                            —HOMER, *Iliad*

Gold

You shall not press down upon the brow of labor this
crown of thorns—you shall not crucify mankind upon a
cross of gold!
                            —W. J. BRYAN, at
                              Democratic National
                              Convention, 1896

Gold begets in brethren hate;
Gold in families debate;
Gold does friendship separate;
Gold does civil wars create.
                            —COWLEY, *Anacreontics*

Gold! Gold! Gold! Gold!
Bright and yellow, hard and cold,
                            —HOOD, *Miss Kilmansegg*

Accursed thirst for gold! what dost thou not compel mortals to do?
                            —VERGIL, *Aeneid*

Golden Rule

What you do not want others to do to you, do not do to others.

—CONFUCIUS, C. 500 B.C.

What thou thyself hatest, do to no man.

—TOBIT. IV. C. 180 B.C.

Do unto the other feller the way he'd like to do unto you an' do it fust.

—EDWARD N. WESTCOTT,
David Harum

My duty towards my neighbor is to love him as myself, and to do to all men as I would they should do unto me.

—BOOK OF COMMON
PRAYER, 1662

Whatsoever thou wouldst that men should not do to thee, do not do that to them.

—HILLEL HA-BABLI, C. 30
B.C.

As ye would that men should do to you, do ye also to them likewise.

—LUKE. VI. 31, C. 75 A.D.

This is the sum of all true righteousness: deal with others as thou wouldst thyself be dealt by. Do nothing to thy neighbor which thou wouldst not have him do to thee hereafter.

—THE MAHABHARATA, C.
150 B.C

We have committed the Golden Rule to memory; let us now commit it to life.

—EDWIN MARKHAM

All things whatsoever ye wou'd that men should do to you, do ye even so to them: for this is the law and the prophets.

—MATTHEW. VII. 12, C.
75 A.D.

Do not do unto others as you would that they should do unto you. Their tastes may not be the same.

— GEORGE BERNARD
SHAW, 1903

Good-Humor

Good-humor makes all things tolerable.

—HENRY WARD BEECHER

The sunshine of the mind.

—BULWER-LYTTON

Good-humor is goodness and wisdom combined.

— OWEN MEREDITH

Goodness

For the cause that lacks assistance,
The wrong that needs resistance,
For the future in the distance,
    And the good that I can do.

— GEORGE LINNAEUS
BANKS, *What I Live
For*

Happy were men if they but understood
There is no safety but in doing good.

—JOHN FOUNTAIN

Can there any good thing come out of Nazareth?
—JOHN. I. 46

Be good, sweet maid, and let who will be clever;
  Do noble things, not dream them all day long;
And so make life, death, and that vast forever
  One grand, sweet song.

—KINGSLEY, *Farewell*

The crest and crowning of all good,
Life's final star, is Brotherhood.

—EDWIN MARKHAM,
Brotherhood

    Since good, the more
Communicated, more abundant grows.

—MILTON, *Paradise Lost*

A glass is good, and a lass is good.
  And a pipe to smoke in cold weather;
The world is good, and the people are good,
  And we're all good fellows together.

—JOHN O'KEEFFE, *Sprigs of
Laurel*

He that does good for good's sake seeks neither praise
nor reward, though sure of both at last.

—WILLIAM PENN

For the Lord Jesus Christ's sake,
Do all the good you can,
To all the people you can,
In all the ways you can,
As long as ever you can.

—Tombstone Inscription in
Shrewsbury, England

Goose

What is sauce for the goose is sauce for the gander.
—VARRO, quoting Gellius

The goose gabbles amid the melodious swans.
—VERGIL, *Ecologues. IX.*
37

Gossip

He that repeateth a matter separateth very friends.
—PROVERBS. XVII. 9

Let the greater part of the news thou hearest be the least part of what thou believest.
—QUARLES

Foul whisperings are abroad.
—SHAKESPEARE, *Macbeth.*
Act V. Sc. 1

I heard the little bird say so.
—SWIFT, *Letter to Stella*

Tattlers also and busy bodies, speaking things which they ought not.
—I TIMOTHY. V. 13

There is only one thing in the world worse than being talked about, and that is not being talked about.
—WILDE, *The Picture of
Dorian Gray*

Government

The safety of the State is the highest law.
—JUSTINIAN

Experience teaches us to be most on our guard to protect liberty when the government's purposes are beneficent.
—BRANDEIS, Olmstead vs.
U. S., 1928

Government is a contrivance of human wisdom to provide for human wants.
—BURKE

Government is a trust, and the officers of the government are trustees; and both the trust and the trustees are created for the benefit of the people.
—HENRY CLAY, Speech.
1829

Though the people support the government the government should not support the people.
—GROVER CLEVELAND

I think we have more machinery of government than is necessary, too many parasites living on the labor of the industrious.
—JEFFERSON, Letter to
William Ludlow

The will of the people is the only legitimate foundation of any government, and to protect its free expression should be our first object.
—JEFFERSON, 1801

Govern a great nation as you would cook a small fish. (Don't overdo it.)

—LAO-TSZE

No man is good enough to govern another man without that other's consent.

—LINCOLN, Speech, 1854

A house divided against itself cannot stand—I believe this government cannot endure permanently half-slave and half-free.

—LINCOLN, Speech, June 17, 1858

The state!—it is I!

—Attributed to Louis XIV of France

Every nation has the government that it deserves.

—JOSEPH DE MAISTRE, Letter, 1811

Democracy is direct self-government, over all the people, for all the people, by all the people.

—THEODORE PARKER, Music Hall, Boston, July 4, 1858

Governments exist to protect the rights of minorities. The loved and the rich need no protection,—they have many friends and few enemies.

—WENDELL PHILLIPS

No man undertakes a trade he has not learned, even the meanest; yet every one thinks himself sufficiently qualified for the hardest of all trades—that of government.

—SOCRATES

It seems to me that government is like a pump, and what it pumps up is just what we are, a fair sample of the intellect, the ethics and the morals of the people, no better, no worse.

—ADLAI STEVENSON,
Speech, September
11, 1952.

Themistocles said, "The Athenians govern the Greeks; I govern the Athenians; you, my wife, govern me; your son governs you."

—PLUTARCH

The basis of our political systems is the right of the people to make and to alter their constitutions of government.

—WASHINGTON, Farewell
Address, 1796

Grace

An outward and visible sign of an inward and spiritual grace.

—BOOK OF COMMON
PRAYER

There, but for the grace of God, goes John Bradford.

—JOHN BRADFORD, on
seeing a condemned
man.

Ye are fallen from grace.

—GALATIANS. V. 4

He does it with a better grace, but I do it more natural.

—SHAKESPEARE, *Twelfth
Night*. Act II. Sc. 3

Gratitude

Gratitude is the heart's memory.
>—FRENCH PROVERB

The gratitude of most men is but a secret desire of receiving greater benefits.
>—LA ROCHEFOUCAULD

He who receives a good turn should never forget it; he who does one should never remember it.
>—CHARRON

Gratitude is a duty which ought to be paid, but which none have a right to expect.
>—ROUSSEAU

Grave

I would rather sleep in the southern corner of a little country churchyard, than in the tombs of the Capulets.
>—BURKE, Letter to Matthew
>Smith

O death, where is thy sting?
O grave, where is thy victory?
>—I CORINTHIANS. XV. 55

Some village Hampden, that, with dauntless breast,
>The little tyrant of his fields withstood,
Some mute inglorious Milton here may rest,
>Some Cromwell guiltless of his country's blood.
>—GRAY, Elegy in a
>Country Churchyard

The house appointed for all living.
>—JOB. XXX. 23

Teach me to live that I may dread
The grave as little as my bed.
>   —BISHOP KEN, *Evening
>   Hymn*

The temple of silence and reconciliation.
>   —MACAULAY

Dust into dust, and under dust, to lie,
Sans wine, sans song, sans singer, and—sans end.
>   —OMAR KHAYYÁM,
>   *Rubaiyat*

Oh, how a small portion of earth will hold us when we
are dead, who ambitiously seek after the whole world
while we are living!
>   —PHILIP, King of Macedon

Is but the threshold of eternity.
>   —SOUTHEY, *Vision of the
>   Maid of Orleans*

Under the wide and starry sky,
Dig the grave and let me lie.
>   —STEVENSON, *Requiem*

Hark! from the tombs a doleful sound.
>   —ISAAC WATTS, *Hymns
>   and Spiritual Songs*

Greatness

All great men come out of the middle classes.
>   —EMERSON

No man ever yet became great by imitation.
>   —SAMUEL JOHNSON

It is the prerogative of great men only to have great defects.

—LA ROCHEFOUCAULD

The nearer we come to great men the more clearly we see that they are only men. They rarely seem great to their valets.

—LA BRUYÈRE

The great are only great because we carry them on our shoulders; when we throw them off they sprawl on the ground.

—MONTANDRÉ

Some are born great, some achieve greatness, and some have greatness thrust upon 'em.

—SHAKESPEARE, *Twelfth Night*. Act II. Sc. 5

The great are great only because we are on our knees. Let us rise!

—STIRNER, *The Ego and His Own*

Greece

Fair Greece! sad relic of departed worth!
Immortal, though no more; though fallen great!
—BYRON, *Childe Harold*

Beware of Greeks bearing gifts.
—LATIN PROVERB

Athens, the eye of Greece, mother of arts
And eloquence.
—MILTON, *Paradise Regained*

The glory that was Greece.
                    —POE, *To Helen*

Grief

It is foolish to tear one's hair in grief, as though sorrow
would be made less by baldness.
                    —CICERO

There is no grief which time does not lessen and soften.
                    —CICERO

Grief is itself a med'cine.
                    —WILLIAM COWPER

The only cure for grief is action.
                    —G. H. LEWES, *The
                    Spanish Drama*

Heavy hearts, like heavy clouds in the sky, are best relieved
by the letting of water.
                    —RIVAROL

Every one can master a grief but he that has it.
                    —SHAKESPEARE, *Much Ado
                    about Nothing*. Act
                    III. Sc. 2

What's gone and what's past help
Should be past grief.
                    —SHAKESPEARE, *Winter's
                    Tale*. Act III. Sc. 2

Guest

No one can be so welcome a guest that he will not annoy
his host after three days.
—PLAUTUS

Unbidden guests
Are often welcomest when they are gone.
—SHAKESPEARE, *Henry* VI.
Pt. I. Act II. Sc. 2

Every guest hates the others, and the host hates them
all.
—ALBANIAN PROVERB

Guilt

Let no guilty man escape, if it can be avoided. No personal consideration should stand in the way of performing
a public duty.
—ULYSSES S. GRANT

Let wickedness escape as it may at the bar, it never fails
of doing justice upon itself; for every guilty person is his
own hangman.
—SENECA

He who flees from trial confesses his guilt.
—SYRUS

Habit

Habit, if not resisted, soon becomes necessity.
—ST. AUGUSTINE

How use doth breed a habit in a man!
> —SHAKESPEARE, *Two
> Gentlemen of
> Verona*. Act V. Sc. 4

Habits are at first cobwebs, then cables.
> —SPANISH PROVERB

The fox changes his skin but not his habits.
> —SUETONIUS

Hair

His hair stood upright like porcupine quills.
> —BOCCACCIO, *Decameron*

Bring down my gray hairs with sorrow to the grave.
> —GENESIS. XLII. 38

Gray hair is a sign of age, not of wisdom.
> —GREEK PROVERB

The very hairs of your head are all numbered.
> —MATTHEW. X. 30

The hoary beard is a crown of glory if it be found in the
way of righteousness.
> —PROVERBS. XVI. 31

There was never a saint with red hair.
> —RUSSIAN PROVERB

Hand

His hand will be against every man, and every man's
hand against him.
> —GENESIS. XVI. 12

The voice is Jacob's voice, but the hands are the hands of Esau.
—GENESIS. XXVII. 22

Let not thy left hand know what thy right hand doeth.
—MATTHEW. VI. 3

Hanging

As well be hanged for a sheep as a lamb.
—ENGLISH PROVERB

So they hanged Haman on the gallows that he had prepared for Mordecai.
—ESTHER. VII. 10

We must all hang together, else we shall all hang separately.

—FRANKLIN, on signing the
Declaration of
Independence

They're hangin' Danny Deever in the morning!
—KIPLING, *Danny Deever*

Happiness

The greatest happiness of the greatest number.
—BECCARIA

What is the worth of anything,
But for the happiness 'twill bring?
—RICHARD OWEN
CAMBRIDGE

Happiness lies, first of all, in health.
>—GEORGE WILLIAM
> CURTIS

Happiness grows at our own firesides, and is not to be picked in strangers' gardens.
>—DOUGLAS JERROLD

We are never so happy, nor so unhappy, as we suppose ourselves to be.
>—LA ROCHEFOUCAULD

What happiness is there which is not purchased with more or less of pain?
>—MARGARET OLIPHANT

I have learned to seek my happiness by limiting my desires, rather than in attempting to satisfy them.
>—JOHN STUART MILL

Everyone speaks of it, few know it.
>—MME. JEANNE P.
> ROLAND

Man is the artificer of his own happiness.
>—THOREAU

Harvest

Whatsoever a man soweth, that shall he also reap.
>—GALATIANS. VI. 7

The harvest truly is plenteous, but the labourers are few.
>—MATTHEW. IX. 37

Dry August and warm,
Doth harvest no harm.
>—TUSSER

Haste

Haste makes waste.

—ENGLISH PROVERB

Take time for all things.

—FRANKLIN

Haste is of the Devil.

—THE KORAN

Make haste slowly.

—LATIN PROVERB

Hate

Whosoever hateth his brother is a murderer.

—I JOHN. III. 15

I like a good hater.

—SAMUEL JOHNSON

But I do hate him as I hate the devil.

—BEN JONSON, *Every Man
out of His Humour*

The hatred we bear our enemies injures their happiness
less than our own.

—J. PETIT-SENN

People hate, as they love, unreasonably.

—THACKERAY

Head

An old head upon young shoulders.

—ENGLISH PHRASE

Two heads are better than one.

—ENGLISH PROVERB

The head is always the dupe of the heart.

—LA ROCHEFOUCAULD

Health

He who has health has hope, and he who has hope has everything.

—ARABIAN PROVERB

Refuse to be ill. Never tell people you are ill; never own it to yourself. Illess is one of those things which a man should resist on principle at the onset.

—BULWER-LYTTON

Health is not a condition of matter, but of Mind.

—MARY BAKER EDDY,
Science and Health

The first wealth is health.

—EMERSON, *The Conduct
of Life*

Health lies in labor, and there is no royal road to it but through toil.

—WENDELL PHILLIPS

The fate of a nation has often depended on the good or bad digestion of a prime minister.

—VOLTAIRE

Hearing

None so deaf as those that will not hear.
—MATTHEW HENRY,
Commentaries. Psalm
LVIII

Little pitchers have wide ears.
—GEORGE HERBERT,
Jacula Prudentum

Went in at the one ear and out at the other.
—JOHN HEYWOOD,
Proverbs

He that hath ears to hear, let him hear.
—MARK. IV. 9

Where more is meant than meets the ear.
—MILTON, *Il Penseroso*

We have two ears and only one tongue in order that we may hear more and speak less.
—DIOGENES

Friends, Romans, countrymen, lend me your ears.
—SHAKESPEARE, *Julius
Caesar*. Act III. Sc. 2.

Heart

My heart's in the Highlands, my heart is not here;
My heart's in the Highlands a-chasing the deer.
—ROBERT BURNS

Maid of Athens, ere we part,
Give, oh, give me back my heart!
                    —BYRON, *Maid of Athens*

Soul of fibre and heart of oak.
                    —CERVANTES, *Don
                        Quixote*

Some people's hearts are shrunk in them, like dried nuts.
You can hear 'em rattle as they walk.
                    —DOUGLAS JERROLD

I caused the widow's heart to sing for joy.
                    —JOB. XXIX. 13

Let not your heart be troubled.
                    —JOHN. XIV. 1

Still stands thine ancient sacrifice—
An humble and a contrite heart.
                    —KIPLING, *Recessional*

No one is so accursed by fate,
No one so utterly desolate,
   But some heart, though unknown,
   Responds unto his own.
                    —LONGFELLOW, *Endymion*

Where your treasure is, there will your heart be also.
                    —MATTHEW. VI. 21

The heart knoweth his own bitterness.
                    —PROVERBS. XIV. 10

A merry heart maketh a cheerful countenance.
                    —PROVERBS. XV. 13

But I will wear my heart upon my sleeve
For daws to peck at; I am not what I am.
                —SHAKESPEARE, *Othello*.
                        Act I. Sc. 1

Heaven

Heaven means to be one with God.
                —CONFUCIUS

All this, and Heaven too!
                —PHILIP HENRY

There the wicked cease from troubling, and there the
weary be at rest.
                —JOB. III. 17

In my father's house are many mansions.
                —JOHN. XIV. 2

A heaven on earth.

                —MILTON, *Paradise Lost*

When Christ ascended
Triumphantly from star to star
He left the gates of Heaven ajar.
                —LONGFELLOW, *Golden
                        Legend*

Lay up for yourselves treasures in heaven.
                —MATTHEW. VI. 20

Earth has no sorrow that heaven cannot heal.
                —MOORE

Heav'n but the Vision of fulfill'd Desire,
And Hell the Shadow from a Soul on fire.
                    —OMAR KHAYYÁM,
                        Rubaiyat

A day in thy courts is better than a thousand. I had
rather be a doorkeeper in the house of my God than to
dwell in the tents of wickedness.
                    —PSALMS. LXXXIV. 10

In Heaven an angel is nobody in particular.
                    —GEORGE BERNARD SHAW

Hell

Hell is paved with good intentions.
                    —Attributed to ST.
                        BERNARD OF
                        CLAIRVAUX

Nor ear can hear nor tongue can tell
The tortures of that inward hell.
                    —BYRON, *The Giaour*

All hell broke loose.

                    —MILTON, *Paradise Lost*

The cunning livery of hell.

                    —SHAKESPEARE, *Measure
                        for Measure*. Act III.
                        Sc. 1

If there is no Hell, a good many preachers are obtaining
money under false pretenses.
                    —WILLIAM A. SUNDAY

Self-love and the love of the world constitute hell.
—SWEDENBORG,
Apocalypse Explained

Help

Light is the task when many share the toil.
—HOMER, *Iliad*

Make two grins grow where there was only a grouch
before.
—ELBERT HUBBARD, *Pig-
Pen Pete*

Art thou lonely, O my brother?
Share thy little with another!
Stretch a hand to one unfriended,
And thy loneliness is ended.
—JOHN OXENHAM, *Lonely
Brother*

Help me, Cassius, or I sink!
—SHAKESPEARE, *Julius
Caesar.* Act I. Sc. 2

God helps those who help themselves.
—ALGERNON SIDNEY

Heredity

It runs in the blood like wooden legs.
—CHESHIRE SAYING

Noble fathers have noble children.
—EURIPIDES

A good tree cannot bring forth evil fruit, neither can a corrupt tree bring forth good fruit.
—MATTHEW. VII. 18

He's a chip o' th' old block.
—WILLIAM ROWLEY, A
Match at Midnight

Clever father, clever daughter; clever mother, clever son.
—RUSSIAN PROVERB

Hero

No man is a hero to his own wife; no woman is a wife to her own hero.
—ANONYMOUS

The boy stood on the burning deck
    Whence all but him had fled;
The flame that lit the battle's wreck,
    Shone round him o'er the dead.
—FELICIA D. HEMANS,
Casabianca

Hero-worship exists, has existed, and will forever exist, universally among mankind.
—CARLYLE, *Sartor Resartus*

No man is a hero to his valet.
—MME. DE CORNUEL

Every hero becomes a bore at last.
—EMERSON

Hail, ye heroes! heaven-born band!
Who fought and bled in Freedom's cause.
—JOSEPH HOPKINSON,
Hail, Columbia!

The idol of today pushes the hero of yesterday out of
our recollection; and will, in turn, be supplanted by his
successor of tomorrow.
—WASHINGTON IRVING,
The Sketch Book

See the conquering hero comes!
Sound the trumpets, beat the drums!
—THOMAS MORELL

History

History is something that never happened, written by a
man who wasn't there.
—ANONYMOUS

History, a distillation of rumor
—CARLYLE, *French
Revolution*

The economic interpretation of history does not necessarily mean that all events are determined solely by economic forces. It simply means that economic facts are
the ever recurring decisive forces, the chief points in the
process of history.
—EDWARD BERNSTEIN,
Evolutionary Socialism

Assassination has never changed the history of the world.
—DISRAELI

There is properly no history, only biography.
—EMERSON, *Essays*

History is indeed little more than the register of the crimes, follies, and misfortunes of mankind.
—GIBBON, *Decline and Fall of the Roman Empire*

What is history but a fable agreed upon?
—NAPOLEON

The historian is a prophet looking backwards.
—SCHLEGEL

All history is a lie!
—SIR ROBERT WALPOLE

Human history is in essence a history of ideas.
—H. G. WELLS, *The Outline of History*

Home

For a man's home is his castle.
—SIR EDWARD COKE

Many a man who thinks to found a home discovers that he has merely opened a tavern for his friends.
—GEORGE NORMAN DOUGLAS, *South Wind*

He is happiest, be he king or peasant who finds peace in his home.
—GOETHE

To Adam Paradise was home. To the good among his descendants home is paradise.
                              —HARE

Peace and rest at length have come,
    All the day's long toil is past;
And each heart is whispering "Home,
    Home at last!"
                              —HOOD, *Home at Last*

The foxes have holes, and the birds of the air have nests, but the Son of Man hath not where to lay his head.
                              —MATTHEW. VII. 20

A man travels the world over in search of what he needs and returns home to find it.
                              —GEORGE MOORE, *The Brook Kerith*

Home is where the heart is.
                              —PLINY

'Mid pleasures and palaces through we may roam,
Be it ever so humble, there's no place like Home.
                              —J. HOWARD PAYNE, *Home Sweet Home*

Those comfortably padded lunatic asylums which are known, euphemistically, as the stately homes of England.
                              —VIRGINIA WOOLF, *The Common Reader*

Honesty

Honesty is the best policy.
                              —CERVANTES, *Don Quixote*

When rogues fall out, honest men get into their own.
>—SIR MATTHEW HALE

An honest man's the noblest work of God.
>—POPE

Ay, sir; to be honest, as this world goes, is to be one man picked out of ten thousand.
>—SHAKESPEARE, *Hamlet*.
>Act II. Sc. 2

I hope I shall always possess firmness and virtue enough to maintain what I consider the most enviable of all titles, the character of an "Honest Man."
>—WASHINGTON, *Moral
>Maxims*

Honor

Dead on the field of honour.
>—Answer given in the
>rollcall of La Tour
>d'Auvergne's regiment
>after his death

Honor lies in honest toil.
>—GROVER CLEVELAND

These were honoured in their generations, and were the glory of the times.
>—ECCLESIASTES. XLIV. 7

I could not love thee, dear, so much,
Loved I not honor more.
>—LOVELACE, *To Lucasta,
>on Going to the Wars*

For Brutus is an honourable man;
So are they all, all honourable men.
—SHAKESPEARE, *Julius
Caesar*. Act III. Sc. 2

Hope

To the sick, while there is life there is hope.
—CICERO

Abandon hope, all ye who enter here.
—DANTE, *Inferno*

A woman's hopes are woven of sunbeams; a shadow annihilates them.
—GEORGE ELIOT

Hope for the best, but prepare for the worst.
—ENGLISH PROVERB

Youth fades; love droops, the leaves of friendship fall;
A mother's secret hope outlives them all.
—HOLMES, *A Mother's
Secret*

Hope says to us constantly, "Go on, go on," and leads us thus to the grave.
—MME. DE MAINTENON

Hope springs eternal in the human breast.
—POPE, *Essay on Man*

Hope deferred maketh the heart sick.
—PROVERBS. XIII. 12

Who against hope believed in hope.
—ROMANS. IV. 18

The sickening pang of hope deferr'd.
—SCOTT, *Lady of the Lake*

Hope is the poor man's bread.
—THALES

Prisoners of hope.
—ZECHARIAH. IX. 12

Horses

You may lead a horse to water but you can't make him drink.
—ENGLISH PROVERB

One white foot—buy him:
Two white feet—try him;
Three white feet—look well about him;
Four white feet—go without him.
—OLD ENGLISH RHYME

A horse! a horse! my kingdom for a horse!
—SHAKESPEARE, *Richard III*. Act V. Sc. 4

Hospitality

Let me live in my house by the side of the road,
    Where the race of men go by;
They are good, they are bad; they are weak, they are
    strong,
    Wise, foolish,—so am I;
Then why should I sit in the scorner's seat,
    Or hurl the cynic's ban?

Let me live in my house by the side of the road,
    And be a friend to man.
                —SAM WALTER FOSS,
                     House by the Side of
                     the Road

For 't is always fair weather
When good fellows get together
With a stein on the table and a good song ringing clear.
                —RICHARD HOVEY, *Spring*

I was an hungered, and ye gave me meat: I was thirsty
and ye gave me drink. I was a stranger, and ye took me
in.
                —MATTHEW. XXV. 35

For I, who hold sage Homer's rule the best,
Welcome the coming, speed the going guest.
                —POPE

Oh that I had in the wilderness a lodging-place of way-
faring men!
                —JEREMIAH. IX. 2

House

Houses are built to live in, and not to look on.
                —BACON, *Essays*

Fools build houses, and wise men buy them.
                —ENGLISH PROVERB

He that lives in a glass house must not throw stones.
                —ENGLISH PROVERB

A foolish man ... built his house upon the sand.
                —MATTHEW. VII. 26

Humanity

Our humanity were a poor thing but for the divinity that
stirs within us.
> —BACON

I love my country better than my family; but I love
humanity better than my country.
> —FÉNELON

W'en you see a man in woe,
Walk right up and say "hullo."
Say "hullo" and "how d'ye do,"
"How's the world a-usin' you?"
> —SAM WALTER FOSS,
> *Hullo*

He held his seat; a friend to human race.
> —HOMER, *Iliad*

Humanitarianism consists in never sacrificing a human
being to a purpose.
> —ALBERT SCHWEITZER

Oh, God! that bread should be so dear,
And flesh and blood so cheap!
> —HOOD, *Song of a Shirt*

Every human heart is human.
> —LONGFELLOW, *Hiawatha*

After all there is but one race—humanity.
> —GEORGE MOORE, *The
> Bending of the Bough*

The world is my country, all mankind are my brethren,
and to do good is my religion.
> —THOMAS PAINE, *Rights of
> Man*

Humanity is the Son of God.
　　　　　　　　—THEODORE PARKER

I am not an Athenian, nor a Greek, but a citizen of the world.
　　　　　　　　—SOCRATES

The age of chivalry has gone; the age of humanity has come.
　　　　　　　　—CHARLES SUMNER

I am a man; I count nothing human foreign to me.
　　　　　　　　—TERENCE

Our true nationality is mankind.
　　　　　　　　—H. G. WELLS, *The Outline of History*

Humility

After crosses and losses, men grow humbler and wiser.
　　　　　　　　—FRANKLIN

'Umble we are, 'umble we have been, 'umble we shall ever be.
　　　　　　　　—DICKENS, *David Copperfield*

In humility imitate Jesus and Socrates.
　　　　　　　　—FRANKLIN

I believe the first test of a truly great man is his humility.
　　　　　　　　—JOHN RUSKIN

Hunger

An empty stomach is not a good political adviser.
—ALBERT EINSTEIN,
Cosmic Religion

If thine enemy be hungry, give him bread to eat.
—PROVERBS

A hungry people listens not to reason, nor cares for justice, nor is bent by any prayers.
—SENECA

Yond Cassius has a lean and hungry look.
—SHAKESPEARE, *Julius Caesar*. Act I. Sc. 2

Husbands

All husbands are alike, but they have different faces so you can tell them apart.
—ANONYMOUS

A good husband should be deaf and a good wife blind.
—FRENCH PROVERB

A good husband is never the first to go to sleep at night or the last to awake in the morning.
—BALZAC, *The Physiology of Marriage*

Husbands, love your wives, even as Christ also loved the church, and gave himself for it.
—EPHESIANS. V. 24

A man should be taller, older, heavier, uglier, and hoarser than his wife.

—E. W. HOWE, *Country Town Sayings*

Men are April when they woo, December when they wed.

—SHAKESPEARE, *As You Like it*. Act IV. Sc. 1

As the husband is, the wife is.

—TENNYSON, *Locksley Hall*

Hypocrisy

Saint abroad, and a devil at home.

—BUNYAN, *Pilgrim's Progress*

Every man is a hypocrite

—FREDERICK IV

Hypocrites do the devil's drudgery in Christ's livery.

—MATTHEW HENRY

Hypocrisy is the homage which vice renders to virtue.

—LA ROCHEFOUCAULD

Who stole the livery of the court of Heaven
To serve the Devil in.

—POLLOK, *Course of Time*

I hope you have not been leading a double life, pretending to be wicked and being really good all the time. That would be hypocrisy.

—WILDE, *Importance of Being Earnest*

Ideas

The material universe exists only in the mind.
                                   —JONATHAN EDWARDS

Ideas must work through the brains and the arms of good
and brave men, or they are no better than dreams.
                                   —EMERSON

No army can withstand the strength of an idea whose
time has come.
                                   —VICTOR HUGO

An idea, to be suggestive, must come to the individual
with the force of a revelation.
                                   —WILLIAM JAMES, *The
                                      Varieties of Religious
                                      Experience*

It is only liquid currents of thought that move men and
the world.
                                   —WENDELL PHILLIPS

Idleness

Some people have a perfect genius for doing nothing,
and doing it assiduously.
                                   —HALIBURTON

Lost time is never found again.
                                   —AUGHEY

Idleness is the holiday of fools.
                                   —CHESTERFIELD

He is not only idle who does nothing, but he is idle who
might be better employed.

> —SOCRATES

For Satan finds some mischief still
>   For idle hands to do.

> —ISAAC WATTS, *Against
>   Idleness*

Ignorance

I am not ashamed to confess that I am ignorant of what
I do not know.

> —CICERO

Ignorance never settles a question.

> —DISRAELI

Where ignorance is bliss,
'Tis folly to be wise.

> —GRAY, *On a Distant
>   Prospect of Eton
>   College.*

Imagination

Imagination is more important than knowledge.

> —ALBERT EINSTEIN, *On
>   Science*

Imagination is the eye of the soul.

> —JOUBERT

He who has imagination without learning has wings but
no feet.

> —JOUBERT

The human race is governed by its imagination.
—NAPOLEON

Imagination disposes of everything; it creates beauty, justice, and happiness, which is everything in this world.
—PASCAL

Imitation

Imitation is the sincerest (form) of flattery.
—COLTON

It is impossible to imitate Voltaire without being Voltaire.
—FREDERICK THE GREAT

He who imitates what is evil always goes beyond the example that is set; on the contrary, he who imitates what is good always falls short.
—GUICCIARDINI, *Storia d' Italia*

A good imitation is the most perfect originality.
—VOLTAIRE

Immortality

What is human is immortal!
—BULWER-LYTTON

A good man never dies.
—CALLIMACHUS

I have been dying for twenty years, now I am going to live.
—JAMES DRUMMOND BURNS, *His Last Words*

Immortality is the glorious discovery of Christianity.
—WILLIAM ELLERY
CHANNING,
Immortality

Then shall the dust return to the earth as it was; and the spirit shall return unto God who gave it.
—ECCLESIASTES, XII. 7

Oh, may I join the choir invisible
Of those immortal dead who live again.
—GEORGE ELIOT, *The
Choir Invisible*

Life is the childhood of our immortality.
—GOETHE

The nearer I approach the end, the plainer I hear around me the immortal symphonies of the worlds which invite me. It is marvelous, yet simple.
—VICTOR HUGO

Our hope of immortality does not come from any religion, but nearly all religions come from that hope.
—INGERSOLL, 1879

I wish to believe in immortality—I wish to live with you forever.
—KEATS, *Letter to Fanny
Brawne*

No one could ever meet death for his country without the hope of immortality.
—CICERO

There is no death! the stars go down to rise upon some fairer shore.

> —J. L. McCREERY, *There
> Is No Death*

For tho' from out our bourne of time and place
>   The flood may bear me far,
I hope to see my Pilot face to face
>   When I have crost the bar.

> —TENNYSON, *Crossing the
> Bar*

Never did Christ utter a single word attesting to a personal resurrection and a life beyond the grave.

> —TOLSOY, *What I Believe*

Imperialism

The mission of the United States is one of benevolent assimilation.

> —WILLIAM MCKINLEY,
> Letter, 1898

Take up the white man's burden—
>   Send forth the best ye breed—
Go bind your sons to exile
>   To serve your captives' need.

> —KIPLING, *The White
> Man's Burden*

The conquest of the earth, which mostly means the taking it away from those who have a different complexion or slightly flatter noses than ourselves, is not a pretty thing when you look into it.

> —JOSEPH CONRAD, *Heart
> of Darkness*

Impossibility

You cannot make a crab walk straight.
—ARISTOPHANES

You can't get blood out of a turnip.
—ENGLISH PROVERB

You can't make a silk purse out of a sow's ear.
—ENGLISH PROVERB

Few things are impossible to diligence and skill.
—SAMUEL JOHNSON,
Rasselas

Never let me hear that foolish word again.
—MIRABEAU

Impossible is a word only to be found in the dictionary of fools.
—NAPOLEON

To the timid and hesitating everything is impossible because it seems so.
—SCOTT

Improvement

It is necessary to try to surpass one's self always; this occupation ought to last as long as life.
—QUEEN CHRISTINA

People seldom improve when they have no other model but themselves to copy after.
—GOLDSMITH

Slumber not in the tents of your fathers. The world is advancing. Advance with it!

—MAZZINI

Independence

I never thrust my nose into other men's porridge. It is no bread and butter of mine: Every man for himself and God for us all.

—CERVANTES, *Don Quixote*

Can anything be so elegant as to have few wants, and to serve them one's self?

—EMERSON

Voyager upon life's sea:—
    To yourself be true,
And whate'er your lot may be,
    Paddle your own canoe.

—EDWARD P. PHILPOTS, *Paddle Your Own Canoe*

I would rather sit on a pumpkin, and have it all to myself, than to be crowded on a velvet cushion.

—THOREAU

Individuality

An institution is the lengthened shadow of one man.

—EMERSON

Every individual has a place to fill in the world, and is important in some respect, whether he chooses to be so or not.

—HAWTHORNE

The worth of a state, in the long run, is the worth of the individuals composing it.

—JOHN STUART MILL

Industry

The bread earned by the sweat of the brow is thrice blessed bread, and it is far sweeter than the tasteless loaf of idleness.

—CROWQUILL

Whatsoever thy hand findeth to do, do it with thy might.

—ECCLESIASTES, IX, 10

The more we do, the more we can do; the more busy we are, the more leisure we have.

—HAZLITT

In this theater of man's life, it is reserved only for God and angels to be lookers on.

—PYTHAGORAS

Influence

I am a part of all that I have met.

—TENNYSON, *Ulysses*

The humblest individual exerts some influence, either for good or evil, upon others.

—HENRY WARD BEECHER

A little leaven leaveneth the whole lump.

—GALATIANS, V. 9

A woman is more influenced by what she divines than by what she is told.
> —NINON DE L'ENCLOS

If the nose of Cleopatra had been shorter, the whole face of the earth would have been changed.
> —PASCAL, *Thoughts*

Thou wert my guide, philosopher, and friend.
> —POPE, *Essay on Man*

Ingratitude

We set ourselves to bite the hand that feeds us.
> —BURKE

Brutes leave ingratitude to man.
> —COLTON

This was the most unkindest cut of all;
For when the noble Caesar saw him stab,
Ingratitude, more strong than traitor's arm,
Quite vanquish'd him; then burst his mighty heart.
> —SHAKESPEARE, *Julius Caesar*. Act III. Sc. 2

Do you know what is more hard to bear than the reverses of fortune? It is the baseness, the hideous ingratitude, of man.
> —NAPOLEON

Injury

The injury we do and the one we suffer are not weighed in the same scales.
> —AESOP, *Fables*

Recompense injury with justice, and recompense kindness with kindness.

— CONFUCIUS

If the other person injures you, you may forget the injury; but if you injure him you will always remember.

—KAHLIL GIBRAN, *Sand and Foam*

In an injury has to be done to a man it should be so severe that his vengeance need not be feared.

—MACHIAVELLI, *The Prince*

There is no ghost so difficult to lay as the ghost of an injury.

—ALEXANDER SMITH

Injustice

There is but one blasphemy, and that is injustice.

—INGERSOLL, Speech, 1880

He who commits injustice is ever made more wretched than he who suffers it.

—PLATO

Innocence

It is better that ten guilty persons escape than that one innocent suffer.

—BLACKSTONE, *Commentaries*

As innocent as a new-laid egg.

—W. S. GILBERT, *Engaged*

They that know no evil will suspect none.
—BEN JOHNSON

Innocence finds not near so much protection as guilt.
—LA ROCHEFOUCAULD

Insanity

No excellent soul is exempt from a mixture of madness.
—ARISTOTLE

Mad as a March hare.
—HALLIWELL, *Archaic Diet*

I teach that all men are mad.
—HORACE

Insanity in individuals is something rare—but in groups, parties, nations, and epochs it is the rule.
—NIETZSCHE

That he is mad, 'tis true; 'tis true 'tis pity;
And pity 'tis 'tis true.
—SHAKESPEARE, *Hamlet*. Act II. Sc. 2

Whom Jupiter would destroy he first drives mad.
—SOPHOCLES, *Antigone*

Though this be madness, yet there is method in 't.
—SHAKESPEARE, *Hamlet*. Act II. Sc. 2

Inspiration

No man was ever great without a touch of divine afflatus.
—CICERO

A writer is rarely so well inspired as when he talks about himself.

—ANATOLE FRANCE

Inspiration and genius—one and the same.

—VICTOR HUGO

Insult

The way to procure insults is to submit to them. A man meets with no more respect than he exacts.

—HAZLITT

Thou hast added insult to injury.

—PHAEDRUS

It is often better not to see an insult than to avenge it.

—SENECA

Intemperance

All the crimes on earth do not destroy so many of the human race, nor alienate so much property, as drunkenness.

—BACON

Bacchus has drowned more men than Neptune.

—GARIBALDI

Of all calamities this is the greatest.

—JEFFERSON, Letter, 1798

The smaller the drink, the clearer the head.

—WILLIAM PENN

Drunkenness is nothing but voluntary madness.

—SENECA

O God, that men should put an enemy in their mouths
to steal away their brains! that we should, with joy, pleas-
ance, revel, and applause, transform ourselves into beasts!

—SHAKESPEARE, *Othello*.
Act II. Sc. 3

Intolerance

The devil loves nothing better than the intolerance of
reformers.

—LOWELL

It were better to be of no church, than to be bitter for
any.

—WILLIAM PENN

Invention

Want, the mistress of invention.

—SUSANNA CENTLIVRE,
The Busy Body

A tool is but the extension of a man's hand, and a machine
is but a complex tool. And he that invents a machine
augments the power of a man and the well-being of mankind.

—HENRY WARD BEECHER

God hath made man upright; but they have sought out
many inventions.

—ECCLESIASTES. VII. 29

Ireland

When Erin first rose from the dark-swelling flood,
God blessed the green island, he saw it was good.
The Emerald of Europe, it sparkled and shone
In the ring of this world, the most precious stone.
—WILLIAM DRENNAN, *Erin*

Ireland is a country in which the probable never happens
and the impossible always does.
—Attributed to J. P.
MAHAFFY

Whether on the scaffold high
Or on the battle-field we die,
Oh, what matter, when for Erin dear we fall.
—T. D. SULLIVAN, *God
Save Ireland*

Italy

You may have the universe if I may have Italy.
—TEMISTOCLE SOLERA,
Verdi's *Attila*

Open my heart and you will see
Graved inside of it, "Italy."
—BROWNING, *Men and
Women*

Beyond the Alps lies Italy.
—ENGLISH SAYING

On desperate seas long wont to roam,
    Thy hyacinth hair, they classic face,
Thy naiad airs have brought me home
    To the glory that was Greece
And the grandeur that was Rome.
                —POE, *Helen*

My soul today
Is far away
Sailing the Vesuvian Bay.
                —THOMAS B. READ,
                    Drifting

Jealousy

He that is not jealous is not in love.
                —ST. AUGUSTINE

In jealousy there is more self-love than love.
                —LA ROCHEFOUCAULD

Jealousy is an awkward homage which inferiority renders to merit.
                —MME. DE PUISIEUX

O jealousy! thou magnifier of trifles.
                —SCHILLER

Jealousy's eyes are green.
                —SHELLEY

Jesting

A man who could make so vile a pun would not scruple to pick a pocket.
—JOHN DENNIS, *The Gentleman's Magazine*

Many a true word is spoken in jest.
—ENGLISH PROVERB

Alas, poor Yorick! I knew him, Horatio: a fellow of infinite jest, of most excellent fancy.
—SHAKESPEARE, *Hamlet.* Act V. Sc. 1

Jesters do often prove prophets.
—SHAKESPEARE, *King Lear.* Act V. Sc. 3

Jew

The Jews were God's chosen people.
—ST. CHRYSOSTOM

I will make of thee a great nation, and I will bless thee, and make thy name great.
—GENESIS. XII. 2

To undo a Jew is charity, and not sin.
—MARLOWE, *The Jew of Malta*

It is not possible for Christians to take part in anti-Semitism. We are Semites spiritually.
—POPE PIUS XI

I am a Jew: Hath not a Jew eyes? hath not a Jew hands, organs, dimensions, senses, affections, passions? fed with the same food, hurt with the same weapons, subject to the same diseases, healed by the same means, warmed and cooled by the same winter and summer, as a Christian is?

—SHAKESPEARE, *Merchant of Venice.* Act III. Sc. 1

Jewel

Neither cast ye your pearls before swine.

—MATTHEW. VII. 6

Pearl of great price.

—MATTHEW. XIII. 46

Journalism

Journalism has already come to be the first power in the land.

—SAMUEL BOWLES

Get your facts first, and then you can distort 'em as much as you please.

—S. L. CLEMENS (MARK TWAIN)

Burke said there were Three Estates in Parliament; but, in the Reporters' gallery yonder, there sat a Fourth Estate more important far than they all.

—CARLYLE, *Heroes and Hero-Worship*

Writing good editorials is chiefly telling the people what they think, not what you think.
—ARTHUR BRISBANE

The best use of a journal is to print the largest practical amount of important truth,—truth which tends to make mankind wiser, and thus happier.
—HORACE GREELEY

Every newspaper editor owes tribute to the devil.
—LA FONTAINE

I fear three newspapers more than a hundred thousand bayonets.
—NAPOLEON

We live under a government of men and morning newspapers.
—WENDELL PHILLIPS

The newspapers! Sir, they are the most villainous—licentious—abominable—infernal—not that I ever read them—no—I make it a rule never to look into a newspaper.
—R. B. SHERIDAN, *The Critic*

Joy

I wish you all the joy that you can wish.
—SHAKESPEARE, *Merchant of Venice.* Act III. Sc. 2

The joyfulness of a man prolongeth his days.
—ECCLESIASTES. XXX. 22

All human joys are swift of wing,
    For heaven doth so allot it;
That when you get an easy thing,
    You find you haven't got it.
                —EUGENE FIELD, *Ways of
                          Life*

A thing of beauty is a joy forever.
                —KEATS

Sweets with sweets war not, joy delights in joy.
                —SHAKESPEARE, *Sonnet*

I have drunken deep of joy,
And I will taste no other wine tonight.
                —SHELLEY, *The Cenci*

Judge

It is better that a judge should lean on the side of compassion than severity.
                —CERVANTES

A Daniel come to judgment! yea, a Daniel!
O wise young judge, how I do honor thee!
                —SHAKESPEARE, *The
                        Merchant of Venice.*
                        Act IV. Sc. 1

Let the judges answer to the question of law, and the jurors to the matter of fact.
                —LAW MAXIM

The cold neutrality of an impartial judge.
                —BURKE

Judges are but men, and are swayed like other men by vehement prejudices. This is corruption in reality, give it whatever other name you please.

—DAVID DUDLEY FIELD

Judges are apt to be naïve, simple-minded men.
—O. W. HOLMES II,
Speech, 1913

Thieves for their robbery have authority
When judges steal themselves.
—SHAKESPEARE, *Measure
for Measure.* Act II.
Sc. 2

Four things belong to a judge: to hear courteously, to answer wisely, to consider soberly, and to decide impartially.

—SOCRATES

Judgment

Thou art weighed in the balances, and art found wanting.
—DANIEL. V. 27

One man's word is no man's word; we should quietly hear both sides.

—GOETHE

Forbear to judge, for we are sinners all.
—SHAKESPEARE, *Henry VI.*
Pt. II. Act III. Sc. 3

I know of no way of judging the future but by the past.
—PATRICK HENRY, 1775

We judge ourselves by what we feel capable of doing,
while others judge us by what we have already done.
—LONGFELLOW, *Kavanagh*

Give your decision, never your reasons; your decisions
may be right, your reasons are sure to be wrong.
—LORD MANSFIELD

Judge not, that ye be not judged.
—MATTHEW. VII. 1

Give every man thine ear, but few thy voice;
Take each man's censure, but reserve thy judgment.
—SHAKESPEARE, *Hamlet*.
Act I. Sc. 3

O judgment! thou are fled to brutish beasts,
And men have lost their reason!
—SHAKESPEARE, *Julius
Caesar*. Act III. Sc. 2

One cool judgment is worth a thousand hasty councils.
The thing to do is to supply light and not heat.
—WOODROW WILSON,
Speech, 1916

Jury

Are you good men and true?
—SHAKESPEARE, *Much Ado
About Nothing*. Act
III. Sc. 2

The jury system puts a ban upon intelligence and honesty, and a premium upon ignorance, stupidity and per-
jury.
—S. L. CLEMENS (MARK
TWAIN), *Roughing It*

The trial of all crimes, except in cases of impeachment, shall be by jury.

—CONSTITUTION OF THE
UNITED STATES

The jury, passing on the prisoner's life,
May in the sworn twelve have a thief or two
Guiltier than him they try.

—SHAKESPEARE, *Measure
for Measure*. Act II.
Sc. 4

Justice

There is no virtue so truly great and godlike as justice.
—ADDISON, *The Guardian*

Thrice is he armed that hath his quarrel just;
And four times he who gets his fist in fust.
—Accredited to JOSH
BILLINGS

The path of the just is as the shining light, that shineth more and more unto the perfect day.
—PROVERBS. IV. 18

There is no such thing as justice—in or out of court.
—CLARENCE DARROW,
1936

Delay of justice is injustice.
—LANDOR

It looks to me to be narrow and pedantic to supply the ordinary ideas of criminal justice to this great public contest. I do not know the method of drawing up an indictment against a whole people.

> —BURKE, Speech on
> Conciliation with
> America

The spirits of just men made perfect.

> —HEBREWS. XII. 23

God's mill grinds slow, but sure.

> —GEORGE HERBERT

The sword of the law should never fall but on those whose guilt is so apparent as to be pronounced by their friends as well as foes.

> —JEFFERSON, Letter, 1801

Render therefore to all their dues.

> —ROMANS. XIII. 7

He who decides a case without hearing the other side, though he decide justly, cannot be considered just.

> —SENECA

This bond is forfeit;
And lawfully by this the Jew may claim
A pound of flesh.

> —SHAKESPEARE, *Merchant
> of Venice*. Act IV. Sc.
> 1

Thrice is he arm'd that hath his quarrel just,
And he but naked, though lock'd up in steel,
Whose conscience with injustice is corrupted.

> —SHAKESPEARE, *Henry* VI.
> Pt. II. Act III. Sc. 2

Let justice be done, though the heavens fall.

> —WILLIAM WATSON, 1602

Kindness

Have you had a kindness shown?
    Pass it on;
'Twas not given for thee alone,
    Pass it on;
Let it travel down the years,
    Let it wipe another's tears,
'Til in Heaven the deed appears—
    Pass it on.

        —REV. HENRY BURTON,
        Pass It On

Their cause I plead—plead it in heart and mind;
A fellow-feeling makes one wondrous kind.
        —DAVID GARRICK, 1776

At little more than kin, and less than kind.
        —SHAKESPEARE, *Hamlet*.
        Act I. Sc. 2

Yet do I fear thy nature;
It is too full o' the milk of human kindness.
        —SHAKESPEARE, *Macbeth*.
        Act I. Sc. 5

Kindness gives birth to kindness.
        —SOPHOCLES

Kiss

Some women blush when they are kissed; some call for
the police, some swear; some bite. But the worst are those
who laugh.
        —ANONYMOUS

Gin a body meets a body
Comin' through the rye,
Gin a body kiss a body
Need a body cry?

—BURNS

Come, lay thy head upon my breast,
And I will kiss thee into rest.

—BYRON, *The Bride of
Abydos*

It was thy kiss, Love, that made me immortal.

—MARGARET FULLER,
Dryad Song

Give me a kisse, and to that kisse a score;
Then to that twenty, adde a hundred more;
A thousand to that hundred; so kisse on,
To make that thousand up a million;
Treble that million, and when that is done,
Let's kisse afresh, as when we first begun.

—HERRICK, *To Anthea*

A long, long kiss, a kiss of youth, and love.

—BYRON, *Don Juan*

Stolen kisses are always sweetest.

—LEIGH HUNT

Jenny kissed me when we met,
    Jumping from the chair she sat in;
Time, you thief, who love to get
    Sweets into your list, put that in.
Say I'm weary, say I'm sad,
    Say that health and wealth have missed me;
Say I'm growing old, but add Jenny kissed me.

—LEIGH HUNT, *Jenny
Kissed Me*

See! the mountains kiss high heaven,
    And the waves clasp one another;
No sister flower would be forgiven
    If it disdained its brother;
And the sunlight clasps the earth,
    And the moonbeams kiss the sea:—
What are all these kissings worth,
    If thou kiss not me?
            —SHELLEY, *Love's*
                  Philosophy

Lord! I wonder what fool it was that first invented kissing.
            —SWIFT, *Polite*
                 Conversation

Drink to me only with thine eyes
    And I will pledge with mine;
Or leave a kiss but in the cup,
    And I'll not look for wine.
            —BEN JONSON, *To Celia*

Soul meets soul on lovers' lips.
            —SHELLEY, *Prometheus*
                  Unbound

Knowledge

Strange how much you've got to know
Before you know how little you know.
            —ANONYMOUS

I take all knowledge to be my province.
            —BACON

Men are four:
He who knows not and knows not he knows not, he is
    a fool—shun him;
He who knows not and knows he knows not, he is
    simple—teach him;
He who knows and knows not he knows, he is asleep—
    wake him;
He who knows and knows he knows, he is wise—follow
    him!
                                        —ARABIC APOTHEGM

To be conscious that you are ignorant is a great step to
knowledge.
                                        —DISRAELI, Sybil

For knowledge, too, is itself a power.
                                        —BACON

The only good is knowledge, and the only evil ignorance.
                                        —DIOGENES

He that increaseth knowledge increaseth sorrow.
                                        —ECCLESIASTES. I. 18

Our knowledge is the amassed thought and experience
of innumerable minds.
                                        —EMERSON, Letters and
                                            Social Aims

One cannot know everything.
                                        —HORACE

Knowledge is of two kinds. We know a subject ourselves,
or we know where we can find information upon it.
                                        —SAMUEL JOHNSON,
                                            Boswell's Life of
                                            Johnson

He who knows others is learned;
    He who knows himself is wise.
              —LAO-TSZE

It ain't the things you don't know what gets you into
trouble; it's the things you know for sure what ain't so.
              —NEGRO SAYING

Better know nothing than half-know many things.
              —NIETZSCHE, *Thus Spake
                Zarathustra*

He that hath knowledge spareth his words.
              —PROVERBS. XVII. 27

Then I began to think, that it is very true which is commonly said, that the one-half of the world knoweth not
how the other half liveth.
              —RABELAIS

We know what we are, but know not what we may be.
              —SHAKESPEARE, *Hamlet.*
                Act IV. Sc. 5

And seeing ignorance is the curse of God,
Knowledge the wing wherewith we fly to heaven.
              —SHAKESPEARE, *Henry VI.*
                Pt. II. Act IV. Sc. 7

Know thyself.
              —SOCRATES

As for me, all I know is that I know nothing.
              —SOCRATES

Labor

They can expect nothing but their labor for their pains.
—CERVANTES, *Don
Quixote*

For as labor cannot produce without the use of land, the
denial of the equal right to use of land is necessarily the
denial of the right of labor to its own produce.
—HENRY GEORGE, *Progress
and Poverty*

The labor of a human being is not a commodity or article
of commerce.
—CLAYTON ANTITRUST
ACT

A truly American sentiment recognises the dignity of
labor and the fact that honor lies in honest toil.
—CLEVELAND

Shall you complain who feed the world?
    Who clothe the world?
    Who house the world?
Shall you complain who are the world,
    Of what the world may do?
    As from this hour
    You use your power,
    The world must follow you!
—CHARLOTTE PERKINS
GILMAN, *To Labor*

Labor conquers all things.
—HOMER

With fingers weary and worn,
    With eyelids heavy and red,
A woman sat in unwomanly rags,
    Plying her needle and thread.
                    —HOOD, *Song of the Shirt*

If we rightly estimate things, what in them is purely
owing to nature, and what to labour, we shall find ninety-
nine parts of a hundred are wholly to be put on the
account of labour.
                    —JOHN LOCKE

The labourer is worthy of his reward.
                    —I TIMOTHY. V. 18

Bowed by the weight of centuries he leans
Upon his hoe and gazes on the ground,
The emptiness of ages in his face,
And on his back the burden of the world.
                    —EDWIN MARKHAM, *The
                    Man with the Hoe*

And all labor without any play, boys,
Makes Jack a dull boy in the end.
                    —H. A. PAGE

Many faint with toil,
That few may know the cares and woe of sloth.
                    —SHELLEY, *Queen Mab*

Labour was the first price, the original purchase money
that was paid for all things.
                    —ADAM SMITH, *Wealth of
                    Nations*

Labour of love.
                    —I THESSALONIANS. I. 3

Lamb

God tempers the wind to the shorn lamb.
—ENGLISH PROVERB

Mary had a little lamb
    Its fleece was white as snow,
And everywhere that Mary went
    The lamb was sure to go.
—MRS. SARAH J. HALE,
    Mary's Little Lamb

Like lambs to the slaughter.
—JEREMIAH. LI. 40

Land

If a man own land, the land owns him.
—EMERSON, *Wealth*

The small landholders are the most precious part of a state.
—JEFFERSON, Letter, 1785

The land shall not be sold for ever: for the land is mine; for ye are strangers and sojourners with me.
—LEVITICUS. XXV. 23

That which is built upon the land goes with the land.
—LEGAL MAXIM

Language

Babel; because the Lord did there confound the language of all the earth.
—GENESIS. XI. 9

But, for my own part, it was Greek to me.
>—SHAKESPEARE, *Julius Caesar*. Act I. Sc. 2

I am the King of Rome, and above grammar.
>—SIGISMUND, At the Council of Constance

Language, as well as the faculty of speech, was the immediate gift of God.
>—NOAH WEBSTER

The whole earth was of one language, and of one speech.
>—GENESIS. XI. 1

No man fully capable of his own language ever masters another.
>— GEORGE BERNARD SHAW, *Maxims for Revolutionists*

Language is not an abstract construction of the learned, or of dictionary-makers, but is something arising out of the work, needs, ties, joys, affections, tastes, of long generations of humanity, and has its bases broad and low, close to the ground.
>—WALT WHITMAN, *Slang in America*

Lark

Rise with the lark, and with the lark to bed.
>—JAMES HURDIS, *The Village Curate*

Hail to thee, blithe Spirit!
    Bird thou never wert,
That from Heaven, or near it,
    Pourest thy full heart
In profuse strains of unpremeditated art.
                —SHELLEY, *To a Skylark*

Laughter

He laughs best who laughs last.
                —OLD ENGLISH PROVERB

To provoke laughter without joining in it greatly heightens the effect.
                —BALZAC

I hasten to laugh at everything, for fear of being obliged to weep.
                —BEAUMARCHAIS

The man who cannot laugh is not only fit for treasons, strategems, and spoils, but his whole life is already a treason and a stratagem.
                —CARLYLE

As the crackling of thorns under a pot, so is the laughter of a fool.
                —ECCLESIASTES. VII. 6

Man is the only creature endowed with the power of laughter.
                —GREVILLE

Man alone suffers so excruciatingly in the world that he was compelled to invent laughter.
                —NIETZSCHE, *The Will to Power*

Laugh and the world laughs with you,
    Weep and you weep alone;
For the sad old earth must borrow its mirth,
    But has trouble enough of its own.
                —ELLA WHEELER WILCOX,
                         Solitude

Nothing is more silly than silly laughter.
                —CATULLUS

Law

Written laws are like spiders' webs, and will like them
only entangle and hold the poor and weak, while the rich
and powerful will easily break through them.
                —ANACHARSIS TO Solon

Law is a bottomless pit.
                —J. ARBUTHNOT, Title of a
                      Pamphlet, 1700

Possession is eleven points in the law.
                —COLLEY CIBBER

After an existence of nearly twenty years of almost innoc-
uous desuetude these laws are brought forth.
                —GROVER CLEVELAND,
                      1886

Reason is the life of the law; nay, the common law itself
is nothing else but reason. The law which is perfection
of reason.
                —SIR EDWARD COKE, *First
                    Institute*

"If the law supposes that," said Mr. Bumble, "the law is
a ass, a idiot."
                —DICKENS, *Oliver Twist*

Be you never so high, the law is above you.
—THOMAS FULLER

Laws too gentle are seldom obeyed; too severe, seldom executed.
—FRANKLIN, *Poor Richard's Almanac*

The English laws punish vice; the Chinese laws do more, they reward virtue.
—GOLDSMITH

Laws grind the poor, and rich men rule the law.
—GOLDSMITH, *The Traveller*

I know no method to secure the repeal of bad or obnoxious laws so effective as their stringent execution.
—ULYSSES S. GRANT, Address, 1869

If the law is upheld only by government officials, then all law is at an end.
—HERBERT HOOVER, Message, 1929

The execution of the laws is more important than the making of them.
—JEFFERSON, Letter, 1789

The laws sometimes sleep, but never die.
—LAW MAXIM

All things obey fixed laws.
—MANILIUS, *Astronomica*

Petty laws breed great crimes.
—OUIDA, *Wisdom, Wit
and Pathos*

Render therefore unto Caesar the things which are Caesar's.
—MATTHEW. XXII. 21

There is no man so good, who, were he to submit all his thoughts and actions to the laws would not deserve hanging ten times in his life.
—MONTAIGNE

Where law ends, there tyranny begins.
—WILLIAM PITT

The law hath not been dead, though it hath slept.
—SHAKESPEARE, *Measure
for Measure.* Act II,
Sc. 2

Lawyer

A lawyer must first get on, then get honor, and then get honest.
—ANONYMOUS

A lawyer starts life giving $500 worth of law for $5, and ends giving $5 worth for $500.
—Attributed to BENJAMIN
H. BREWSTER

Our wrangling lawyers are so litigious and busy here on earth, that I think they will plead their clients' causes hereafter, some of them in hell.
—BURTON

It is a secret worth knowing that lawyers rarely go to law.

—MOSES CROWELL

A lawyer's opinion is worth nothing unless paid for.
—ENGLISH PROVERB

The first thing we do, let's kill all the lawyers.
—SHAKESPEARE, *Henry VI.*
Pt. II. Act IV. Sc. 2

Most good lawyers live well, work hard, and die poor.
—DANIEL WEBSTER

Leadership

When we think we lead we most are led.
—BYRON, *The Two Foscari*

An army of stags led by a lion would be better than an army of lions led by a stag.
—LATIN PROVERB

If the blind lead the blind, both shall fall into the ditch.
—MATTHEW. XV. 14

Reason and judgment are the qualities of a leader.
—TACITUS

Learning

Much learning doth make thee mad.
—ACTS. XXVI. 24

It is always in season for old men to learn.
—AESCHYLUS, *Agamemnon*

All wish to be learned, but no one is willing to pay the price.

—JUVENAL

Reading maketh a full man; conference a ready man; and writing an exact man.

—BACON, *Essays*

The three foundations of learning: Seeing much, suffering much, and studying much.

—CATHERALL

Wear your learning like your watch, in a private pocket; and do not pull it out and strike it, merely to show that you have one.

—CHESTERFIELD

And still they gazed, and still the wonder grew,
That one small head should carry all it knew.

—GOLDSMITH, *The
Deserted Village*

They have learned nothing, and forgotten nothing.

—CHEVALIER DE PANAT

A little learning is a dangerous thing;
Drink deep, or taste not the Pierian spring;
Their shallow draughts intoxicate the brain,
And drinking largely sobers us again.

—POPE, *Essay on Criticism*

A learned man is an idler who kills time by study.

—GEORGE BERNARD
SHAW, *Maxims for
Revolutionists*

Men learn while they teach.

—SENECA

Leisure

Increased means and increased leisure are the two civilizers of man.

—DISRAELI, Speech, 1872

The wisdom of a learned man cometh by opportunity of leisure.

—ECCLESIASTES. XXXVIII.
24

Leisure is the mother of philosophy.

—THOMAS HOBBES,
Leviathan

Lending

If you lend you either lose the money or gain an enemy.

—ALBANIAN PROVERB

Better give a shilling than lend and lose half a crown.

—THOMAS FULLER

A good man showeth favor, and lendeth.

—PSALMS. CXII. 5

Letter

In a man's letters his soul lies naked.

—SAMUEL JOHNSON

I have made this letter longer than usual because I lack the time to make it shorter.

—PASCAL

I have received no more than one or two letters in my life that were worth the postage.

—THOREAU, *Walden*

Liberal

One who has both feet firmly planted in the air.

—ANONYMOUS

Liberalism is trust of the people tempered by prudence; conservatism, distrust of the people tempered by fear.

—GLADSTONE

A liberal is a man who is willing to spend somebody else's money.

—CARTER GLASS, 1938

Liberality

Liberality consists less in giving much than in giving at the right moment.

—LA BRUYÉRE

The liberal soul shall be made fat.

—PROVERBS. XI. 25

What's mine is yours, and what is yours is mine.

—SHAKESPEARE, *Measure for Measure*. Act V. Sc. 1

Liberty

The tree of liberty grows only when watered by the blood of tyrants.

—BARÈRE

The people never give up their liberties but under some delusion.

—BURKE

Liberty's in every blow!
Let us do or die.

—BURNS, *Bruce to His Men at Bannockburn*

Where the spirit of the Lord is, there is Liberty.

—II CORINTHIANS. III. 17

Eternal vigilance is the price of liberty.

—JOHN PHILPOT CURRAN, Dublin, 1808

Those who would give up essential liberty to purchase a little temporary safety deserve neither liberty nor safety.

—FRANKLIN

Give me liberty, or give me death.

—PATRICK HENRY

The God who gave us life, gave us liberty at the same time.

—JEFFERSON

Give me your tired, your poor,
Your huddled masses, yearning to breathe free,
The wretched refuse of your teeming shore.
Send these, the homeless, tempest tossed, to me:
I lift my lamp beside the golden door.

—EMMA LAZARUS, Inscription on Statue of Liberty, New York Harbor

Proclaim liberty throughout all the land unto all the inhabitants thereof.

> —LEVITICUS. XXV. 10.,
> Inscription on Liberty
> Bell at Philadelphia

Give me the liberty to know, to think, to believe, and to utter freely according to conscience, above all other liberties.

> —MILTON

O liberty! how many crimes are committed in thy name!
> —MME. JEANNE ROLAND

Liberty is the only thing you cannot have unless you are willing to give it to others.

> —WILLIAM ALLEN WHITE,
> 1940

Liberty *and* Union, now and for ever, one and inseparable!

> —WEBSTER, Speech, 1830

I have always in my own thought summed up individual liberty, and business liberty, and every other kind of liberty, in the phrase that is common in the sporting world, "A free field and no favor."

> —WOODROW WILSON

Life

Ofttimes the test of courage becomes rather to live than to die.

> —ALFIERI, *Orestes*

Every man's life is a fairy-tale written by God's fingers.
> —HANS CHRISTIAN
> ANDERSEN

Life is a jig saw puzzle with most of the pieces missing.
—ANONYMOUS

I expect to pass through this world but once. Any good therefore that I can do, or any kindness that I can show to any fellow creature, let me do it now. Let me not defer or neglect it, for I shall not pass this way again.
—ANONYMOUS

We come and we cry, and that is life; we yawn and we depart, and that is death!
—AUSONE DE CHANCEL,
Lines in an Album

It matters not how long we live, but how.
—BAILEY, *Festus*

Life is a long lesson in humility.
—BARRIE, *Little Minister*

It is a misery to be born, a pain to live, a trouble to die.
—ST. BERNARD OF
CLAIRVAUX

Life is but a day at most.
—BURNS, *Friars' Carse
Hermitage*

One life—a little gleam of Time between two Eternities.
—CARLYLE

Hurried and worried until we're buried, and there's no
    curtain call,
Life's a very funny proposition, after all.
—GEORGE M. COHAN

For life in general, there is but one decree: youth is a blunder, manhood a struggle, old age a regret.
—DISRAELI

Out of sleeping a waking,
Out of waking a sleep.

—EMERSON, *The Sphinx*

Our whole life is like a play.

—BEN JONSON

No one is to be despaired of as long as he breathes. (While there is life there is hope.)

—ERASMUS

Dost thou love life? Then do not squander time, for that is the stuff life is made of.

—FRANKLIN, *Poor Richard*

A useless life is an early death.

—GOETHE

All that a man hath will he give for his life.

—JOB. II. 4

Life is a tragedy for those who feel, and a comedy for those who think.

—LA BRUYÈRE

Every life is many days, day after day. We walk through ourselves, meeting robbers, ghosts, giants, old men, young men, wives, widows, brothers-in-love. But always meeting ourselves.

—JAMES JOYCE, *Ulysses*

Tell me not, in mournful numbers,
    Life is but an empty dream!

—LONGFELLOW, *A Psalm
    of Life*

Christian life consists in faith and charity.

—LUTHER

Strait is the gate and narrow is the way which leadeth
unto life.

—MATTHEW. VII. 14

My candle burns at both ends;
    It will not last the night;
But, ah, my foes, and, oh, my friends—
    It gives a lovely light.

—EDNA ST. VINCENT
    MILLAY, *Figs from
    Thistles*

Ah Love! could you and I with him conspire
    To grasp this sorry Scheme of Things entire
    Would we not shatter it to bits—and then
Re-mould it nearer to the Heart's Desire?

—OMAR KHAYYÁM,
    Rubaiyat

Life is the game that must be played:
This truth at least, good friends, we know;
So live and laugh, nor be dismayed
As one by one the phantoms go.

—EDWIN ARLINGTON
    ROBINSON, *Ballade by
    the Fire*

I wish to preach not the doctrine of ignoble ease, but the
doctrine of the strenuous life.

—THEODORE ROOSEVELT

As is a tale, so is life: not how long it is, but how good
it is, is what matters.

—SENECA

His saying was: live and let live.

—SCHILLER

Out, out, brief candle!
Life's but a walking shadow.

> —SHAKESPEARE, *Macbeth*.
> Act V. Sc. 5

May you live all the days of your life.

> —SWIFT

Let your life lightly dance on the edges of Time like dew
on the tip of a leaf.

> —TAGORE, *Gardener*

The white flower of a blameless life.

> —TENNYSON, *Idylls of the
> King*

Life is a game of whist. From unseen sources
The cards are shuffled, and the hands are dealt.

• • •

I do not like the way the cards are shuffled,
But yet I like the game and want to play.

> —EUGENE F. WARE, *Whist*

Men know life too early, women know life too late.

> —WILDE, *A Woman of No
> Importance*

All the things I really like to do are either immoral, illegal
or fattening.

> —ALEXANDER WOOLLCOTT

Light

And God said, Let there be light: and there was light.

> —GENESIS. I. 3

The true light, which lighteth every man that cometh
into the world.
—JOHN. I. 9

He was a burning and a shining light.
—JOHN. V. 35

Lead, kindly Light, amid the encircling gloom,
Lead Thou me on!
The night is dark, and I am far from home—
Lead Thou me on!
Keep Thou my feet; I do not ask to see
The distant scene,—one step enough for me.
—JOHN HENRY NEWMAN

And this I know; whether the one True Light
Kindle to Love, or Wrath consume me quite,
One flash of it within the Tavern caught
Better than in the temple lost outright.
—OMAR KHAYYÁM,
Rubaiyat

Nature and Nature's laws lay hid in night:
God said, "Let Newton be!" and all was light.
—POPE, Epitaph for Sir
Isaac Newton

Like

Birds of a feather flock together.
—ENGLISH PROVERB

Like mother, like daughter.
—ENGLISH PROVERB

One crow will not pick out another crow's eyes.
—ENGLISH PROVERB

Like will to like, each creature loves his kind.
                                    —HERRICK, *Hesperides*

Like father, like son.

                                    —LATIN PROVERB

I shall not look upon his like again.
                                    —SHAKESPEARE, *Hamlet*.
                                        Act I. Sc. 2

Lincoln

His heart was as great as the world, but there was no
room in it to hold the memory of a wrong.
                                    —EMERSON, *Letters and
                                            Social Aims*

> Nature, they say, doth dote,
> And cannot make a man
> Save on some worn-out plan
> Repeating us by rote:
> For him her Old World moulds aside she threw
> And, choosing sweet clay from the breast
> Of the unexhausted West,
> With stuff untainted shaped a hero new.
>   —LOWELL, *A Hero New*

Honesty rare as a man without self-pity,
Kindness as large and plain as a prairie wind.
                                    —STEPHEN VINCENT
                                        BENÉT, *John Brown's
                                        Body*

O captain! my captain! our fearful trip is done;
The ship has weather'd every rack; the prize we sought
    is won;

The port is near, the bells I hear, the people all exulting,
While follow eyes the steady keel, the vessel grim and
        daring;
But O heart! heart! heart!
        O the bleeding drops of red,
Where on the deck my captain lies,
        Fallen cold and dead.

—WALT WHITMAN, *O
        Captain! My Captain!*

Lion

The lion is not so fierce as they paint him.
            —HERBERT

Do not pluck the beard of a dead lion.
            —MARTIAL

A lion among ladies is a most dreadful thing.
            —SHAKESPEARE, *A Mid-
            summer Night's
            Dream.* Act III. Sc. 1

It is not good to wake a sleeping lion.
            —PHILIP SIDNEY, *Arcadia*

Listening

From listening comes wisdom, and from speaking repentance.
            —ITALIAN PROVERB

A good listener is not only popular everywhere, but after
a while he knows something.
            —WILSON MIZNER

Literature

The great standard of literature as to purity and exactness of style is the Bible.

>—HUGH BLAIR

The man who writes about himself and his own time is the only man who writes about all people and about all time.

>—GEORGE BERNARD
>SHAW, *The Sanity of
>Art*

Literature is my Utopia. Here I am not disfranchised. No barrier of the senses shuts me out from the sweet, gracious discourse of my book-friends. They talk to me without embarrassment or awkwardness.

>—HELEN KELLER, *The
>Story of My Life*

The classics are only primitive literature. They belong to the same class as primitive machinery and primitive music and primitive medicine.

>—STEPHEN LEACOCK,
>*Homer and Humbug*

The republic of letters.

>—MOLIÈRE

The difference between literature and journalism is that journalism is unreadable, and literature is not read.

>—WILDE, *The Critic as
>Artist*

LOGIC • LOVE / 265

Logic

Logic is logic. That's all I say.
>   —HOLMES, *The One-Hoss
>   Shay*

Logic is neither a science nor an art, but a dodge.
>   —BENJAMIN JOWETT

Grammar is the logic of speech, even as logic is the grammar of reason.
>   —TRENCH

London

A mighty mass of brick, and smoke, and shipping,
    Dirty and dusty, but as wide as eye
Could reach, with here and there a sail just skipping
    In sight, then lost amidst the forestry
Of masts; a wilderness of steeples peeping
    On tiptoe through their sea-coal canopy;
A huge, dun cupola, like a fools-cap crown
    On a fool's head—and there is London Town.
>   —BYRON, *Don Juan*

London is a roost, for every bird.
>   —DISRAELI, *Lothair*

Love

The sweetest joy, the wildest woe is love.
>   —BAILEY, *Festus*

Man loves little and often, woman much and rarely.
>   —BASTA

Love in France is a comedy; in England a tragedy; in Italy an opera seria; and in Germany a melodrama.
—MARGUERITE
BLESSINGTON

Our first and last love is—self-love.
—BOVEE

The first sigh of love is the last of wisdom.
—ANTOINE BRET

Oh my luve's like a red, red rose,
    That's newly sprung in June;
Oh my luve's like the melodie
    That's sweetly played in tune.
—BURNS, *Red, Red Rose*

Man's love is of man's life a thing apart,
    'Tis woman's whole existence.
—BYRON, *Don Juan*

Of all the girls that are so smart
    There's none like pretty Sally;
She is the darling of my heart,
    And lives in our alley.
—HENRY CAREY, *Sally in
Our Alley*

There's no love lost between us.
—CERVANTES, *Don
Quixote*

All thoughts, all passions, all delights,
    Whatever stirs this mortal frame,
All are but ministers of Love,
    And feed his sacred flame.
—COLERIDGE, *Love*

Heaven has no rage like love to hatred turned.
—CONGREVE

How wise are they that are but fools in love!
—JOSHUA COOKE

Love with men is not a sentiment, but an idea.
—MME. DE GIRARDIN

Love is an ocean of emotions, entirely surrounded by expenses.
—LORD DEWAR

We are all born for love,
... It is the principle of existence and its only end.
—DISRAELI, *Sybil*

If yet I have not all thy love, love
Dear, I shall never have it all.
—JOHN DONNE

I have found it impossible to carry the heavy burden of responsibility and to discharge my duties as King as I would wish to do without the help and support of the woman I love.
—EDWARD VIII, (later the Duke of Windsor), in his farewell address, 1936

But one always returns to one's first loves.
—ÉTIENNE, *Joconde*

If you would be loved, love and be lovable.
—FRANKLIN

It's love, it's love that makes the world go round.
—FRENCH SONG

All mankind love a lover.
>
> —EMERSON, *Essays*

Young men wish: love, money and health. One day, they'll
say: health, money and love.
>
> —PAUL GERALDY

Man begins by loving love and ends by loving a woman.
Woman begins by loving a man and ends by loving love.
>
> —REMY DE GOURMONT

Whom the Lord loveth he chasteneth.
>
> —HEBREWS. XII. 6

You say to me-ward's your affection's strong;
Pray love me little, so you love me long.
>
> —HERRICK

Love is a conflict between reflexes and reflections.
>
> —MAGNUS HIRSCHFELD,
> *Sex in Human
> Relationship*

Pale hands I loved beside the Shalimar,
>   Where are you now? Who lies beneath your spell?
Whom do you lead on Rapture's roadway, far,
>   Before you agonize them in farewell?
>
> —LAURENCE HOPE,
> *Kashmiri Song*

There is no fear in love; but perfect love casteth out fear.
>
> —I JOHN. IV. 18

Love's like the measles—all the worse when it comes late
in life.
>
> —DOUGLAS JERROLD

Greater love hath no man than this, that a man lay down his life for his friends.

—JOHN. XV. 13

Love in a hut, with water and a crust,
Is—Love, forgive us!—cinders, ashes, dust.

—KEATS, *Lamia*

Sing, for faith and hope are high—
    None so true as you and I—
Sing the Lovers' Litany:
    "Love like ours can never die!"

—KIPLING, *Lovers' Litany*

The reason why lovers and their mistresses never tire of being together is that they are always talking of themselves.

—LA ROCHEFOUCAULD

I could not love thee, dear, so much
    Loved I not honour more.

—LOVELACE, *To Lucasta,
    on Going to the Wars*

I love a lassie, a bonnie, bonnie lassie,
She's as pure as the lily in the dell.
    She's as sweet as the heather,
The bonnie, bloomin' heather,
    Mary, ma Scotch Blue-bell.

—HARRY LAUDER and
    GERALD GRAFTON

He who loves not wine, woman, and song,
Remains a fool his whole life long.

—Attributed to LUTHER

Come live with me, and be my love,
And we will all the pleasures prove,
That valleys, groves, or hills, or fields,
Or woods and steepy mountains, yield.
>   —MARLOWE, *The
>   Passionate Shepherd to
>   His Love*

He who for love hath undergone
>   The worst that can befall,
Is happier thousandfold than one
>   Who never loved at all.
>   —RICHARD MONCKTON
>   MILNES, *To Myrzha*

So dear I love him, that with him all deaths
I could endure, without him live no life.
>   —MILTON, *Paradise Lost*

Love is often a fruit of marriage.
>   —MOLIÈRE

But there's nothing half so sweet in life
As love's young dream.
>   —MOORE

The only victory over love is flight.
>   —NAPOLEON

Love—a grave mental disease.
>   —PLATO

Everybody in love is blind.
>   —PROPERTIUS

Better is a dinner of herbs where love is, than a stalled
ox and hatred therewith.
>   —PROVERBS. XV. 17

As one who cons at evening o'er an album all alone,
And muses on the faces of the friends that he has known,
So I turn the leaves of Fancy, till in shadowy design
I find the smiling features of an old sweetheart of mine.
—JAMES WHITCOMB RILEY,
*An Old Sweetheart of
Mine*

Love must have wings to fly away from love,
And to fly back again.
—EDWIN ARLINGTON
ROBINSON, *Tristram*

Love is the fulfilling of the law.
—ROMANS. XIII. 10

The hours I spent with thee, dear heart,
     Are as a string of pearls to me;
I could them over, every one apart,
     My rosary, my rosary.
—ROBERT CAMERON
ROGERS, *My Rosary*

And love is loveliest when embalm'd in tears.
—SCOTT, *Lady of the Lake*

Men have died from time to time, and worms have eaten
them—but not for love.
—SHAKESPEARE, *As You
Like It*. Act IV. Sc. 1

Ay me! for aught that I ever could read,
Could ever hear by tale or history,
The course of true love never did run smooth.
—SHAKESPEARE,
*Midsummer Night's
Dream*. Act 1. Sc. 1

Give me my Romeo; and, when he shall die.
Take him, and cut him out in little stars,
And he will make the face of heaven so fine,
That all the world will be in love with night,
And pay no worship to the garish sun.

—SHAKESPEARE, *Romeo
and Juliet*. Act III. Sc. 2

Whither thou goest, I will go; and where thou lodgest,
I will lodge; thy people shall be my people, and thy God
my God.

—RUTH. I. 16

Love sought is good, but given unsought is better.

—SHAKESPEARE, *Twelfth
Night*. Act III. Sc. 1

The fickleness of the woman I love is equalled by the
infernal constancy of the women who love me.

—GEORGE BERNARD
SHAW, *The
Philanderer*

Love is strong as death; jealousy is cruel as the grave.

—SONG OF SOLOMON.
VIII. 6

Many waters cannot quench love, neither can the floods
drown it.

—SONG OF SOLOMON.
VIII. 7

Blue eyes say, "Love me or I die"; black eyes say, "Love
me or I kill thee."

—SPANISH PROVERB

To love her was a liberal education.
>—STEELE, *Of Lady*
>Elizabeth Hastings

Some pray to marry the man they love,
>My prayer will somewhat vary:
I humbly pray to Heaven above
>That I love the man I marry.
>>—ROSE PASTOR STOKES,
>>*My Prayer*

'Tis better to have loved and lost,
Than never to have loved at all.
>—TENNYSON, *In Memoriam*

"I'm sorry that I spell'd the word;
>I hate to go above you,
Because"—the brown eyes lower fell,—
>"Because, you see, I love you!"
>>—WHITTIER, *In School-
>>Days*

Werther had a love for Charlotte,
>Such as words could never utter;
Would you know how first he met her?
>She was cutting bread and butter.
>>—THACKERAY, *The Sorrows
>>of Werther*

Love in its essence is spiritual fire.
>—SWEDENBORG, *True
>Christian Religion*

Luck

Good luck is a lazy man's estimate of a worker's success.
>—ANONYMOUS

Throw a lucky man into the sea, and he will come up
with a fish in his mouth.
                              —ARAB PROVERB

As ill-luck would have it.
                              —CERVANTES, *Don
                                 Quixote*

A pound of pluck is worth a ton of luck.
                              —JAMES A. GARFIELD

Behind bad luck comes good luck.
                              —GIPSY PROVERB

Lullaby

Hush, my dear, lie still and slumber,
     Holy angels guard thy bed!
Heavenly blessings without number
     Gently falling on thy head.
                              —ISAAC WATTS

Rock-a-bye baby, on the tree top,
When the wind blows the cradle will rock;
When the bough breaks the cradle will fall;
Down will come baby, cradle and all.
                              —ENGLISH NURSERY
                                 RHYME

Sweet and low, sweet and low,
     Wind of the western sea,
Low, low, breathe and blow,
     Wind of the western sea!
Over the rolling waters go,
Come from the dying moon, and blow,
     Blow him again to me;
While my little one, while my pretty one sleeps.
                              —TENNYSON, *The Princess*

Lying

Peter said, Ananias, why hath Satan filled thine heart to lie to the Holy Ghost? . . . And Ananias hearing these words fell down, and gave up the ghost.

—ACTS. III. 3–5

And after all, what is a lie?
    'Tis but
The truth in masquerade.

—BYRON, *Don Juan*

A liar is not believed even though he tell the truth.

—CICERO

Any fool can tell the truth, but it requires a man of some sense to know how to lie well.

—SAMUEL BUTLER, *Note-Books*

Terminological inexactitude

—WINSTON CHURCHILL, Speech, 1906

A good memory is needed once we have lied.

—CORNEILLE

Show me a liar, and I will show thee a thief.

—HERBERT

Who dares think one thing, and another tell,
My heart detests him as the gates of hell.

—HOMER, *Iliad*

The liar's punishment is not in the least that he is not believed, but that he cannot believe anyone else.

—GEORGE BERNARD SHAW

That a lie which is half a truth is ever the blackest of
    lies;
That a lie which is all a lie may be met and fought with
    outright—
But a lie which is part a truth is a harder matter to fight.
               —TENNYSON, *The*
                 Grandmother

Machine

A tool is but the extension of a man's hand, and a machine
is but a complex tool. He that invents a machine augments the power of a man and the well being of mankind.
               —HENRY WARD BEECHER

Man is a tool-using animal.
               —CARLYLE, *Sartor Resartus*

One machine can do the work of fifty ordinary men. No
machine can do the work of one extraordinary man.
               —ELBERT HUBBARD

Men have become the tools of their tools.
               —THOREAU, *Walden*

Majority

One with the law is a majority.
               —CALVIN COOLIDGE,
                 Speech, 1920

A minority may be right; a majority is always wrong.
               —IBSEN, *An Enemy of the*
                 People

It is my principle that the will of the majority should
always prevail.
—JEFFERSON, Letter, 1787

One, on God's side, is a majority.
—WENDELL PHILLIPS

Mammon

Cursed Mammon be, when he with treasures
    To restless action spurs our fate!
—GOETHE, *Faust*

Ye cannot serve God and mammon.
—MATTHEW. VI. 24

What treasures here do Mammon's sons behold!
Yet know that all that which glitters is not gold.
—QUARLES

Man

There never was such beauty in another man.
Nature made him, and then broke the mould.
—ARIOSTO, *Orlando
Furioso*

Let each man think himself an act of God.
His mind a thought, his life a breath of God.
—BAILEY, *Festus*

A man's a man for a' that!

—BURNS, *For A' That and
A' That*

Man!
Thou pendulum betwixt a smile and tear.
—BYRON, *Childe Harold*

We are the miracle of miracles, the great inscrutable mystery of God.

—CARLYLE

Man's inhumanity to man
Makes countless thousands mourn!
—BURNS, *Man Was Made
to Mourn*

Every man is a volume, if you know how to read them.
—WILLIAM ELLERY
CHANNING

There are times when one would like to hang the whole human race, and finish the farce.
—S. L. CLEMENS (MARK
TWAIN), *A
Connecticut Yankee at
King Arthur's Court*

I am made all things to all men.
—I CORINTHIANS. IX. 22

The first man is of the earth, earthy.
—I CORINTHIANS. XV. 47

His tribe were God Almighty's gentlemen.
—DRYDEN, *Absalom and
Achitophel*

Man wants but little here below,
Nor wants that little long.
—GOLDSMITH, *The Hermit*

Man is the only animal that laughs and weeps; for he is the only animal that is struck with the difference between what things are, and what they ought to be.

—HAZLITT

Man is a piece of the universe made alive.

—EMERSON

I decline to accept the end of men . . . I believe that man will not merely endure: he will prevail. He is immortal not because he alone among creatures has an inexhaustible voice but because he has a soul, a spirit capable of compassion and sacrifice and endurance.

—WILLIAM FAULKNER,
Acceptance Speech for
Nobel Prize in
Literature, 1949

God give us men. A time like this demands
Strong minds, great hearts, true faith and ready hands!
Men whom the lust of office does not kill,
Men whom the spoils of office cannot buy,
Men who possess opinions and a will,
Men who love honor, men who cannot lie.

—J. G. HOLLAND

Man passes away; his name perishes from record and recollection; his history is as a tale that is told, and his very monument becomes a ruin.

—WASHINGTON IRVING,
The Sketch Book

Cease ye from man, whose breath is in his nostrils.

—ISAIAH, II. 22

If you can keep your head when all about you
Are losing theirs and blaming it on you,
If you can trust yourself when all men doubt you,
But make allowance for their doubting too;
Yours is the Earth and everything that's in it,
And—which is more—you'll be a man, my son!
—KIPLING, *If*

Man that is born of a woman is of few days, and full of trouble.
—JOB. XIV. I

Though I've belted you and flayed you,
By the livin' Gawd that made you,
You're a better man than I am, Gunga Din.
—KIPLING, *Gunga Din*

Make ye no truce with Adam-zad—the Bear that walks like a man.
—KIPLING, *The Truce of the Bear*

It is easier to know mankind in general than man individually.
—LA ROCHEFOUCAULD

Men, in general, are but great great children.
—NAPOLEON

I teach you beyond Man (superman). Man is something that shall be surpassed. What have you done to surpass him?
—NIETZSCHE, *Thus Spake Zarathustra*

Man's the bad child of the universe.
—JAMES OPPENHEIM, *Laughter*

Does man differ from the other animals? Only in posture.
The rest are bent, but he is a wild beast who walks
upright.

—PHILEMON

We must laugh at man, to avoid crying for him.

—NAPOLEON

Know then thyself, presume not God to scan;
The proper study of mankind is man.

—POPE, *Essay on Man*

Man is the measure of all things.

—PROTAGORAS

Thou hast made him a little lower than the angels.

—PSALMS. VIII. 5

Mark the perfect man, and behold the upright.

—PSALMS. XXXVII. 37

The forgotten man at the bottom of the economic pyr-
amid.

—F. D. ROOSEVELT,
Speech, 1932

Quit yourselves like men.

—I SAMUEL. IV. 9

A man after his own heart.

—I SAMUEL. XIII. 14

Thou art the man.

—II SAMUEL. XII. 7

What a piece of work is a man! how noble in reason! how infinite in faculty! in form and moving how express and admirable! in action how like an angel! in apprehension how like a god! the beauty of the world! the paragon of animals! And, yet, to me, what is this quintessence of dust? man delights not me: no, nor woman neither, though by your smiling, you seem to say so.

—SHAKESPEARE, *Hamlet.*
Act II. Sc. 2

Man is a social animal.

—SENECA

He was a man, take him for all in all, I shall not look upon his like again.

—SHAKESPEARE, *Hamlet.*
Act I. Sc. 2

His life was gentle, and the elements
So mix'd in him that Nature might stand up,
And say to all the world, This was a man!

—SHAKESPEARE, *Julius
Caesar.* Act V. Sc. 5

Manners

He was the mildest manner'd man
That ever scuttled ship or cut a throat.

—BYRON, *Don Juan*

Now as to politeness . . . I would venture to call it benevolence in trifles.

—LORD CHATHAM

Manners must adorn knowledge and smooth its way through the world.

—CHESTERFIELD

"What sort of a doctor is he?" "Well, I don't know much about his ability; but he's got a very good bedside manner."
—*Punch,,* March 15, 1884.

Men make laws; women make manners.
—DE SEGUR

They asked Lucman, the fabulist, From whom did you learn manners? He answered: From the unmannerly.
—SADI

What once were vices are now manners.
—SENECA

Politeness goes far, yet costs nothing.
—SAMUEL SMILES

Good manners is the art of making those people easy with whom we converse. Whoever makes the fewest persons uneasy, is the best bred in the company.
—SWIFT

Suit your manner to the man.
—TERENCE, *Adelphi*

Marriage

Marriage is a romance in which the hero dies in the first chapter.
—ANONYMOUS

It is better for a woman to marry a man who loves her than a man she loves.
—ARAB PROVERB

He that hath a wife and children hath given hostages to fortune; for they are impediments to great enterprises, either of virtue or mischief.

—BACON, *Essays*

A man finds himself seven years older the day after his marriage.

—BACON

A woman must be a genius to create a good husband.

—BALZAC

To have and to hold from this day forward, for better, for worse, for richer, for poorer, in sickness, and in health, to love and to cherish, till death us do part.

—BOOK OF COMMON
PRAYER

To love, cherish, and to obey.

—BOOK OF COMMON
PRAYER

With this ring I thee wed, with my body I thee worship, and with all my worldly goods I thee endow.

—BOOK OF COMMON
PRAYER

Thus grief still treads upon the heels of pleasure,
Marry'd in hast, we may repent at leisure.

—CONGREVE, *The Old
Bachelor*

A deaf husband and a blind wife are always a happy couple.

—DANISH PROVERB

To marry once is a duty, twice a folly, thrice is madness.

—DUTCH PROVERB

There is a French saying: "Love is the dawn of marriage, and marriage is the sunset of love."
—DE FINOD

It destroys one's nerves to be amiable every day to the same human being.
—DISRAELI

Every woman should marry—and no man.
—DISRAELI, *Lothair*

Is not marriage an open question, when it is alleged, from the beginning of the world, that such as are in the institution wish to get out, and such as are out wish to get in.
—EMERSON, *Representative Men*

Where there's marriage without love, there will be love without marriage.
—FRANKLIN, *Poor Richard*

Keep thy eyes wide open before marriage; and half shut afterward.
—THOMAS FULLER, *Introductio ad Prudentiam*

It is not good that the man should be alone.
—GENESIS. II. 18

Bone of my bones, and flesh of my flesh.
—GENESIS. II 23

Weeping bride, laughing wife; laughing bride, weeping wife.
—GERMAN PROVERB

Matrimony,—the high sea for which no compass has yet
been invented.

—HEINE

Marriage is something you have to give your whole mind
to.

—IBSEN, *The League of
Youth*

Heaven will be no heaven to me if I do not meet my wife
there.

—ANDREW JACKSON

What therefore God hath joined together let not man put
asunder.

—MATTHEW. XIX. 6

Something old, something new,
Something borrowed, something blue.

—OLD ENGLISH RHYME
(The wedding dress)

If thou wouldst marry wisely, marry thine equal.

—OVID

The woman cries before the wedding; the man afterward.

—POLISH PROVERB

A prudent wife is from the Lord.

—PROVERBS, XIX. 14

Marriage is a lottery in which men stake their liberty,
and women their happiness.

—MME. DE RIEUX

Men are April when they woo, December when they wed; maids are May when they are maids, but the sky changes when they are wives.
—SHAKESPEARE, *As You Like It.* Act IV. Sc. 1

Advice to persons about to marry—Don't.
—*Punch's Almanack, 1845*

The whole world is strewn with snares, traps, gins and pitfalls for the capture of men by women.
—GEORGE BERNARD SHAW, *Man and Superman*

Marriages are made in Heaven.
—TENNYSON, *Aylmer's Field*

Remember, it is as easy to marry a rich woman as a poor woman.
—THACKERAY, *Pendennis*

Marriage is the one subject on which all women agree and all men disagree.
—WILDE

Men marry because they are tired, women because they are curious: both are disappointed.
—WILDE

Medicine

The physician heals, Nature makes well.
—ARISTOTLE

Nature, time, and patience are the three great physicians.
—H. G. BOHN

The best doctor is the one you run for and can't find.
—DIDEROT

I find the medicine worse than the malady.
—BEAUMONT AND
FLETCHER, Love's
Cure

An apple a day keeps the doctor away.
—ENGLISH PROVERB

God heals and the doctor takes the fee.
—FRANKLIN, Poor Richard's
Almanac

He's the best physician that knows the worthlessness of the most medicines.
—FRANKLIN, Poor Richard's
Almanac

I firmly believe that if the whole *materia medica* as now used, could be sunk to the bottom of the sea, it would be all the better for mankind and all the worse for the fishes.
—HOLMES, Lecture,
Medical Society

Physician, heal thyself.
—LUKE. IV. 23

Doctors are men who prescribe medicines of which they know little, to cure diseases of which they know less, in human beings of whom they know nothing.
—VOLTAIRE

A sound mind in a sound body is a thing to be prayed for.
—JUVENAL

Memory

Time whereof the memory of man runneth not to the contrary.

> —BLACKSTONE,
> *Commentaries*

To live in hearts we leave behind,
Is not to die.

> —CAMPBELL, *Hallowed
> Ground*

Vanity plays lurid tricks with our memory.

> —JOSEPH CONRAD, *Lord
> Jim*

Don't you remember sweet Alice Ben Bolt?
    Sweet Alice, whose hair was so brown;
Who wept with delight when you gave her a smile,
    And trembl'd with fear at your frown!

> —THOMAS DUNN
> ENGLISH, *Ben Bolt*

I remember, I remember,
    The house where I was born,
The little window where the sun
    Came peeping in at morn;
He never came a wink too soon,
    Nor brought too long a day,
But now, I often wish the night
    Had borne my breath away!

> —HOOD, *I Remember, I
> Remember*

We must always have old memories and young hopes.

> —ARSÈNE HOUSSAYE

The true art of memory is the art of attention.

> —SAMUEL JOHNSON

All to myself I think of you,
Think of the things we used to do,
Think of the things we used to say,
Think of each happy bygone day,
Sometimes I sigh, and sometimes I smile,
But I keep each olden, golden while
All to myself.

> —WILBUR D. NESBIT, *All
> to Myself*

Women and elephants never forget.

> —DOROTHY PARKER,
> *Ballade of Unfortunate
> Mammals*

If I do not remember thee, let my tongue cleave to the
roof of my mouth.

> —PSALMS. CXXXVII. 6

The Right Honorable gentleman is indebted to his memory for his jests and to his imagination for his facts.

> —R. B. SHERIDAN

Mercy

Among the attributes of God, although they are all equal,
mercy shines with even more brilliancy than justice.

> —CERVANTES

The mercy of the Lord is from everlasting to everlasting
upon them that fear Him.

> —PSALMS. CIII. 17

The quality of mercy is not strain'd,
It droppeth as the gentle rain from heaven
Upon the place beneath: it is twice blest;
It blesseth him that gives and him that takes;

'Tis mightiest in the mightiest; it becomes
The throned monarch better than his crown;
His sceptre shows the force of temporal power,
The attribute to awe and majesty,
Wherein doth sit the dread and fear of kings;
But mercy is above this sceptred sway;
It is enthroned in the hearts of kings,
It is an attribute to God himself;
And earthly power doth then show likest God's
When mercy seasons justice.

> —SHAKESPEARE, *Merchant
> of Venice*. Act IV.
> Sc. 1

Being all fashioned of the self-same dust.
Let us be merciful as well as just.

> —LONGFELLOW, *Tales of a
> Wayside Inn*

Merriment

A source of innocent merriment!
   Of innocent merriment.

> —W. S. GILBERT, *The
> Mikado*

Merry have we met, and merry have we been;
Merry let us part, and merry meet again;
With our merry sing-song, happy gay, and free,
With a merry ding-dong, happy let us be!

> —OLD ENGLISH RHYME

A merry heart doeth good like a medicine.

> —PROVERBS. XVII. 22

Let us eat, and be merry.

> —LUKE, XV. 23

Nothing is more hopeless than a scheme of merriment.
—SAMUEL JOHNSON, The
Idler

Midnight

The dreadful dead of dark midnight.
—SHAKESPEARE, The Rape
of Lucrece

Once upon a midnight dreary, while I pondered weak
and weary,
Over many a quaint and curious volume of forgotten lore.
—POE, The Raven

Mind

God is Mind, and God is infinite; hence all is Mind.
—MARY BAKER EDDY,
Science and Health

The true, strong, and sound mind is the mind that can
embrace equally great things and small.
—SAMUEL JOHNSON,
Boswell's Life of
Johnson

What is mind? No matter. What is matter? Never mind.
—T. H. KEY

The mind is its own place, and in itself
Can make a heaven of hell, a hell of heaven.
—MILTON, Paradise Lost

A feeble body weakens the mind.
—ROUSSEAU, Émile

'Tis but a base, ignoble mind
That mounts no higher than a bird can soar.
—SHAKESPEARE, *Henry* V.
Act IV. Sc. 1

Misery

He that is down need fear no fall.
—BUNYAN

Misery loves company.
—ENGLISH PROVERB

Fire tries gold, misery tries brave men.
—SENECA

Misery acquaints a man with strange bedfellows.
—SHAKESPEARE, *Tempest*.
Act II. Sc. 2

Misfortune

Misfortunes always come in by a door that has been left open for them.
—CZECH PROVERB

Little minds are tamed and subdued by misfortune; but great minds rise above it.
—WASHINGTON IRVING

We have all of us sufficient fortitude to bear the misfortunes of others.
—LA ROCHEFOUCAULD

Let us be of good cheer, however, remembering that the misfortunes hardest to bear are those which never come.

—LOWELL, *Democracy and Addresses*

The worst is not
So long as we can say "This is the worst."

—SHAKESPEARE, *King Lear.*
Act IV. Sc. 1

Mobs

The mob is man voluntarily descending to the nature of the beast.

—EMERSON

The mob is a sort of bear; while your ring is through its nose, it will even dance under your cudgel; but should the ring slip, and you lose your hold, the brute will turn and rend you.

—JANE PORTER

It has been very truly said that the mob has many heads, but no brains.

—RIVAROL

Moderation

It is best to rise from life as from a banquet, neither thirsty nor drunken.

—ARISTOTLE

To live long, it is necessary to live slowly.

—CICERO

A thing moderately good is not so good as it ought to be. Moderation in temper is always a virtue; but moderation in principle is always a vice.
—THOMAS PAINE

In everything the middle course is best: all things in excess bring trouble to men.
—PLAUTUS

Give me neither poverty nor riches.
—PROVERBS. XXX. 8

Modesty

Modesty is the conscience of the body.
—BALZAC

Modesty is the only sure bait when you angle for praise.
—CHESTERFIELD

Modesty died when false modesty was born.
—S. L. CLEMENS (MARK TWAIN)

Man is the only animal that blushes. Or needs to.
—S. L. CLEMENS (MARK TWAIN)

A modest man never talks of himself.
—LA BRUYÈRE

With people of only moderate ability modesty is mere honesty; but with those who possess great talent it is hypocrisy.
—SCHOPENHAUER

Money

Money is a good servant but a bad master.
—Quoted by BACON

Money makes the man.
—ARISTODEMUS

A fool and his money are soon parted.
—GEORGE BUCHANAN

Penny wise, pound foolish.
—BURTON

Wine maketh merry: but money answereth all things.
—ECCLESIASTES. X. 19

If you would know the value of money, go and try to
borrow some.
—FRANKLIN, *Poor Richard's
Almanac*

Never ask of money spent
Where the spender thinks it went.
Nobody was ever meant
To remember or invent
What he did with every cent.
—ROBERT FROST, *The
Hardship of
Accounting*

The almighty dollar, that great object of universal devotion throughout our land, seems to have no genuine devo-
tees in these peculiar villages.
—WASHINGTON IRVING,
Creole Village

Jesus went into the temple ... overthrew the tables of the
money changers, and the seats of them that sold doves.
—MARK. XI. 15

When I had money everyone called me brother.
—POLISH PROVERB

Take care of the pence, and the pounds will take care of
themselves.

—WILLIAM LOWNDES

Ah, take the Cash, and let the Credit go,
Nor heed the rumble of a distant Drum!
—OMAR KHAYYÁM,
Rubaiyat

When money speaks the truth is silent.
—RUSSIAN PROVERB

Money is not required to buy one necessity of the soul.
—THOREAU

Not greedy of filthy lucre.
—I TIMOTHY. III. 3

The love of money is the root of all evil.
—I TIMOTHY. VI. 10

Months

October turned my maple's leaves to gold;
The most are gone now; here and there one lingers;
Soon these will slip from out the twig's weak hold,
Like coins between a dying miser's fingers.
—T. B. ALDRICH, *Maple
Leaves*

If cold December gave you birth,
The month of snow and ice and mirth,
Place on your hand a turquoise blue,
Success will bless what'er you do.
                              —ANONYMOUS

Thirty days hath September,
April, June, and November;
All the rest have thirty-one
Excepting February alone:
Which hath but twenty-eight, in fine,
Till leap year gives it twenty-nine.
                              —ANONYMOUS

O sweet September, thy first breezes bring
        The dry leaf's rustle and the squirrel's laughter,
The cool fresh air whence health and vigor spring
        And promise of exceeding joy hereafter.
                              —GEORGE ARNOLD,
                                September Days

Oh, to be in England
Now that April's there.
                              —BROWNING, *Home
                                Thoughts from Abroad*

March comes in like a lion and goes out like a lamb.
                              —ENGLISH PROVERB

If February give much snow
A fine Summer it doth foreshow.
                              —ENGLISH PROVERB

No park—no ring—no afternoon gentility—
No company—no nobility—
No warmth, no cheerfulness, no healthful ease.
No comfortable feel in any member—

No shade, no shine, no butterflies, no bees,
No fruits, no flowers, no leaves, no birds,
    November!
                    —HOOD, *November*

And what is so rare as a day in June?
    Then, if ever, come perfect days;
Then Heaven tries earth if it be in tune,
    And over it softly her warm ear lays.
                    —LOWELL, *Vision of Sir
                    Launfal*

As full of spirit as the month of May.
                    —SHAKESPEARE, *King
                    Henry IV.* Pt. I. Act
                    IV. Sc. 1

Among the changing months,
May stands confest
The sweetest, and in fairest colors dressed.
                    —JAMES THOMSON, *On
                    May*

Sweet April showers
Do bring May flowers.
                    —TUSSER, *Five Hundred
                    Points of Good
                    Husbandry*

Oh, the lovely fickleness of an April day!
                    —W. H. GIBSON, *Pastoral
                    Days*

The ides of March are come.
                    —SHAKESPEARE, *Julius
                    Caesar.* Act III. Sc. 1

January grey is here,
 Like a sexton by her grave;
February bears the bier,
 March with grief doth howl and rave,
And April weeps—but, O ye hours!
Follow with May's fairest flowers.

    —SHELLEY, *Dirge for the
    Year*

Monuments

Those only deserve a monument who do not need one.
    —HAZLITT

Monuments! what are they? the very pyramids have forgotten their builders, or to whom they were dedicated.
Deeds, not stones, are the true monuments of the great.
    —MOTLEY

Soldiers, forty centuries are looking down upon you from
these pyramids.

    —NAPOLEON

Moon

How like a queen comes forth the lonely Moon
From the slow opening curtains of the clouds
Walking in beauty to her midnight throne!
    —GEORGE CROLY, *Diana*

He should, as he list, be able to prove the moon is green
cheese.

    —SIR THOMAS MORE,
    English Works

That orbed maiden, with white fire laden,
Whom mortals call the moon.
—SHELLEY, *The Cloud*

Morality

Morality is a private and costly luxury.
—HENRY B. ADAMS, *The
Education of Henry
Adams*

"Tut, tut, child," said the Duchess. "Everything's got a
moral if only you can find it."
—LEWIS CARROLL, *Alice in
Wonderland*

I never did, or countenanced, in public life, a single act
inconsistent with the strictest good faith; having never
believed there was one code of morality for a public, and
another for a private man.
—JEFFERSON, 1809

Dr. Johnson's morality was as English an article as a
beefsteak.
—HAWTHORNE, *Our Old
Home*

To give a man full knowledge of true morality, I would
send him to no other book than the New Testament.
—LOCKE

We know no spectacle so ridiculous as the British public
in one of its periodical fits of morality.
—MACAULAY, *On Moore's
Life of Lord Byron*

Morality is the best of all devices for leading mankind by the nose.

—NIETZSCHE, *The Antichrist*

Do not be too moral. You may cheat yourself out of much life so. Aim above morality. Be not simply good; be good for something.

—THOREAU

Morning

Now the frosty stars are gone:
I have watched them one by one,
Fading on the shores of Dawn.
Round and full the glorious sun
Walks with level step the spray,
Through his vestibule of Day.

—BAYARD TAYLOR, *Ariel in the Cloven Pine*

The grey-ey'd morn smiles on the frowning night,
Chequering the eastern clouds with streaks of light.

—SHAKESPEARE, *Romeo and Juliet*. Act I. Sc. 1

Lose an hour in the morning, and you will be all day hunting for it.

—WHATELY

Mortality

All flesh shall perish together, and man shall turn again unto dust.

—JOB. XXXIV. 15

Oh, why should the spirit of mortal be proud?
Like a fast-flitting meteor, a fast-flying cloud,
A flash of the lightning, a break of the wave,
He passes from life to his rest in the grave.
                              —WILLIAM KNOX,
                                  Mortality

The lilies of the field whose bloom is brief;—
      We are as they;
      Like them we fade away
As doth a leaf.

                              —CHRISTINA G. ROSSETTI,
                                  Consider

Mother

The mother of all living.
                              —GENESIS. III. 20

She's somebody's mother, boys, you know,
For all she's aged and poor and slow.
                              —MARY DOW BRINE,
                                  Somebody's Mother

A mother is a mother still,
The holiest thing alive.
                              —COLERIDGE, *The Three
                                  Graves*

Men are what their mothers made them.
                              —EMERSON

What is home without a mother?
                              —ALICE HAWTHORNE.
                                  Title of a Poem

There is none,
In all this cold and hollow world, no fount
Of deep strong, deathless love, save that within
A mother's heart.
> —FELICIA D. HEMANS,
> *Siege of Valencia*

If I were hanged on the highest hill,
Mother o' mine, O mother o' mine!
I know whose love would follow me still,
Mother o' mine, O mother o' mine!
> —KIPLING, *Mother o' Mine*

All that I am or hope to be,
I owe to my angel mother.
> —Attributed to LINCOLN

I arose a mother in Israel.
> —JUDGES. V. 7

The bravest battle that ever was fought;
   Shall I tell you where and when?
On the maps of the world you will find it not;
   It was fought by the mothers of men.
> —JOAQUIN MILLER, *The
> Bravest Battle*

Who ran to help me when I fell,
And would some pretty story tell,
Or kiss the place to make it well?
   My Mother.
> —ANNE TAYLOR, *My
> Mother*

For the hand that rocks the cradle
   Is the hand that rules the world.
> —WILLIAM ROSS
> WALLACE, *What
> Rules the World*

Sure I love the dear silver that shines in your hair,
And the brow that's all furrowed, and wrinkled with care.
I kiss the dear fingers, so toil-worn for me,
Oh, God bless you and keep you, Mother Machree.
—RIDA JOHNSON YOUNG,
Mother Machree

Her children arise up and call her blessed.
—PROVERBS. XXXI. 28

Mountain

'Tis distance lends enchantment to the view,
And robes the mountain in its azure hue.
—CAMPBELL, *Pleasures of
Hope*

To make a mountain of a mole-hill.
—HENRY ELLIS, *Original
Letters*

If the mountain won't come to Mohammed, Mohammed
must go to the mountain.
—ENGLISH PROVERB

The mountain was in labour, and Jove was afraid, but it
brought forth a mouse.
—TACHOS, King of Egypt

Mourning

Blessed are they that mourn: for they shall be comforted.
—MATTHEW. V. 4

By the waters of Babylon we sat down and wept,
    Remembering thee.
                —SWINBURNE, *Super*
                    Flumina Babylonis

He mourns the dead who lives as they desire.
            —YOUNG, *Night Thoughts*

Mouse

The mouse that hath but one hole is quickly taken.
            —HERBERT

Mousetrap

If a man write a better book, preach a better sermon, or
make a better mousetrap than his neighbor, though he
build his house in the woods, the world will make a
beaten path to his door.
            —MRS. SARAH S. B. YULE,
                credits the quotation to
                Emerson in her
                Borrowings (1889)

Murder

Thou shalt not kill.
            —EXODUS. XX. 13

Murder most foul, as in the best it is;
But this most foul, strange and unnatural.
            —SHAKESPEARE, *Hamlet*.
              Act I. Sc. 5

For murder, though it have no tongue, will speak
With most miraculous organ.
                              —SHAKESPEARE, *Hamlet*.
                                    Act II. Sc. 2

Music

Music should strike fire from the heart of man, and bring
tears from the eyes of woman.
                              —BEETHOVEN

Music hath charms to soothe the savage breast.
                              —WILLIAM CONGREVE,
                                    The Mourning Bride

Soprano, basso, even the contralto
Wished him five fathom under the Rialto.
                              —BYRON, *Beppo*

Music is well said to be the speech of angels.
                              —CARLYLE, *Essays*

Why should the devil have all the good tunes?
                              —ROWLAND HILL, *Sermons*

The musician who always plays on the same string, is
laughed at.
                              —HORACE

When the morning stars sang together, and all the sons
of God shouted for joy.
                              —JOB. XXXVII. 7

Music is the universal language of mankind.
                              —LONGFELLOW, *Outre-Mer*

All of heaven we have below.
                    —ADDISON

Such sweet compulsion doth in music lie.
                    —MILTON, *Arcades*

Let me die to the sounds of delicious music.
                    —Last words of MIRABEAU

The harp that once through Tara's halls
        The soul of music shed,
Now hangs as mute on Tara's walls,
        As if that soul were fled.
                    —MOORE, *Harp That Once*
                        Through Tara's Halls

Wagner's music is better than it sounds.
                    —BILL NYE

Seated one day at the organ,
        I was weary and ill at ease,
And my fingers wandered idly
        Over the noisy keys.

I do not know what I was playing,
        Or what I was dreaming then,
But I struck one chord of music
        Like the sound of a great Amen.
                    —ADELAIDE A. PROCTER,
                        Lost Chord

Light quirks of music, broken and uneven,
Make the soul dance upon a jig to Heav'n.
                    —POPE, *Moral Essays*

The man that hath no music in himself,
Nor is no moved with concord of sweet sounds,
Is fit for treasons, stratagems and spoils.
> —SHAKESPEARE, *Merchant
> of Venice.* Act V. Sc. 1

Hell is full of musical amateurs.
> — GEORGE BERNARD
> SHAW, *Man and
> Superman*

Mystery

There was the door to which I found no key,
There was the veil through which I might not see.
> —OMAR KHAYYÁM,
> *Rubaiyat*

There be three things which are too wonderful for me,
yea, four which I know not: the way of an eagle in the
air; the way of a serpent upon a rock; the way of a ship
in the midst of the sea; and the way of a man with a
maid.
> —PROVERBS. XXX. 18–19

Mystery is the wisdom of blockheads.
> —HORACE WALPOLE

Name

Sticks and stones will break my bones, but names will
never hurt me.
> —ENGLISH PROVERB

Father calls me William, sister calls me Will,
Mother calls me Willie, but the fellows call me Bill!
—EUGENE FIELD, *Jest 'Fore
Christmas*

Adam gave names to all cattle, and to the fowl of the air,
and to every beast of the field.
—GENESIS. II. 20

A nickname is the hardest stone that the devil can throw
at a man.

—Quoted by HAZLITT

And, lo! Ben Adhem's name led all the rest.
—LEIGH HUNT, *Abou Ben
Adhem*

He left the name at which the world grew pale,
To point a moral, or adorn a tale.
—SAMUEL JOHNSON,
*Vanity of Human
Wishes*

A good name is rather to be chosen than great riches.
—PROVERBS. XXII. 1

I cannot tell what the dickens his name is.
—SHAKESPEARE, *Merry
Wives of Windsor.* Act
III. Sc. 2

My name is Legion.

—MARK. V. 9

Good name in man and woman, dear my lord,
Is the immediate jewel of their souls:
Who steals my purse steals trash; 'tis something, nothing;
'Twas mine, 'tis his, and has been slave to thousands;

But he that filches from me my good name
Robs me of that which not enriches him,
And makes me poor indeed.

> —SHAKESPEARE, *Othello*.
> Act III. Sc. 3

What's in a name? that which we call a rose
By any other name would smell as sweet.

> —SHAKESPEARE, *Romeo
> and Juliet*. Act II. Sc. 1

Nationalism

Nationalism is an infantile disease.
It is the measles of mankind.

> —ALBERT EINSTEIN

Born in inquity and conceived in sin, the spirit of nationalism has never ceased to bend human institutions to the
service of dissension and distress.

> —VEBLEN, *Absentee
> Ownership*

Nature

Earth's crammed with Heaven,
And every common bush afire with God.

> —E. B. BROWNING, *Aurora
> Leigh*

To him who in the love of Nature holds
Communion with her visible forms, she speaks
A various language.

> —BRYANT, *Thanatopsis*

I love not man the less, but nature more.
> —BYRON, *Childe Harold*

For Art may err, but Nature cannot miss.
> —DRYDEN, *Fables*

The woods were made for the hunter of dreams,
  The brooks for the fishes of song.
> —SAM WALTER FOSS,
>   *Bloodless Sportsman*

Nature is a volume of which God is the author.
> —HARVEY

Nature, like a kind and smiling mother, lends herself to
our dreams and cherishes our fancies.
> —VICTOR HUGO

Accuse not Nature, she hath done her part;
Do thou but thine!
> —MILTON, *Paradise Lost*

Grass is the forgiveness of nature—her constant benediction. . . . Forests decay, harvests perish, flowers vanish, but grass is immortal.
> —INGALLS, Speech, 1874

Speak to the earth, and it shall teach thee.
> —JOB. XII. 8

Everything in nature acts in conformity with law.
> —IMMANUEL KANT

Nature abhors a vacuum.
> —RABELAIS, *Gargantua*

To hold, as 't were, the mirror up to nature.
> —SHAKESPEARE, *Hamlet*.
>   Act. III. Sc. 2

I chatter, chatter, as I flow
    To join the brimming river,
For men may come and men may go,
    But I go on forever.
            —TENNYSON, *The Brook*

When I would recreate myself, I seek the darkest wood, the thickest and most interminable, and to the citizen, most dismal swamp. I enter a swamp as a sacred place— a *sanctum sanctorum*. There is the strength, the marrow of Nature.

            —THOREAU

One touch of nature makes the whole world kin.
            —SHAKESPEARE, *Troilus
               and Cressida*. Act III.
               Sc. 3

Nature has always had more force than education.
            —VOLTAIRE, *Life of Molière*

Navigation

O pilot! 'tis a fearful night,
There's danger on the deep.
            —THOMAS HAYNES BAYLY,
               The Pilot

The winds and waves are always on the side of the ablest navigators.
            —GIBBON, *Decline and
               Fall of the Roman
               Empire*

Oh, I am a cook and a captain bold
    And the mate of the *Nancy* brig,
And a bo'sun tight and a midshipmate
    And the crew of the captain's gig.
                —W. S. GILBERT, *Yarn of
                the "Nancy Bell"*

Thus, I steer my bark, and sail
On even keel, with gentle gale.
                —MATTHEW GREEN,
                Spleen

Navy

Hearts of oak are our ships,
Hearts of oak are our men.
                —GARRICK

Now landsmen all, whoever you may be,
If you want to rise to the top of the tree,
If your soul isn't fettered to an office stool,
Be careful to be guided by this golden rule—
Stick close to your desks and *never go to to sea*,
And you may all be Rulers of the Queen's Navee.
                —W. S. GILBERT, *H.M.S.
                Pinafore*

Tell that to the Marines—the sailors won't believe it.
                —Old saying quoted by
                SCOTT

Necessity

Necessity has no law.
                —ANONYMOUS

Necessity, the mother of invention.
—ANONYMOUS

Necessity is often the spur to genius.
—BALZAC

Necessity is the plea for every infringement of human freedom. It is the argument of tyrants; it is the creed of slaves.

—WILLIAM PITT

Necessity makes even the timid brave.
—SALLUST

Negroes

Not for myself I make this prayer,
    But for this race of mine
That stretches forth from shadowed places
    Dark hands for bread and wine.
—COUNTEE CULLEN,
Pagan Prayer

The image of God cut in ebony.
—THOMAS FULLER

O black and unknown bards of long ago,
How came your lips to touch the sacred fire?
How, in your darkness, did you come to know
The power and beauty of the minstrel's lyre?
—JAMES WELDON
JOHNSON, O Black
and Unknown Bards

In the Negro countenance you will often meet with strong traits of benignity. I have felt yearnings of tenderness towards some of these faces.
—LAMB

The best way to uncolor the Negro is to give the white man a white heart.
—PANIN

The Negro is an exotic of the most gorgeous and superb countries of the world, and he has deep in his heart a passion for all that is splendid, rich and fanciful.
—HARRIET BEECHER
STOWE

Neighbors

Thou salt not bear false witness against they neighbor.
—EXODUS. XX. 16

We can live without our friends but not without our neighbors.
—THOMAS FULLER

When your neighbor's house is afire your own property is at stake.
—HORACE

Thou shalt love thy neighbor as thyself.
—LEVITICUS. XIX. 18

The crop always seems better in our neighbor's field, and our neighbor's cow gives more milk.
—OVID

In the field of world policy I would dedicate this nation to the policy of the good neighbor.
—F. D. ROOSEVELT,
Inaugural Address,
1933

Neutrality

The cold neutrality of an impartial judge.
— BURKE

Neutrality, as a lasting principle, is an evidence of weakness.
— KOSSUTH

A wise neuter joins with neither, but uses both, as his honest interest leads him.
— WILLIAM PENN

The heart is never neutral.
— SHAFTESBURY

A plague o' both your houses.
— SHAKESPEARE, *Romeo and Juliet*. Act III. Sc. 1

Newness

There is nothing new except what is forgotten.
— MILLE. ROSE BERTIN (Milliner to Marie Antoinette)

Spick and span new.
— CERVANTES, *Don Quixote*

There is no new thing under the sun.
— ECCLESIASTES. I. 9

Is there anything whereof it may be said, See, this is new? It hath been already of old time, which was before us.

—ECCLESIASTES. I. 10

What is valuable is not new, and what is new is not valuable.

—DANIEL WEBSTER

New York City

I like to visit New York, but I wouldn't live there if you gave it to me.

—AMERICAN SAYING

If there ever was an aviary overstocked with jays it is that Yaptown-on-the-Hudson, called New York.

—O. HENRY, *The Gentle Grafter*

Vulgar of manner, overfed,
Overdressed and underbred;
Heartless, Godless, hell's delight,
Rude by day and lewd by night;
Bedwarfed the man, o'ergrown the brute,
Ruled by boss and prostitute;
Purple-robed and pauper-clad,
Raving, rotting, money-mad;
A squirming herd in Mammon's mesh,
A wilderness of human flesh;
Crazed with avarice, lust and rum,
New York, thy name's Delirium.

—BYRON R. NEWTON, *Ode to New York*

News

If a man bites a dog, that is news.
—JOHN BOGART

By evil report and good report.
—II CORINTHIANS. VI. 8

As cold waters to a thirsty soul, so is good news from a
far country.
—PROVERBS. XXV. 25

There's villainous news abroad.
—SHAKESPEARE, *Henry IV.*
Pt. I. Act II. Sc. 4

When we hear news we should always wait for the sac-
rament of confirmation.
—VOLTAIRE

Newspapers

Newspapers are the world's mirrors.
—JAMES ELLIS

Were it left to me to decide whether we should have a
government without newspapers or newspapers without
government, I should not hesitate a moment to prefer the
latter.
—JEFFERSON, Letter, 1787

Every editor of newspapers pays tribute to the devil.
—LA FONTAINE

Four hostile newspapers are more to be feared than a
thousand bayonets.
—NAPOLEON

Let me make the newspapers, and I care not what is preached in the pulpit or what is enacted in Congress.
—WENDELL PHILLIPS

All I know is what I see in the papers.
—WILL ROGERS

Night

The Night has a thousand eyes,
    The Day but one;
Yet the light of the bright world dies
    With the dying sun.
—F. W. BOURDILLON, *Light*

For the night
Shows stars and women in a better light.
—BYRON, *Don Juan*

Night's black Mantle covers all alike.
—DU BARTAS

Watchman, what of the night?
—ISAIAH, XXI. 11

Night, when deep sleep falleth on men.
—JOB. IV. 13

The night cometh when no man can work.
—JOHN, IX. 4

And the night shall be filled with music
    And the cares, that infest the day,
Shall fold their tents, like the Arabs,
    And as silently steal away.
—LONGFELLOW, *The Day
Is Done*

In a real dark night of the soul it is always three o'clock
in the morning.
> —F. SCOTT FITZGERALD,
> *The Crackup*

The nearer the dawn the darker the night.
> —LONGFELLOW, *Tales of a*
> *Wayside Inn*

The night is dark, and I am far from home.
> —JOHN HENRY NEWMAN,
> *Lead, Kindly Light*

To all, to each, a fair good night,
And pleasing dreams; and slumbers light.
> —SCOTT, *Marmion*

Making night hideous.
> —SHAKESPEARE, *Hamlet.*
> Act I. Sc. 4

Nightingales

It is the hour when from the boughs
    The nightingale's high note is heard;
It is the hour when lovers' vows
    Seem sweet in every whisper'd word.
> —BYRON

  Hark! that's the nightingale,
  Telling the self-same tale
Her song told when this ancient earth was young:
So echoes answered when her song was sung
  In the first wooded vale.
> —CHRISTINA G. ROSSETTI,
> *Twilight Calm*

The angel of spring, the mellow-throated nightingale.
—SAPPHO

Nobility

Send your noble blood to market and see what it will bring.

—THOMAS FULLER

Noble blood is an accident of fortune; noble actions characterize the great.

—GOLDONI, *Pamela*

Be noble in every thought
And in every deed!

—LONGFELLOW, *Christus*

This was the noblest Roman of them all.

—SHAKESPEARE, *Julius Caesar*. Act V. Sc. 5

Nonsense

A little nonsense now and then
Is relished by the wisest men.

—ANONYMOUS

The Owl and the Pussy-Cat went to sea
In a beautiful pea-green boat.

—EDWARD LEAR, *The Owl and the Pussy-Cat*

No one is exempt from talking nonsense; the misfortune is to do it solemnly.

—MONTAIGNE

Nose

Plain as a nose in a man's face.
—RABELAIS

Give me a man with a good allowance of nose, . . . when
I want any good head-work done I choose a man—pro-
vided his education has been suitable—with a long nose.
—NAPOLEON, Related in
Notes on Noses

If the nose of Cleopatra had been a little shorter the whole
face of the world would have been changed.
—PASCAL

Nothingness

Nothing to do but work,
    Nothing to eat but food,
Nothing to wear but clothes,
    To keep one from going nude.
—BEN KING, *The Pessimist*

Nothing's new, and nothing's true, and nothing matters.
—Attributed to LADY
MORGAN

Blessed be he who expects nothing, for he shall never be
disappointed.
—POPE, Letter

They laboriously do nothing.
—SENECA

A life of nothing's nothing worth,
From that first nothing ere his birth,
To that last nothing under earth.
—TENNYSON, *Two Voices*

Oath

You can have no oath registered in heaven to destroy the Government; while I shall have the most solemn one to "preserve, protect, and defend" it.

—LINCOLN, First Inaugural
Address

'Tis not the many oaths that makes the truth,
But the plain single vow that is vow'd true.

—SHAKESPEARE, *All's Well
That Ends Well*. Act
IV. Sc. 2

I'll take thy word for faith, not ask thine oath;
Who shuns not to break one will sure crack both.

—SHAKESPEARE, *Pericles*.
Act I. Sc. 2

Obedience

Obedience alone gives the right to command.

—EMERSON

Let they child's first lesson be obedience, and the second will be what thou wilt.

—FRANKLIN

Women are perfectly well aware that the more they seem to obey the more they rule.

—MICHELET

Let them obey that know not how to rule.

—SHAKESPEARE, *Henry VI*.
Pt. II. Act V. Sc. 1

The eye that mocketh at his father, and despiseth to obey his mother, the ravens of the valley shall pick it out, and the young eagles shall eat it.

—PROVERBS. XXX. 17

Obscurity

I give the fight up; let there be an end,
A privacy, an obscure nook for me,
I want to be forgotten even by God.

—BROWNING, *Paracelsus*

Full many a flower is born to blush unseen,
And waste its sweetness on the desert air.

—GRAY, *Elegy in a
Country Churchyard*

How happy is the blameless vestal's lot!
The world forgetting, by the world forgot.

—POPE, *Eloisa to Abélard*

How many a rustic Milton has passed by,
Stifling the speechless longings of his heart
In unremitting drudgery and care!
How many a vulgar Cato has compelled
His energies, no longer tameless then,
To mold a pin, or fabricate a nail!

—SHELLEY, *Queen Mab*

Thus let me live, unseen, unknown,
        Thus unlamented let me die;
Steal from the world, and not a stone
        Tell where I lie.

—POPE, *Ode on Solitude*

Obstinacy

Obstinacy and vehemency in opinion are the surest proofs of stupidity.

—BERNARD BARTON

An obstinate man does not hold opinions, but they hold him.

—POPE

Occupation

I hold every man a debtor to his profession; from the which as men of course do seek to receive countenance and profit, so ought they of duty to endeavor themselves, by way of amends, to be a help and ornament thereunto.

—BACON, *Maxims of the Law*

The crowning fortune of a man is to be born to some pursuit which finds him employment and happiness, whether it be to make baskets, or broadswords, or canals, or statues, or songs.

—EMERSON

The ugliest of trades have their moments of pleasure. Now, if I were a grave-digger, or even a hangman, there are some people I could work for with a great deal of enjoyment.

—DOUGLAS JERROLD, *Ugly Trades*

Ocean

Full many a gem of purest ray serene,
  The dark unfathomed caves of ocean bear.

—GRAY, *Elegy in a Country Churchyard*

The breaking waves dashed high
    On a stern and rock-bound coast,
And the woods against a stormy sky,
    Their giant branches toss'd.
        —FELICIA D. HEMANS, *The Landing of the Pilgrim Fathers in New England*

Love the sea? I dote upon it—from the beach.
        —DOUGLAS JERROLD, *Love of the Sea*

Praise the sea, but keep on land.
        —GEORGE HERBERT

Rocked in the cradle of the deep,
I lay me down in peace to sleep.
        —EMMA WILLARD, *The Cradle of the Deep*

Office

The very essence of a free government consists in considering offices as public trusts, bestowed for the good of the country, and not for the benefit of an individual or a party.
        —CALHOUN, Speech, 1835

If a due participation of office is a matter of right, how are vacancies to be obtained? Those by death are few: by resignation, none.
        —JEFFERSON, Letter, 1801

This struggle and scramble for office, for a way to live without work, will finally test the strength of our institutions.
        —LINCOLN, 1861

Every time I fill a vacant place I make a hundred mal-
contents and one ingrate.

> —Attributed to Louis XIV of
> France

Public office is the last refuge of the incompetent.

> —Attributed to BOISE
> PENROSE

The insolence of office.

> —SHAKESPEARE, *Hamlet*.
> Act III. Sc. 1

Opinion

It were not best that we should all think alike; it is difference of opinion that makes horseraces.

> —S. L. CLEMENS (MARK
> TWAIN), *Pudd'n-head
> Wilson*

Stiff in opinion, always in the wrong.

> —DRYDEN, *Absalom and
> Achitophel*

It is rare that the public sentiment decides immorally or
unwisely, and the individual who differs from it ought
to distrust and examine well his own opinion.

> —JEFFERSON, Letter, 1801

Those who never retract their opinions love themselves
more than they love truth.

> —JOUBERT

Public opinion, though often formed upon a wrong basis,
yet generally has a strong underlying sense of justice.

> —LINCOLN

Opinions cannot survive if one has no chance to fight for them.

—THOMAS MANN, *The Magic Mountain*

The foolish and the dead alone never change their opinion.

—LOWELL

Force and not opinion is the queen of the world; but it it opinion that uses the force.

—PASCAL

Public opinion is a compound of folly, weakness, prejudice, wrong feeling, right feeling, obstinacy, and newspaper paragraphs.

—ROBERT PEEL

The feeble tremble before opinion, the foolish defy it, the wise judge it, the skillful direct it.

—MME. JEANNE ROLAND

I know where there is more wisdom than is found in Napoleon, Voltaire, or all the ministers present and to come—in public opinion.

—TALLEYRAND, In the Chamber of Peers

Opportunity

Do not suppose opportunity will knock twice at your door.

—CHAMFORT

Make hay while the sun shines.

—ENGLISH PROVERB

Plough deep while sluggards sleep.
—BENJAMIN FRANKLIN

There is an hour in each man's life appointed
To make his happiness, if then he seize it.
—BEAUMONT and
FLETCHER

There is a tide in the affairs of men,
Which, taken at the flood, leads on to fortune.
—SHAKESPEARE, *Julius
Caesar*. Act IV. Sc. 3

The opportunity for doing mischief is found a hundred
times a day, and of doing good once in a year.
—VOLTAIRE, *Zadig*

Optimism

Optimism: A cheerful frame of mind that enables a tea
kettle to sing though in hot water up to its nose.
—ANONYMOUS

An optimist sees an opportunity in every calamity; a
pessimist sees a calamity in every opportunity.
—ANONYMOUS

To look up and not down,
To look forward and not back,
To look out and not in, and
To lend a hand.
—EDWARD EVERETT HALE

Two men look out through the same bars:
One sees the mud, and one the stars.
—FREDERICK LANGBRIDGE

Keep your face to the sunshine and you cannot see the shadow.

—HELEN KELLER

Oratory

Oratory is the power to talk people out of their sober and natural opinions.

—CHATFIELD

Glittering generalities! They are blazing ubiquities.
—EMERSON, Remark on
Choate's words

I am not fond of uttering platitudes
In stained-glass attitudes.
—W. S. GILBERT, *Patience*.
Bunthorne's Song

The object of oratory is not truth, but persuasion.
—MACAULAY, *The
Athenian Orators*

What the orators want in depth, they give you in length.
—MONTESQUIEU

Order

Have a place for everything and have everything in its place.

—ANONYMOUS

Set thine house in order.
—ISAIAH. XXXVIII. 1

Order is Heaven's first law.
—POPE, *An Essay on Man*

Let all things be done decently and in order.
                              —I CORINTHIANS. XIV. 40

Oyster

It is unseasonable and unwholesome in all months that
have not an R in their names to eat an oyster.
                              —WILLIAM BUTLER

The world's mine oyster,
Which I with sword will open.
                              —SHAKESPEARE, *The Merry
                              Wives of Windsor.* Act
                              II. Sc. 2

He was a bold man that first ate an oyster.
                              —SWIFT, *Polite
                              Conversation*

Pain

Man endures pain as an undeserved punishment; woman
accepts it as a natural heritage.
                              —ANONYMOUS

Pain and pleasure, like light and darkness, succeed each
other.
                              —LAURENCE STERNE

Nothing begins, and nothing ends,
     That is not paid with moan;
For we are born in others' pain,
     And perish in our own.
                              —FRANCIS THOMPSON,
                              Daisy

The pain of the mind is worse than the pain of the body.
                              —SYRUS

Painting

If we could but paint with the hand as we see with the eye!
                              —BALZAC

Pictures must not be too picturesque.
                              —EMERSON, *Essays*

The fellow mixes blood with his colors.
                              —GUIDO RENI (about
                                    Rubens)

A picture is a poem without words.
                              —HORACE

I mix them with my brains, sir.
                              —JOHN OPIE, when asked
                                    with what he mixed
                                    his colors.

Paradise

A book of Verses underneath the Bough,
A Jug of Wine, a Loaf of Bread—and Thou
Beside me singing in the Wilderness—
Oh, Wilderness were Paradise enow!
                              —OMAR KHAYYÁM,
                                    Rubaiyat

In this fool's paradise, he drank delight
                              —CRABBE, *The Borough
                                    Players*

Unto you is paradise opened.

—II Esdras, VIII. 52

Parent

There is no friendship, no love, like that of the parent for the child.

—Henry Ward Beecher

The first half of our lives is ruined by our parents and the second half by our children.

—Clarence S. Darrow

Next to God, thy parents.

—William Penn

Parting

Oh has thou forgotten how soon we must sever?
    Oh hast thou forgotten this day we must part?
It may be for years and it may be forever;
    Oh why art thou silent, thou voice of my heart?

—Julia Crawford,
Kathleen Mavourneen

Excuse me, then! you know my heart;
But darest friends, alas! must part.

—Gay, *The Hare and
Many Friends*

Fare thee well! and if for ever,
Still for ever, fare thee well.

—Byron, *Fare Thee Well*

Departure should be sudden.

—Disraeli

The sweetest flower that blows,
    I give you as we part.
For you it is a rose
    For me it is my heart.
              —FREDERICK PETERSON,
                  At Parting

Good-night, good-night! parting is such sweet sorrow,
That I shall say good-night till it be morrow.
              —SHAKESPEARE, *Romeo*
                  and Juliet. Act II. Sc.
                  2

Party

Political parties serve to keep each other in check, one
keenly watching the other.
              —HENRY CLAY

I always voted at my party's call,
And I never thought of thinking for myself at all.
              —W. S. GILBERT, *H.M.S.*
                  Pinafore

He serves his party best who serves the country best.
              —R. B. HAYES, Inaugural
                  Address, 1877

If I could not go to Heaven but with a party I would not
go there at all.
              —JEFFERSON, 1789

Party honesty is party expediency.
              —GROVER CLEVELAND,
                  1889

Now is the time for all good men to come to the aid of
the party.

> —CHARLES E. WELLER,
> 1867 (Originated as a
> typing exercise.)

Passion

Passion is universal humanity. Without it religion, history, romance and art would be useless.

> —BALZAC

Knowledge of mankind is a knowledge of their passions.

> —DISRAELI, *The Young
> Duke*

Passions unguided are for the most part mere madness.

> —THOMAS HOBBES,
> *Leviathan*

Take heed lest passion sway
Thy judgment to do aught, which else free will
Would not admit.

> —MILTON, *Paradise Lost*

The ruling passion, be it what it will,
The ruling passion conquers reason still.

> —POPE, *Moral Essays*

Give me that man
That is not passion's slave.

> —SHAKESPEARE, *Hamlet*,
> Act III. Sc. 2

Past

The present contains nothing more than the past, and what is found in the effect was already in the cause.
——HENRI BERGSON,
Creative Evolution

Gone—glimmering through the dream of things that were.
——BYRON, *Childe Harold*

O God! Put back Thy universe and give me yesterday.
——HENRY ARTHUR JONES,
Silver King

Weep no more, lady, weep no more,
    Thy sorrow is in vain,
For violets plucked, the sweetest showers
    Will ne'er make grow again.
——THOMAS PERCY

I tell you the past is a bucket of ashes.
——CARL SANDBURG, *Prairie*

Those who cannot remember the past are condemned to repeat it.
——GEORGE SANTAYANA

The best prophet of the future is the past.
——JOHN SHERMAN, *Speech,*
1890

Patience

A handful of patience is worth more than a bushel of brains.
——DUTCH PROVERB

Adopt the pace of nature: her secret is patience.
———EMERSON

He that can have patience can have what he will.
———FRANKLIN

By time and toil we sever
What strength and rage could never.
———LA FONTAINE

All things come round to him who will but wait.
———LONGFELLOW, *Tales of a*
Wayside Inn

And makes us rather bear those ills we have
Than fly to others that we know not of?
———SHAKESPEARE, *Hamlet.*
Act III. Sc. 1

How poor are they that have not patience!
What wound did ever heal but by degrees?
———SHAKESPEARE, *Othello.*
Act II. Sc. 3

Patience is the art of hoping.
———VAUVENARGUES

Patriotism

Swim or sink, live or die, survive or perish with my
country was my unalterable determination.
———JOHN ADAMS, *Works*

Our country! In her intercourse with foreign nations,
may she always be in the right; but our country, right
or wrong.
———STEPHEN DECATUR

No man can be a patriot on an empty stomach.
—W. C. BRANN, *Old Glory*

I realize that patriotism is not enough. I must have no hatred toward any one.
—EDITH CAVELL

Den I wish I was in Dixie, Hooray! Hooray!
In Dixie Land I'll take my stand
To lib and die in Dixie.
—DANIEL D. EMMETT,
Dixie Land

I only regret that I have but one life to lose for my country.
—NATHAN HALE, Last
Words, 1776

I am not a Virginian but an American.
—PATRICK HENRY

Patriotism is the last refuge of a scoundrel.
—SAMUEL JOHNSON

Breathes there the man with soul so dead,
Who never to himself hath said,
This is my own, my native land!
—SCOTT, *Lay of the Last
Minstrel*

The world is my country, all mankind are my brethren, and to do good is my religion.
—THOMAS PAINE, *Rights of
Man*

Millions for defense, but not one cent for tribute.
—CHARLES C. PINCKNEY

Peace

I prefer the most unfair peace to the most righteous war.
—CICERO

Peace rules the day, where reason rules the mind.
—WILLIAM COLLINS,
Eclogue II

Even peace may be purchased at too high a price.
—FRANKLIN

Peace be with you.

—GENESIS. XLIII. 23

I have never advocated war, except as a means of peace.
—ULYSSES S. GRANT

They shall beat their swords into ploughshares, and their spears into pruninghooks; nation shall not lift up sword against nation neither shall they learn war any more.
—ISAIAH. II. 4

The wolf also shall dwell with the lamb, and the leopard shall lie down with the kid.
—ISAIAH. XI. 6

I am a man of peace, God knows how I love peace; but I hope I shall never be such a coward as to mistake oppression for peace.

—KOSSUTH

Peace at any price.

—LAMARTINE

Glory to God, in the highest, and on earth peace, good will toward men.
—LUKE. II. 14

Peace be to this house.
—LUKE. X. 5

Peace hath her victories,
No less renowned than war.
—MILTON

If they want peace, nations should avoid the pin-pricks that precede cannon-shots.
—NAPOLEON

Her ways are ways of pleasantness, and all her paths are peace.
—PROVERBS. III. 17

Mercy and truth are met together: righteousness and peace have kissed each other.
—PSALMS. LXXXV. 10

Peace be within thy walls, and prosperity within they palaces.
—PSALMS. CXXII. 7

If peace cannot be maintained with honor, it is no longer peace.
—LORD RUSSELL

The peace of God, which passeth all understanding.
—PHILIPPIANS. IV. 7

Peace won by compromise is usually a short-lived achievement.
—WINFIELD SCOTT

If the pursuit of peace is both old and new, it is also both complicated and simple. It is complicated, for it has to do with people, and nothing in this universe baffles man as much as man himself.

—ADLAI STEVENSON,
Speech, October 24,
1952

The war-drum throbb'd no longer, and the battleflags
were furl'd
In the parliament of man, the federation of the world.
—TENNYSON, *Locksley Hall*

To be prepared for war is one of the most effectual means of preserving peace.

—WASHINGTON

Pen

The pen is mightier than the sword.
—BULWER-LYTTON

If you give me six lines written by the hand of the most honest of men, I will find something in them which will hang him.

—RICHELIEU

People

The voice of the people is the voice of God.
—ALCUIN, *Epistles*

The people are the only sure reliance for the preservation of our liberty.

—JEFFERSON, 1787

We here highly resolve that these dead shall not have died in vain; that this nation, under God, shall have a new birth of freedom, and that government of the people, by the people, and for the people, shall not perish from the earth.

—LINCOLN, *Gettysburg Address*

God must have loved the plain people: He made so many of them.

—LINCOLN

You can fool some of the people all of the time, and all of the people some of the time, but you cannot fool all of the people all the time.

—LINCOLN

The second, sober thought of the people is seldom wrong, and always efficient.

—MARTIN VAN BUREN

The two kinds of people on earth that I mean
Are the people who lift and the people who lean.

—ELLA WHEELER WILCOX, *To Lift or to Lean*

Perfection

The very pink of perfection.

—GOLDSMITH, *She Stoops to Conquer*

There are many lovely women, but no perfect ones.

—VICTOR HUGO

Trifles make perfection, and perfection is no trifle.

—MICHELANGELO

Whoever thinks a faultless piece to see,
Thinks what ne'er was, nor is, nor e'er shall be.
>   —POPE, *Essay on Criticism*

Perseverance

The waters wear the stones.
>   —JOB. XIV. 19

Victory belongs to the most persevering.
>   —NAPOLEON

Many strokes, though with a little axe,
Hew down and fell the hardest-timber'd oak.
>   —SHAKESPEARE, *Henry VI.*
>   Pt. III. Act II. Sc. 1

Do what you love. Know your own bone; gnaw at it,
bury it, unearth it, and gnaw it still.
>   —THOREAU

Pessimism

A pessimist is one who feels bad when he feels good for
fear he'll feel worse when he feels better.
>   —ANONYMOUS

How happy are the pessimists! What joy is theirs when
they have proved there is no joy.
>   —MARIE EBNER-
>   ESCHENBACH

A pessimist? A man who thinks everybody as nasty as
himself, and hates them for it.
>   —GEORGE BERNARD SHAW

Philanthropy

Philanthropies and charities have a certain air of quackery.

—EMERSON, *The Transcendentalist*

Steal the hog, and give the feet for alms.
—HERBERT

I was eyes to the blind, and feet was I to the lame.
—JOB. XXIX. 15

To pity distress is but human; to relieve it is Godlike.
—HORACE MANN, *Lectures on Education*

Take heed that ye do not your alms before men, to be seen of them.
—MATTHEW. VI. 1

When thou doest alms, let not thy left hand know what they right hand doeth.
—MATTHEW. VI. 3

Philosophy

A little philosophy inclineth man's mind to atheism; but depth in philosophy bringeth men's minds about to religion.

—BACON, *Essays*

The philosophy of one century is the common sense of the next.

—HENRY WARD BEECHER

Philosophy: A route of many roads leading from nowhere to nothing.

—BIERCE, *The Devil's Dictionary*

Queen of arts, and daughter of heaven.

—BURKE

In philosophy, it is not the attainment of the goal that matters, it is the things that are met with by the way.

—HAVELOCK ELLIS, *The Dance of Life*

Philosophy goes no further than probabilities, and in every assertion keeps a doubt in reserve.

—FROUDE

Whence? wither? why? how?—these questions cover all philosophy.

—JOUBERT

There are more things in heaven and earth, Horatio,
Than are dreamt of in your philosophy.

—SHAKESPEARE, *Hamlet*. Act I. Sc. 5

There was never yet philosopher
That could endure the toothache patiently.

—SHAKESPEARE, *Much Ado About Nothing*. Act V. Sc. 1

The philosopher is Nature's pilot. And there you have our difference: to be in hell is to drift: to be in heaven is to steer.

—GEORGE BERNARD SHAW, *Man and Superman*

The discovery of what is true and the practice of that which is good are the two most important objects of philosophy.

—VOLTAIRE

Pity

More helpful than all wisdom is one draught of simple human pity that will not forsake us.

—GEORGE ELIOT, *The Mill on the Floss*

He that hath pity upon the poor lendeth unto the Lord; and that which he hath given will he pay him again.

—PROVERBS. XIX. 17

Pity is the feeling which arrests the mind in the presence of whatsoever is grave and constant in human sufferings and unites it with the human sufferer.

—JAMES JOYCE, *A Portrait of the Artist as a Young Man*

A book or poem which has no pity in it had better not be written.

—WILDE

Plagiarism

They lard their lean books with the fat of others' works.

—BURTON, *Anatomy of Melancholy*

Most plagiarists, like the drone, have neither taste to select, industry to acquire, nor skill to improve, but impudently pilfer the honey ready prepared, from the hive.

—COLTON

Goethe said there would be little left of him if he were to discard what he owed to others.

—CHARLOTTE CUSHMAN

When Shakespeare is charged with debts to his authors, Landor replies, "Yet he was more original than his originals. He breathed upon dead bodies and brought them into life."

—EMERSON, *Letters and
Social Aims*

Pleasure

The great pleasure in life is doing what people say you cannot do.

—WALTER BAGEHOT,
Literary Studies

The rule of my life is to make business a pleasure, and pleasure my business.

—AARON BURR, Letter to
Pichon

There is no pleasure without a tincture of bitterness.
—HAFIZ

Fly the pleasure that bites tomorrow.
—HERBERT

Follow pleasure, and then will pleasure flee,
Flee pleasure, and pleasure will follow thee.
—HEYWOOD, *Proverbs*

We tire of those pleasures we take, but never of those we give.

—J. PETIT-SENN

He that loveth pleasure shall be a poor man.
—PROVERBS. XXI. 17

Poet

No man was ever yet a great poet, without at the same time being a profound philosopher.
—COLERIDGE

All men are poets at heart.
—EMERSON, *Literary Ethics*

Modern poets mix too much water with their ink.
—GOETHE

The man is either mad or he is making verses.
—HORACE

All that is best in the great poets of all countries is not what is national in them, but what is universal.
—LONGFELLOW, *Kavanagh*

Every man is a poet when he is in love.
—PLATO, *Symposium*

Poets have a license to lie.
—PLINY THE YOUNGER

Villon, our sad bad glad mad brother's name.
—SWINBURNE, *Ballad of François Villon*

Poetry

Poetry, the eldest sister of all arts, and parent of most.
—CONGREVE

Poetry is the Devil's wine.
—ST. AUGUSTINE

Poetry, therefore, we will call Musical Thought.
—CARLYLE, *Heroes and Hero-Worship*

All that is not prose passes for poetry.
—CRABBE

Oh love will make a dog howl in rhyme.
—JOHN FLETCHER, *Queen of Corinth*

Poetry is truth dwelling in beauty.
—GILFILLAN

Let your poem be kept nine years.
—HORACE

With me poetry has not been a purpose, but a passion.
—POE

I consider poetry very subordinate to moral and political science.
—SHELLEY, Letter to Thomas L. Peacock

The reader who is illuminated is, in a real sense, the poem.
—H. M. TOMLINSON, *Between the Lines*

One merit of poetry few persons will deny: it says more
and in fewer words than prose.
—VOLTAIRE, *A*
Philosophical
Dictionary

Publishing a volume of verse is like dropping a rose-petal
down the Grand Canyon and waiting for the echo.
—DON MARQUIS, *The Sun*
Dial

I was promised on a time,
To have reason for my rhyme;
From that time unto this season,
I received nor rhyme nor reason.
—SPENSER, *Lines on His*
Promised Pension

Poison

One man's meat is another's poison.
—ENGLISH PROVERB

The man recover'd of the bite,
    The dog it was that died.
—GOLDSMITH, *Elegy on*
the Death of a Mad
Dog

Policy

It is easier to catch flies with honey than with vinegar.
—ENGLISH PROVERB

Don't throw a monkey-wrench into the machinery.
—PHILANDER JOHNSON

Politics

A politican is an animal who can sit on a fence and yet keep both ears to the ground.
—ANONYMOUS

All political parties die at last of swallowing their own lies.
—JOHN ARBUTHNOT

Man is by nature a civic animal.
—ARISTOTLE

Politics is not an exact science.
—BISMARCK, Speech, 1863

A politician thinks of the next election; a statesman, of the next generation.
—JAMES FREEMAN CLARKE

It is a *condition* which confronts us—not a theory.
—GROVER CLEVELAND,
Annual Message, 1877

A majority is always better than the best repartee.
—DISRAELI

Damned Neuters, in their Middle way of Steering,
Are neither Fish, nor Flesh, nor good Red Herring.
—DRYDEN, *Duke of Guise*

I always voted at my party's call,
And I never thought of thinking for myself at all.
—W. S. GILBERT, *H.M.S.
Pinafore*

The purification of politics is an iridescent dream.
—INGALLS, *Epigram*

Like an armed warrior, like a plumed knight, James G. Blaine marched down the halls of American Congress and threw his shining lance full and fair against the brazen foreheads of the defamers of his country, and the maligners of his honor.

> —INGERSOLL, on
> nomination of Blaine
> for President, 1876

If a due participation of office is a matter of right, how are vacancies to be obtained? Those by death are few; by resignation, none.

> —JEFFERSON, 1801

Nothing is politically right which is morally wrong.
> —DANIEL O'CONNELL

Politics is but the common pulsebeat, of which revolution is the feverspasm.

> —WENDELL PHILLIPS,
> Speech, 1853

The Republicans have their splits right after election and Democrats have theirs just before an election.
> —WILL ROGERS

The statesman shears the sheep, the politician skins them.
> —AUSTIN O'MALLEY

My hat's in the ring. The fight is one and I'm stripped to the buff.

> —THEODORE ROOSEVELT,
> 1912

Something is rotten in the state of Denmark.
> —SHAKESPEARE, *Hamlet.*
> Act I. Sc. 4

If nominated I will not accept; if elected I will not serve.
—WILLIAM TECUMSEH
SHERMAN, 1884

Who is the dark horse he has in his stable?
—THACKERAY, *Adventures
of Philip*

As long as I count the votes what are you going to do about it?
—WILLIAM M. TWEED

Popularity

Popular applause veers with the wind.
—JOHN BRIGHT

The actor's popularity is evanescent; applauded today, forgotten tomorrow.
—EDWIN FORREST

Possession

As having nothing, and yet possessing all things.
—II CORINTHIANS. VI. 10

When we have not what we love, we must love what we have.
—BUSSY-RABUTIN, 1667

Of a rich man who was mean and niggardly, he said, "That man does not possess his estate, but his estate possesses him."
—DIOGENES

Property has its duties as well as its rights.
>   —DRUMMOND

Wouldst thou both eat they cake and have it?
>   —HERBERT

Unto every one that hath shall be given, and he shall have abundance; but from him that hath not shall be taken away even that which he hath.
>   —MATTHEW. XXV. 29

Possession, they say, is eleven points of the law.
>   —SWIFT

Post

A strange volume of real life in the daily packet of the postman. Eternal love and instant payment!
>   —DOUGLAS JERROLD, *The Postman's Budget*

Neither snow, nor rain, nor heat, nor night stays these couriers from the swift completion of their appointed rounds.
>   —HERODOTUS, Inscription on Postoffice, New York City

A woman seldom writes her Mind, but in her Postscript.
>   —STEELE, *Spectator*

Go, little letter, apace, apace,
Fly;
Fly to the light in the valley below—
    Tell my wish to her dewy blue eye.
>   —TENNYSON, *The Letter*

Posterity

Think of your forefathers!
Think of your posterity!

—JOHN QUINCY ADAMS,
1802

People will not look forward to posterity who never look
backward to their ancestors.

—EDMUND BURKE

As to posterity, I may ask what has it ever done to oblige
me?

—GRAY, Letter to Dr.
Wharton

Pottery

Hath not the potter power over the clay, of the same
lump to make one vessel unto honour, and another unto
dishonour?

—ROMANS. IX. 21

All this of Pot and Potter—Tell me then,
Who is the Potter, pray, and who the Pot?

—OMAR KHAYYÁM,
Rubaiyat

Poverty

Over the hill to the poor-house I'm trudgin' my weary
way.

—WILL CARLETON, *Over
the Hill to the Poor-
House*

He is now fast rising from affluence to poverty.
—S. L. CLEMENS (MARK
TWAIN)

The greatest man in history was the poorest.
—EMERSON, *Domestic Life*

As poor as a church mouse.
—ENGLISH PHRASE

That amid our highest civilization men faint and die with
want is not due to the niggardliness of nature, but to the
injustice of man.
—HENRY GEORGE, *Progress
and Poverty*

I am as poor as Job, my lord, but not so patient.
—SHAKESPEARE, *Henry IV*
Pt. II. Act I. Sc. 2

Poverty is no sin.
—HERBERT

O God! that bread should be so dear,
And flesh and blood so cheap!
—HOOD, *The Song of the
Shirt*

The poor always ye have with you.
—JOHN. XII. 8

He that hath pity upon the poor lendeth unto the Lord.
—PROVERBS. XIX. 17

Blessed is he that considereth the poor.
—PSALMS. XLI. 1

It is life near the bone, where it is sweetest.
> —THOREAU, *Walden*

Power

Give me a lever long enough
And a prop strong enough,
I can single-handed move the world.
> —ARCHIMEDES

Iron hand in a velvet glove.
> —CHARLES V

Patience and gentleness is power.
> —LEIGH HUNT

Power will intoxicate the best hearts, as wine the strongest heads. No man is wise enough nor good enough to be trusted with unlimited power.
> —COLTON

I have never been able to conceive how any rational being could propose happiness to himself from the exercise of power over others.
> —JEFFERSON, Letter, 1811

Wherever I found a living creature, there I found the will to power.
> —NIETZSCHE, *Thus Spake Zarathustra*

Power is ever stealing from the many to the few.
> —WENDELL PHILLIPS

Unlimited power corrupts the possessor.
> —WILLIAM PITT, 1770

The powers that be are ordained of God.
—ROMANS. XIII. 1

He who has great power should use it lightly.
—SENECA

Lust of power is the most flagrant of all the passions.
—TACITUS

Praise

I praise loudly; I blame softly.
—CATHERINE II OF RUSSIA

A refusal of praise is a desire to be praised twice.
—LA ROCHEFOUCAULD

I would have praised you more had you praised me less.
—LOUIS XIV

Approbation from Sir Hubert Stanley is praise indeed.
—THOMAS MORTON, *Cure
for the Heartache*

Praise the wise man behind his back, but a woman to
her face.
—WELCH PROVERB

As the Greek said, "Many men know how to flatter, few
men know how to praise."
—WENDELL PHILLIPS

With faint praises one another damn.
—WYCHERLEY, *Plain
Dealer*

The sweetest of all sounds is praise.
—XENOPHON

Prayer

A prayer, in its simplest definition, is merely a wish turned heavenward.

—PHILLIPS BROOKS

They never sought in vain that sought the Lord aright!
—BURNS, *The Cotter's
Saturday Night*

Prayer is the voice of faith.

—HORNE

Prayer is not to be used as a confessional, to cancel sin. Such an error would impede true religion. Sin is forgiven only as it is destroyed by Christ—Truth and Light.
—MARY BAKER EDDY,
Science and Health

You pray in your distress and in your need; would that you might pray also in the fullness of your joy and in your days of abundance.
—KAHLIL GIBRAN, *The
Prophet*

At church, with meek and unaffected grace,
His looks adorn'd the venerable place;
Truth from his lips prevailed with double sway,
And fools, who came to scoff, remain'd to pray.
—GOLDSMITH, *The
Deserted Village*

He that will learn to pray, let him go to Sea.
—HERBERT

O God, if in the day of battle I forget Thee, do not Thou forget me.

—WILLIAM KING

If I am right, Thy grace impart,
  Still in the right to stay;
If I am wrong, O teach my heart
  To find that better way!
                    —POPE, *Universal Prayer*

Our Father, which art in heaven, Hallowed be thy Name.
Thy kingdom come. Thy will be done in earth as it is
in heaven. Give us this day our daily bread. And forgive
us our debts, as we forgive our debtors. And lead us not
into temptation, but deliver us from evil: For thine is the
kingdom and the power and the glory, for ever. Amen.
                    —MATTHEW, VI. 9–13
                      (The Lord's Prayer)

God warms his hands at man's heart when he prays.
                    —MASEFIELD, *Widow in
                      the Bye Street*

Every one that asketh receiveth; and he that seeketh
findeth.
                    —MATTHEW. VII. 8

Now I lay me down to take my sleep,
I pray thee, Lord, my soul to keep;
If I should die before I wake,
I pray thee, Lord, my soul to take.
                    —NEW ENGLAND PRIMER,
                      1814

Our prayers should be for blessings in general, for God
knows best what is good for us.
                    —SOCRATES

The Lord's Prayer contains the sum total of religion and
morals.
                    —DUKE OF WELLINGTON

Ask, and it shall be given you; seek and ye shall find; knock, and it shall be opened unto you.

— MATTHEW. VII. 7

Pray as if everything depended on God, and work as if everything depended upon man.

— FRANCIS CARDINAL
SPELLMAN

Give us the strength to encounter that which is to come, that we may be brave in peril, constant in tribulation, temperate in wrath, and in all changes of fortune, and down to the gates of death, loyal and loving one to anther.

— ROBERT LOUIS
STEVENSON

Preaching

The Christian ministry is the worst of all trades, but the best of all professions.

— NEWTON

Do as we say, and not as we do.

— BOCCACCIO, *Decameron*

Alas for the unhappy man that is called to stand in the pulpit, and *not* give the bread of life.

— EMERSON

I would have every minister of the gospel address his audience with the zeal of a friend, with the generous energy of a father, and with the exuberant affection of a mother.

— FÉNELON

The test of a preacher is that his congregation goes away saying, not What a lovely sermon, but, I will do something!

—St. Francis de Sales

But in his duty prompt at every call,
He watch'd and wept, he pray'd and felt for all.
—Goldsmith, *Deserted Village*

Sir, a woman preaching is like a dog's walking on his hind legs. It is not done well: but you are surprised to find it done at all.

—Samuel Johnson

Some plague the people with too long sermons; for the faculty of listening is a tender thing, and soon becomes weary and satiated.

—Luther

I have taught you, my dear flock, for above thirty years how to live; and I will show you in a very short time how to die.

—Sandys.

Sermons in stones and good in every thing.
—Shakespeare, *As You Like It*. Act II. Sc. I

Preach the word; be instant in season, out of season; reprove, rebuke, exhort with all long suffering and doctrine.

—II Timothy. IV. 2

The minister's brain is often the "poor-box" of the church.
—Whipple

Prejudice

He hears but half who hears one party only.
—AESCHYLUS

A fox should not be of the jury at a goose's trial.
—THOMAS FULLER

He who never leaves his country is full of prejudices.
—GOLDONI, *Pamela*

Prejudice is the child of ignorance.
—HAZLITT

Opinions founded on prejudice are always sustained with the greatest violence.
—JEFFREY

Preparedness

To lead an untrained people to war is to throw them away.
—CONFUCIUS

In fair weather prepare for foul.
—THOMAS FULLER

Keep the munition, watch the way, make thy loins strong, fortify thy power mightily.
—NAHUM. II. 1

We should lay up in peace what we shall need in war.
—SYRUS

To be prepared for war is one of the most effectual means of preserving peace.

> —WASHINGTON, Address, 1790

Presidency

If you are as happy, my dear sir, on entering this house as I am in leaving it and returning home, you are the happiest man in this country.

> —BUCHANAN, To Lincoln, 1861

I would rather be right than President.

> —HENRY CLAY, Speech, 1850

No man will ever bring out of the Presidency the reputation which carries him into it.

> —JEFFERSON, Letter, 1796

If forced to choose between the penitentiary and the White House for four years, I would say the penitentiary, thank you.

> —WILLIAM TECUMSEH SHERMAN

They pick a President and then for four years they pick on him.

> —ADLAI STEVENSON, Speech, August 28, 1952

My movements to the chair of government will be accompanied by feelings not unlike those of a culprit who is going to the place of his execution.

> —WASHINGTON, Letter, 1789

Press

Congress shall make no law abridging the freedom of speech or of the press.

—CONSTITUTION OF THE
UNITED STATES

Our liberty depends on the freedom of the press, and that cannot be limited without being lost.

—JEFFERSON, Letter, 1786

The freedom of the press is one of the great bulwarks of liberty and can never be restrained but by despotic governments.

—GEORGE MASON,
*Virginia Declaration of
Rights*

Freedom of conscience, of education, of speech, of assembly are among the very fundamentals of democracy and all of them would be nullified should freedom of the press ever be successfully challenged.

—F. D. ROOSEVELT

Freedom of the press is the staff of life, for any vital democracy.

—WENDELL L. WILLKIE

Pride

They are proud in humility, proud in that they are not proud.

—BURTON, *Anatomy of
Melancholy*

Pride ruined the angels.

—EMERSON, *The Sphinx*

Pride that dines on vanity, sups on contempt.
—FRANKLIN

The proud hate pride—in others.
—FRANKLIN, *Poor Richard's Almanac*

Oh! Why should the spirit of mortal be proud?
Like a swift-fleeing meteor, a fast flying cloud,
A flash of the lightning, a break of the wave,
Man passes from life to his rest in the grave.
—WILLIAM KNOX, *Mortality*

Pride and weakness are Siamese twins.
—LOWELL

Pride goeth before destruction, and an haughty spirit before a fall.
—PROVERBS. XVI. 18

In pride, in reas'ning pride, our error lies;
All quit their sphere and rush into the skies.
Pride still is aiming at the bless'd abodes,
Men would be angels, angels would be gods.
—POPE, *Essay on Man*

The infinitely little have pride infinitely great.
—VOLTAIRE

Principle

Principles become modified in practise by facts.
—COOPER, *The American Democrat*

If principle is good for anything, it is worth living up to.
——FRANKLIN

Important principles may and must be flexible.
——LINCOLN, Speech, 1865

Prison

Stone walls do not a prison make,
    Nor iron bars a cage,
Minds innocent and quiet take
    That for an hermitage.
——LOVELACE, *To Althea,*
            from Prison

In durance vile here must I wake and weep,
And all my frowsy couch in sorrow steep.
——BURNS

While we have prisons it matters little which of us occupy
the cells.
——GEORGE BERNARD
            SHAW, *Maxims for*
            Revolutionists

Under a government which imprisons any unjustly, the
true place for a just man is also a prison.
——THOREAU

I know not whether laws be right,
Or whether laws be wrong;
All that we know who lie in gaol
Is that the wall is strong;
And that each day is like a year,
A year whose days are long.
——WILDE, *The Ballad of*
            Reading Gaol

Progress

What we call progress is the exchange of one Nuisance for another Nuisance.

—HAVELOCK ELLIS

Every step of progress which the world has made has been from scaffold to scaffold, and from stake to stake.

—WENDELL PHILLIPS

So long as all the increased wealth which modern progress brings, goes but to build up great fortunes, to increase luxury, and make sharper the contest between the House of Have and the House of Want, progress is not real and cannot be permanent.

—HENRY GEORGE, *Progress and Poverty*

Progress—the stride of God!

—VICTOR HUGO

If you strike a thorn or rose,
    Keep a-goin!
If it hails or if it snows,
    Keep a-goin!
'Tain't no use to sit and whine
'Cause the fish ain't on your line;
Bait your hook an' keep on tryin'.
    Keep a-goin!

—FRANK I. STANTON, *Keep a-goin!*

Promise

An acre of performance is worth the whole world of promise.

—JAMES HOWELL

He who is the most slow in making a promise is the most faithful in the performance of it.

—ROUSSEAU

Promise and pie-crust are made to be broken.

—SWIFT, *Polite
Conversation*

Undertake not what you cannot perform but be careful to keep your promise.

—WASHINGTON

Proof

You may prove anything by figures.

—Quoted by CARLYLE

The burden of proof lies on the plaintiff.

—LEGAL MAXIM

You cannot demonstrate an emotion or prove an aspiration.

—JOHN MORLEY, *Rousseau*

Prove all things; hold fast that which is good.

—I. THESSALONIANS. V. 21

I come from a State that raises corn and cotton and cockleburs and Democrats, and frothy eloquence neither convinces nor satisfies me. I am from Missouri. You have got to show me.

—WILLARD D. VANDIVER,
Speech, 1899

Property

Mine is better than ours.

> —FRANKLIN, *Poor Richard's Almanac*

There can be to the ownership of anything no rightful title which is not derived from the title of the producer and does not rest upon the natural right of the man to himself.

> —HENRY GEORGE, *Progress and Poverty*

The instinct of ownership is fundamental in man's nature.

> —WILLIAM JAMES

The reason why men enter into society is the preservation of their property.

> —LOCKE, *Treatise on Government*

Is it not lawful for me to do what I will with mine own?

> —MATTHEW. XX. 15

Property is theft.

> —PROUDHON

Property exists by grace of the law. It is not a fact, but a legal fiction.

> —STIRNER, *The Ego and His Own*

The highest law gives a thing to him who can use it.

> —THOREAU

Prophecy

I shall always consider the best guesser the best prophet.
                    —CICERO

We know in part, and we prophesy in part.
                    —I. CORINTHIANS. XIII. 9

A prophet is not without honour, save in his own country,
and in his own house.
                    —MATTHEW. XIII. 57

Prosperity

It requires a strong constitution to withstand repeated
attacks of prosperity.
                    —J. L. BASFORD

The desert shall rejoice, and blossom as the rose.
                    —ISAIAH. XXXV. 1

They shall sit every man under his vine and under his
fig-tree.
                    —MICAH. IV. 4

Prosperity makes some friends and many enemies.
                    —VAUVENARGUES

Providence

He that doth the ravens feed.
Yea, providently caters for the sparrow.
Be comfort to my age!
                    —SHAKESPEARE, *As You
                    Like It.* Act. II. Sc. 3

And pleas'd th' Almighty's orders to perform.
Rides in the whirlwind and directs the storm.
—ADDISON, *The Campaign*

Fear not, but trust in Providence,
Wherever thou may'st be.
—THOMAS HAYNES BAYLY,
The Pilot

There is a divinity that shapes our ends,
Rough-hew them how we will.
—SHAKESPEARE, *Hamlet*.
Act V. Sc. 2

Prudence

Put your trust in God, my boys, and keep your powder
dry.
—COL. VALENTINE
BLACKER

Dine on little, and sup on less.
—CERVANTES

I recommend you to take care of the minutes, for the
hours will take care of themselves.
—CHESTERFIELD

People who live in glass houses should not throw stones.
—ENGLISH PROVERB

The first years of man must make provision for the last.
—SAMUEL JOHNSON

He that fights and runs away
Will live to fight another day.
—OLD ENGLISH RHYME

I won't quarrel with my bread and butter.
—SWIFT, *Polite
Conversation*

Public

We would not listen to those who were wont to say the voice of the people is the voice of God, for the voice of the mob is near akin to madness.
—ALCUIN

The public! why, the public's nothing better than a great baby.
—THOMAS CHALMERS

The public! the public! How many fools does it take to make up a public?
—CHAMFORT

The public have neither shame nor gratitude.
—HAZLITT

It is to the middle class we must look for the safety of England.
—THACKERAY, *Four
Georges*

The public be damned.
—W. H. VANDERBILT

Pun

I never knew an enemy to puns who was not an ill-natured man.
—LAMB

Of puns it has been said that those most dislike who are least able to utter them.
—POE, *Marginalia*

He that would pun would pick a pocket.
—POPE

Punctuality

Unfaithfulness in the keeping of an appointment is an act of clear dishonesty. You may as well borrow a person's money as his time.
—HORACE MANN

I have always been a quarter of an hour before my time, and it has made a man of me.
—NELSON

Punishment

Let them stew in their own grease (or juice).
—BISMARCK

Eye for eye, tooth for tooth, hand for hand, foot for foot.
—DEUTERONOMY. XIX. 21

My punishment is greater than I can bear.
—GENESIS. IV. 13

My object all sublime
I shall achieve in time—
To let the punishment fit the crime.
—W. S. GILBERT, *Mikado*

Whoso sheddeth man's blood, by a man shall his blood
be shed.

—GENESIS. IX. 6

It is more dangerous that even a guilty person should be
punished without the forms of law than that he should
escape.

—JEFFERSON, 1788

One man meets an infamous punishment for that crime
which confers a diadem upon another.

—JUVENAL

No one should be twice punished for one crime.

—LEGAL MAXIM

It were better for him that a millstone were hanged about
his neck, and he cast into the sea.

—LUKE. XVII. 2

The object of punishment is, prevention from evil; it
never can be made impulsive to good.

—HORACE MANN

He that spareth his rod hateth his son.

—PROVERBS. XIII. 24

The punishment of criminals should be of use; when a
man is hanged he is good for nothing.

—VOLTAIRE

Quality

The best is the cheapest.

—FRANKLIN

Quality, not quantity, is my measure.
—DOUGLAS JERROLD

Many individuals have, like uncut diamonds, shining
qualities beneath a rough exterior.
—JUVENAL

Ye are the salt of the earth: but if the salt have lost his
savour, wherewith shall it be salted?
—MATTHEW. V. 13

Nothing endures but personal qualities.
—WALT WHITMAN, *Leaves
of Grass*

Quarreling

Those who in quarrels interpose,
Must often wipe a bloody nose.
—GAY, *Fables*

In quarreling the truth is always lost.
—SYRUS

Question

A fool may ask more questions in an hour than a wise
man can answer in seven years.
—ENGLISH PROVERB

It is not every question that deserves an answer.
—SYRUS

Ask me no questions, and I'll tell you no fibs.
—GOLDSMITH, *She Stoops
to Conquer*

Questioning is not the mode of conversation among gentlemen.
—SAMUEL JOHNSON

Race

God hath made of one blood all nations of men.
—ACTS. XVII. 26

The race to which we belong is the most arrogant and rapacious, the most exclusive and indomitable in history. All other races have been its enemies or its victims.
—INGALLS, Speech, 1890

Rain

After the rain cometh the fair weather.
—AESOP, *Fables*

Nature, like man, sometimes weeps for gladness.
—DISRAELI

It never rains but it pours.
—ENGLISH PROVERB

The rain cometh down, and the snow from heaven, and returneth not thither, but watereth the earth, and maketh it bring forth and bud, that it may give seed to the sower, and bread to the eater.
—ISAIAH. LV. 10

Be still, sad heart, and cease repining;
Behind the clouds is the sun still shining;
Thy fate is the common fate of all,
Into each life some rain must fall,
Some days must be dark and dreary.
—LONGFELLOW, *The Rainy
Day*

He shall come down like rain upon the mown grass.
—PSALMS. LXXII. 6

I know Sir John will go, though he was sure it would
rain cats and dogs.
—SWIFT, *Polite
Conversation*

Vexed sailors curse the rain for which poor shepherds
prayed in vain.
—EDMUND WALLER

Rainbow

Look upon the rainbow, and praise him that made it.
—ECCLESIASTES, XLIII. 11

A rainbow in the morning
Is the Shepherd's warning;
But a rainbow at night
Is the Shepherd's delight.
—OLD WEATHER RHYME

Reading

Reading makcth a full man.
—BACON, *Of Studies*

Reading is to the mind, what exercise is to the body.
—ADDISON, *The Tatler*

Read, mark, learn, and inwardly digest.
—BOOK OF COMMON
PRAYER

In science, read, by preference, the newest works; in literature, the oldest. The classic literature is always modern.
—BULWER-LYTTON

My early and invincible love of reading, I would not exchange for the treasures of India.
—GIBBON, *Memoirs*

When I am reading a book, whether wise or silly, it seems to me to be alive and talking to me.
—SWIFT

Read the best books first, or you may not have a chance to read them at all.
—THOREAU

Reason

Reason is the mistress and queen of all things.
—CICERO

He who will not reason, is a bigot; he who cannot is a fool; and he who dares not, is a slave.
—WILLIAM DRUMMOND

Reasons are not like garments, the worse for wearing.
—EARL OF ESSEX, 1598

Reason can in general do more than blind force.
— GALLUS

If I go to heaven I want to take my reason with me.
— INGERSOLL

Come now, and let us reason together.
— ISAIAH. I. 18

Error of opinion may be tolerated where reason is left free to combat it.

— JEFFERSON, Inaugural
Address, 1801

Human reason is like a drunken man on horseback; set it up on one side, and it tumbles over on the other.
— LUTHER

You know, my friends, with what a brave carouse
I made a second marriage in my house;
    Divorced old barren reason from my bed,
And took the daughter of the vine to spouse.
— OMAR KHAYYÁM,
Rubaiyat

The feast of reason and the flow of soul.
— POPE

Every why hath a wherefore.
— SHAKESPEARE, Comedy of
Errors. Act. II. Sc. 2

I have no other but a woman's reason.
I think him so because I think him so.
— SHAKESPEARE, Two
Gentlemen of Verona.
Act I. Sc. 2

Many are destined to reason wrongly; others, not to reason at all: and others to persecute those who do reason.
                              —VOLTAIRE

Rebellion

Rebellion to tyrants is obedience to God.
                              —Motto on JEFFERSON'S
                                seal

A little rebellion now and then . . . is a medicine necessary for the sound health of government.
                              —JEFFERSON, Letter to
                                Madison

The only justification of rebellion is success.
                              —THOMAS B. READ,
                                Speech, 1878

Reform

Reforms should begin at home and stay there.
                              —ANONYMOUS

At twenty a man is full of fight and hope. He wants to reform the world. When he's seventy he still wants to reform the world, but he knows he can't.
                              —CLARENCE S. DARROW

We are reformers in Spring and Summer; in Autumn and Winter we stand by the old; reformers in the morning, conservers at night.
                              —EMERSON, The
                                Conservative

Reform must come from within, not from without. You
cannot legislate for virtue.

—JAMES CARDINAL
GIBBONS

The hole and the patch should be commensurate.
—JEFFERSON, Letter, 1787

To make a crooked stick straight, we bend it the contrary
way.

—MONTAIGNE

An indefinable something is to be done, in a way nobody
knows how, at a time nobody knows when, that will
accomplish nobody knows what.

—THOMAS B. READ

Relative

And so do his sisters and his cousins and his aunts!
His sisters and his cousins
Whom he reckons up by dozens,
    And his aunts!

—W. S. GILBERT, *H. M. S.
Pinafore*

No man will be respected by others who is despised by
his own relatives.

—PLAUTUS

The worst hatred is that of relatives.
—TACITUS

Relations are simply a tedious pack of people who haven't
got the remotest knowledge of how to live, nor the smallest instinct about when to die.

—WILDE, *The Importance
of Being Earnest*

Religion

There was never law, or sect, or opinion did so much magnify goodness, as the Christian religion doth.
—BACON, *Essays*

One religion is as true as another.
—BURTON, *Anatomy of Melancholy*

His religion at best is an anxious wish,—like that of Rebelais, a great Perhaps.
—CARLYLE, *Burns*

Men will wrangle for religion; write for it; fight for it; die for it; anything but—live it.
—COLTON, *Lacon*

Religion, if in heavenly truths attired,
Needs only to be seen to be admired.
—COWPER, *Expostulation*

If men are so wicked with religion, what would they be without it?
—FRANKLIN

A good life is the only religion.
—THOMAS FULLER

The best religion is the most tolerant.
—MME. DE GIRARDIN

My creed is this:
    Happiness is the only good.
    The place to be happy is here.
    The time to be happy is now.
    The way to be happy is to help make others so.
—INGERSOLL

To be of no Church is dangerous.

—SAMUEL JOHNSON, *Life of Milton*

Religion is the opium of the people.

—KARL MARX, *A Criticism of Hegelian Philosophy*

Religion is nothing else but love to God and man.

—WILLIAM PENN

He that hath no cross deserves no crown.

—QUARLES, *Esther*

The world is my country, all mankind are my brethren, and to do good is my religion.

—THOMAS PAINE, *The Age of Reason*

Republic

Republics are ungrateful.

—ANONYMOUS

A monarchy is a merchantman which sails well, but will sometimes strike on a rock, and go to the bottom; a republic is a raft which will never sink, but then your feet are always in water.

—FISHER AMES, Speech, 1795

It is of great importance in a republic not only to guard against the oppression of its rulers, but to guard one part of society against the injustice of the other part.

—ALEXANDER HAMILTON, *The Federalist*

A republican government is slow to move, yet when once in motion, its momentum becomes irresistible.
—JEFFERSON, Letter, 1815

Republics are brought to their ends by luxury; monarchies by poverty.
—MONTESQUIEU, *The Spirit of the Laws*

Reputation

When I did well, I heard it never;
When I did ill, I heard it ever.
—OLD ENGLISH RHYME

The purest treasure mortal times afford
Is spotless reputation; that away,
Men are but gilded loam or painted clay.
—SHAKESPEARE, *Richard II*.
Act I. Sc. 1

Associate with men of good quality, if you esteem your own reputation; for it is better to be alone than in bad company.
—WASHINGTON

Resignation

Welcome death, quoth the rat, when the trap fell.
—THOMAS FULLER

A wise man cares not for what he cannot have.
—HERBERT

The Lord gave, and the Lord hath taken away; blessed
be the name of the Lord.
—JOB. I. 21

    That's best
Which God sends. 'Twas His will: it is mine.
—OWEN MEREDITH, *Lucile*

Job feels the rod,
Yet blesses God.

—NEW ENGLAND PRIMER

Resolution

I will sit down now, but the time will come when you
will hear me.

—DISRAELI, Maiden Speech
in the House of
Commons

I am in earnest—I will not equivocate—I will not
excuse—I will not retreat a single inch *and I will be heard.*
—WILLIAM LLOYD
GARRISON, Salutatory
of the Liberator, 1831

I propose to fight it out on this line if it takes all Summer.
—ULYSSES S. GRANT,
Dispatch to Lincoln

Tell your master that if there were as many devils at
Worms as tiles on its roofs, I would enter.
—LUTHER

Never tell your resolution beforehand.
—JOHN SELDEN, *Table Talk*

Rest

He that can take rest is greater than he that can take cities.

—FRANKLIN, *Poor Richard's Almanac*

On the seventh day God ended his work which he had made; and he rested on the seventh day.

—GENESIS. II. 2

Come unto me, all ye that labor and are heavy laden, and I will give you rest.

—MATTHEW. XI. 28

Result

They have sown the wind, and they shall reap the whirl-wind.

—HOSEA. VIII. 7

By their fruits ye shall know them.

—MATTHEW. VII. 20

Whoso diggeth a pit shall fall therein.

—PROVERBS. XXVI. 27

Resurrection

Earth to earth, ashes to ashes, dust to dust, in sure and certain hope of the resurrection.

—BOOK OF COMMON PRAYER

For as in Adam all die, even so in Christ shall all be made alive.

—I CORINTHIANS. XV. 22

Many of them that sleep in the dust of the earth shall awake, some to everlasting life, and some to shame and everlasting contempt.

—DANIEL. XII. 2

Retribution

The mills of the gods grind slowly, but they grind exceedingly fine.

—ENGLISH PROVERB

The way of transgressors is hard.

—PROVERBS. XIII. 15

Revenge

In taking revenge a man is but equal to his enemy, but in passing it over he is his superior.

—BACON

Vengeance is a dish that should be eaten cold.

—ENGLISH PROVERB

Revenge is sweeter than life itself. So think fools.

—JUVENAL

Vengeance is sweet.

—WILLIAM PAINTER, *The Palace of Pleasure*

Not to be provoked is best; but if moved, never correct till the fume is spent; for every stroke our fury strikes is sure to hit ourselves at last.

—WILLIAM PENN

Revenge is an inhuman word.

—SENECA

Revolution

Revolutions are not about trifles, but spring from trifles.

—ARISTOTLE, *Politics*

A reform is a correction of abuses; a revolution is a transfer of power.

—BULWER-LYTTON

Do you think then that revolutions are made with rose water?

—CHAMFORT to
Marmontel, on the
excesses of the
Revolution

At last I perceive that in revolutions the supreme power finally rests with the most abandoned.

—DANTON

It is impossible to predict the time and progress of revolution. It is governed by its own more or less mysterious laws. But when it comes it moves irresistibly.

—LENIN, 1918

It is not a revolt, it is a revolution.

—DUC DE LIANCOURT to
Louis XVI, July 14,
1789

This country, with its institutions, belongs to the people who inhabit it. Whenever they shall grow weary of the existing government they can exercise their constitutional right of amending it, or their revolutionary right to dismember or overthrow it.

—LINCOLN, Inaugural
Address, 1861

Let the ruling classes tremble at a Communist revolution. The proletarians have nothing to lose but their chains. They have a world to win. Working men of all countries, unite!

—KARL MARX and
FRIEDRICH ENGLES,
*The Communist
Manifesto*

Revolutions are not made; they come.
—WENDELL PHILLIPS

If I were an American, as I am an Englishman, while a foreign troop was landed in my country I never would lay down my arms,—never! never! never!

—WILLIAM PITT, Speech,
1777

Riches

A little house well filled, a little land well tilled, and a little wife well willed, are great riches.
—ANONYMOUS

Ah, if the rich were rich as the poor fancy riches!
—EMERSON

The pleasures of the rich are bought with the tears of the poor.

—THOMAS FULLER

I am rich beyond the dreams of avarice.

—EDWARD MOORE, *The Gamester*

Lay not up for yourselves treasures upon earth, where moth and rust doth corrupt, and where thieves break through and steal.

—MATTHEW. VI. 19

A man's true wealth is the good he does in this world.

—MOHAMMED

It is the wretchedness of being rich that you have to live with rich people.

—LOGAN PEARSALL SMITH

Nothing is so hard for those who abound in riches as to conceive how others can be in want.

—SWIFT

That man is the richest whose pleasures are the cheapest.

—THOREAU

Ridicule

Cervantes smiled Spain's chivalry away.

—BYRON

He will laugh thee to scorn.

—ECCLESIASTES. XIII. 7

Resort is had to ridicule only when reason is against us.

—JEFFERSON, Letter, 1813

There is only one step from the sublime to the ridiculous.
—NAPOLEON

Right

Sir, I would rather be right than be President.
—HENRY CLAY, Speech,
1850

He will hew to the line of right, let the chips fly where
they may.
—ROSCOE CONKLING,
Speech, 1880

Be sure you are right, then go ahead.
—DAVID CROCKETT

Two wrongs can never make a right.
—ENGLISH PROVERB

Let us have faith that Right makes Might, and in that
faith let us to the end dare to do our duty as we understand it.
—LINCOLN, Second
Inaugural Address

Right is the eternal sun; the world cannot delay its coming.
—WENDELL PHILLIPS

One truth is clear, Whatever is is right.
—POPE, *Essay on Man*

Heaven itself has ordained the right.
—WASHINGTON

Rights

We hold these truths to be self-evident,—that all men
are created equal; that they are endowed by their Creator
with certain unalienable rights; that among these are Life,
Liberty, and the pursuit of happiness.

> —DECLARATION OF
> INDEPENDENCE

Wherever there is a human being, I see God-given rights
inherent in that being, whatever may be the sex or complexion.

> —WILLIAM LLOYD
> GARRISON

The equal right of all men to the use of land is as clear
as their equal right to breathe the air—it is a right pro-
claimed by the fact of their existence. For we cannot
suppose that some men have a right to be in this world,
and others no right.

> —HENRY GEORGE, *Progress
> and Poverty*

Equal rights for all, special privileges for none.

> —JEFFERSON

Rome

All roads lead to Rome; but our antagonists think we
should choose different paths.

> —LA FONTAINE

The grandeur that was Rome.

> —POE, *To Helen*

If you are at Rome live in the Roman style; if you are elsewhere live as they live elsewhere.

> —ST. AMBROSE to St.
> Augustine

Rome was not built in a day.

> —ANONYMOUS

Royalty

The king reigns but does not govern.

> —BISMARCK

That the king can do no wrong is a necessary and fundamental principle of the English constitution.

> —BLACKSTONE

Every noble crown is, and on Earth will forever be, a crown of thorns.

> —CARLYLE, *Past and Present*

Who made thee a prince and a judge over us?

> —EXODUS. II. 14

The trappings of a monarchy would set up an ordinary commonwealth.

> —SAMUEL JOHNSON, *Life of Milton*

I am the State.

> —LOUIS XIV of France

The King is dead! Long live the King!

> —PARDOE, *Life of Louis XIV*

Put not your trust in princes.
—Psalms. CXLVI. 3

Here lies our sovereign lord, the king,
    Whose word no man relies on,
Who never said a foolish thing,
    And never did a wise one.
—Earl of Rochester, *To Charles II*

Uneasy lies the head that wears a crown.
—Shakespeare, *Henry IV*. Pt. II. Act III. Sc. 1

Ay, every inch a king.
—Shakespeare, *King Lear*. Act IV. Sc. 6

Rumor

"They say so" is half a lie.
—Thomas Fuller

I cannot tell how the truth may be;
I say the tale as 'twas said to me.
—Scott, *Lay of the Last Minstrel*

Tattlers also and busybodies, speaking things which they ought not.
—I. Timothy. V. 13

What some invent the rest enlarge.
—Swift

Sabbath

Remember the sabbath day, to keep it holy. Six days shalt thou labor, and do all thy work: but the seventh day is the sabbath of the Lord thy God.
—EXODUS. XX. 8–11

God blessed the seventh day, and sanctified it: because that in it he had rested from all his work which God created and made.
—GENESIS. II. 3

Day of the Lord, as all our days should be!
—LONGFELLOW, *Christus*

The Sabbath was made for man, and not man for the Sabbath.
—MARK. II. 27

Safety

It is better to be safe than sorry.
—AMERICAN PROVERB

The trodden path is the safest.
—LEGAL MAXIM

Sailor

They that go down to the sea in ships, that do business in great waters; these see the works of the Lord, and his wonders in the deep.
—PSALMS. XVII. 23–24

The wind that blows, the ship that goes
And the lass that loves a sailor.

—OLD ENGLISH TOAST

Science

Art is I; science is we.

—CLAUDE BERNARD

Every great advance in science has issued from a new audacity of imagination.

—JOHN DEWEY, *The Quest for Certainty*

Steam is no stronger now than it was a hundred years ago, but it is put to better use.

—EMERSON

Science and art belong to the whole world, and before them vanish the barriers of nationality.

—GOETHE

Science is simply common sense at its best—that is, rigidly accurate in observation, and merciless to fallacy in logic.

—T. H. HUXLEY

Science is nothing but developed perception, interpreted intent, common sense rounded out, and minutely articulated.

—SANTAYANA, *The Life of Reason*

Science is the systematic classification of experience.

—GEORGE HENRY LEWES

Science is nothing but perception.

—PLATO

Science is organized knowledge.

—SPENCER, *Education*

Science falsely so called.

—I TIMOTHY. VI. 20

Scotland

Give me but one hour of Scotland,
Let me see it ere I die.

—WILLIAM E. AYTOUN

O Caledonia! stern and wild,
Meet nurse for a poetic child!
Land of brown heath and shaggy wood,
Land of the mountain and the flood,
Land of my sires! what mortal hand
Can e'er untie the filial band,
That knits me to thy rugged strand!

—SCOTT, *Lay of the Last
Ministrel*

Scripture

A glory gilds the sacred page,
    Majestic like the sun,
It gives a light to every age,
    It gives, but borrows none.

—COWPER, *Olney Hymns*

Thy word is a lamp unto my feet and a light unto my
path.

—PSALMS. CXIX. 105

We search the world for truth; we cull
The good, the pure, the beautiful,
From all old flower fields of the soul;
And, weary seekers of the best,
We come back laden from our quest,
To find that all the sages said
Is in the Book our mothers read.
                    —WHITTIER, *Miriam*

Sculpture

Madam de Staël pronounced architecture to be frozen
music; so is statuary crystalized spirituality.
                    —ALCOTT

Then marble, soften'd into life, grew warm.
                    —POPE, *Second Book of*
                                Horace

Sea

All the rivers run into the sea, yet the sea is not full.
                    —ECCLESIASTES. I. 7

Praise the sea; on shore remain.
                    —JOHN FLORIO

He that will learn to pray, let him go to sea.
                    —HERBERT

I must go down to the seas again, to the lonely sea and
    the sky,
And all I ask is a tall ship and a star to steer her by.
                    —MASEFIELD, *Sea-Fever*

The sea hath no king but God alone.
>   —ROSSETTI, *The White
>   Ship*

Break, break, break,
On thy cold gray stones, O sea!
And I would that my tongue could utter
The thoughts that arise in me.
>   —TENNYSON

Seasons

Autumn to winter, winter into spring,
Spring into summer, summer into fall,—
So rolls the changing year, and so we change;
Motion so swift, we know not that we move.
>   —DINAH MULOCK CRAIK,
>   *Immutable*

Spring is a virgin, Summer a mother,
Autumn a widow, and Winter a stepmother.
>   —POLISH PROVERB

Secrecy

There is a skeleton in every house.
>   —ANONYMOUS

A man can hide all things, excepting twain—
That he is drunk, and that he is in love.
>   —ANTIPHANES

The secret things belong unto the Lord our God.
>   —DEUTERONOMY, XXIX.

29

Nothing is secret which shall not be made manifest.
—LUKE. VIII. 17

Tell it not in Gath; publish it not in the streets of Askelon.
—II SAMUEL. I. 20

If you would wish another to keep your secret, first keep it yourself.

—SENECA

Selfishness

The force of selfishness is as inevitable and as calculable as the force of gravitation.
—HAILLIARD

The same people who can deny others everything are famous for refusing themselves nothing.
—LEIGH HUNT

That man who lives for self alone
Lives for the meanest mortal known.
—JOAQUIN MILLER, *Walker in Nicaragua*

Selfishness is the only real atheism; aspiration, unselfishness, the only real religion.
—ZANGWILL, *Children of the Ghetto*

Self-Knowledge

He who knows himself best esteems himself least.
—H. G. BOHN

Thales was asked what was most difficult to man; he
answered: "To know one's self."

> —DIOGENES

Oh, wad some power the giftie gie us
To see oursels as ithers see us!
It wad frae monie a blunder free us,
> And foolish notion.

> —ROBERT BURNS, *To a
> Louse*

We know what we are, but know not what we may be.
> —SHAKESPEARE, *Hamlet*.
> Act IV. Sc. 5

Know thyself.

> —Attributed to SOCRATES

Self-Love

He was like a cock who thought the sun had risen to hear
him crow.

> —GEORGE ELIOT, *Adam
> Bede*

He that falls in love with himself will have no rivals.
> —FRANKLIN

Self-love is the greatest of all flatterers.
> —LA ROCHEFOUCAULD

All men love themselves.

> —PLAUTUS

I to myself am dearer than a friend.
> —SHAKESPEARE, *Two
> Gentlemen of Verona*.
> Act II. Sc. 6

To love one's self is the beginning of a life-long romance.
—WILDE

Self-Made

He is a self-made man, and worships his creator.
—JOHN BRIGHT, referring to
Disraeli.

Every man is the architect of his own fortune.
—ENGLISH PROVERB

Self-Praise

God hates those who praise themselves.
—ST. CLEMENT

If you wish in this world to advance
Your merits you're bound to enhance;
    You must stir it and stump it,
    And blow your own trumpet,
Or, trust me, you haven't a chance.
—W. S. GILBERT,
Ruddigore

Let another man praise thee, and not thine own mouth.
—PROVERBS. XXVII. 2

Self-Reliance

A man is a lion in his own cause.
—SCOTTISH PROVERB

For they can conquer who believe they can.
—VERGIL

I have ever held it as a maxim never to do that through another which it was possible for me to execute myself.
—MONTESQUIEU

Doubt whom you will, but never yourself.
—BOVEE

No man should part with his own individuality and become that of another.
—CHANNING

Think wrongly, if you please, but in all cases think for yourself.
—LESSING

Self-Sacrifice

Greater love hath no man than this, that a man lay down his life for his friends.
—JOHN. XV. 13

Then out spake brave Horatius,
    The captain of the gate:
"To every man upon this earth
    Death cometh soon or late.
And how can man die better
    Than facing fearful odds,
For the ashes of his fathers
    And the temples of his gods?"
—MACAULAY, *Lays of
Ancient Rome*

Service

They also serve who only stand and wait.
—MILTON, *On His
Blindness*

Servant of God, well done.
> —MILTON, *Paradise Lost*

They serve God well,
Who serve his creatures.
> —CAROLINE NORTON, *The Lady of La Garaye*

My heart is ever at your service.
> —SHAKESPEARE, *Timon of Athens.* Act I. Sc. 2

He profits most who serves best.
> —ARTHUR F. SHELDON, Motto for Rotary International

Shadow

What shadows we are, what shadows we pursue!
> —BURKE, Speech, 1775

Coming events cast their shadows before.
> —CAMPBELL, *Lochiel's Warning*

Shadows are in reality, when the sun is shining, the most conspicuous thing in a landscape, next to the highest lights.
> —RUSKIN, *Painting*

Shakespeare

He was not of an age, but for all time!
> —BEN JONSON, *Line to the Memory of Shakespeare*

Shakespeare has had neither equal nor second.
—MACAULAY

Shame

Shame is an ornament to the young; a disgrace to the old.
—ARISTOTLE

I count him lost, who is lost to shame.
—PLAUTUS

We live in an atmosphere of shame. We are ashamed of everything that is real about us; ashamed of ourselves, of our relatives, of our incomes, of our accents, of our opinion, of our experience, just as we are ashamed of our naked skins.
—GEORGE BERNARD SHAW, *Man and Superman*

O shame! Where is they blush?
—SHAKESPEARE, *Hamlet*. Act III. Sc. 4

Sheep

A leap year
Is never a good sheep year.
—OLD ENGLISH SAYING

Baa, baa, black sheep,
    Have you any wool?
Yes, marry, have I
    three bags full:

One for the master,
    And one for my dame,
And one for the little boy
    Who lives in the lane.

            —NURSERY RHYME

Ships

Don't give up the ship!

            —JAMES LAWRENCE,
                Commander of the
                Chesapeake, 1813

Ships that pass in the night.

            —LONGFELLOW, *Tales of a*
                Wayside Inn, 1893

They that go down to the sea in ships, that do business in great waters.

            —PSALMS. CVII. 23

Ships are but boards, sailors but men.

            —SHAKESPEARE, *The*
                Merchant of Venice.
                Act I. Sc. 3

There breaks in every Gloucester wave
A windowed woman's heart.

            —ELIZABETH WARD,
                Gloucester Harbor

Shoemaking

Him that makes shoes go barefoot himself.

            —BURTON, *Anatomy of*
                Melancholy

I can tell where my own shoe pinches me.
—CERVANTES, *Don
Quixote*

Shoemaker, stick to your last.
—Proverb quoted by PLINY
THE ELDER

Sickness

Be not slow to visit the sick.
—ECCLESIASTES. VII. 35

Sickness is a belief, which must be annihilated by the
divine Mind.
—MARY BAKER EDDY,
Science and Health

Prevention is better than cure.
—ERASMUS, *Adagia*

The whole head is sick, and the whole heart faint.
—ISAIAH. I. 5

Silence

Silence gives consent.
—POPE BONIFACE VIII

Silence is more eloquent than words.
—CARLYLE, *Heroes and
Hero-Worship*

Silence is the unbearable repartee.
—CHESTERTON

Speech is silver; silence is golden.
> —GERMAN PROVERB

Still waters run deep.
> —ENGLISH PROVERB

Vessels never give so great a sound as when they are empty.
> —BISHOP JOHN JEWELL

It is a great misfortune neither to have enough wit to talk well nor enough judgment to be silent.
> —LA BRUYÈRE

Keep quiet and people will think you a philosopher.
> —LATIN PROVERB

Blessed are they who have nothing to say, and who cannot be persuaded to say it.
> —LOWELL

Be silent and safe—silence never betrays you.
> —JOHN BOYLE O'REILLY,
> *Rules of the Road*

He that keepeth his mouth keepeth his life; but he that openeth wide his lips shall have destruction.
> —PROVERBS. XIII. 3

The rest is silence.
> —SHAKESPEARE, *Hamlet*.
> Act V. Sc. 2

Smooth runs the water where the brook is deep.
> —SHAKESPEARE, *Henry* VI.
> Pt. II. Act III. Sc. 1

I regret often that I have spoken; never that I have been silent.

—SYRUS

Simplicity

Nothing is more simple than greatness; indeed, to be simple is to be great.

—EMERSON, *Literary Ethics*

Simplicity of character is the natural result of profound thought.

—HAZLITT

Affected simplicity is refined imposture.

—LA ROCHEFOUCAULD

The fewer our wants, the nearer we resemble the gods.

—SOCRATES

Sin

O sin, what hast thou done to this fair earth!

—R. H. DANA

He that falls into sin is a man; that grieves at it, is a saint; that boasteth of it, is a devil.

—THOMAS FULLER, *Holy State*

Proverty and wealth are comparative sins.

—VICTOR HUGO

He that is without sin among you, let him cast the first stone.

—JOHN. VIII. 7

The sin they do by two and two they must pay for one by one.
> —KIPLING, *Tomlinson*

So many laws argue so many sins.
> —MILTON, *Paradise Lost*

It is not alone what we do, but also what we do not do, for which we are accountable.
> —MOLIÈRE

In Adam's Fall
We sinned all.

> —NEW ENGLAND PRIMER

O thou, who didst with pitfall and with gin
Beset the road I was to wander in,
   Thou wilt not with predestin'd evil round
Enmesh, and then impute my fall to sin.
> —OMAR KHAYYÁM,
> *Rubaiyat*

My son, if sinners entice thee, consent thou not.
> —PROVERBS. I. 10

The way of transgressors is hard.
> —PROVERBS. XIII. 15

The wages of sin is death.
> —ROMANS. VI. 23

I am a man
More sinn'd against than sinning.
> —SHAKESPEARE, *King Lear.*
> Act III. Sc. 2

Sincerity

Of all the evil spirits abroad at this hour in the world, insincerity is the most dangerous.

—FROUDE, *Short Stories on Great Subjects*

There is no greater delight than to be conscious of sincerity on self-examination.

—MENCIUS

A little sincerity is a dangerous thing, and a great deal of it is absolutely fatal.

—WILDE, *The Critic as Artist*

Skepticism

Skepticism means, not intellectual doubt alone, but moral doubt.

—CARLYLE, *Heroes and Hero-Worship*

With most people, doubt about one thing is simply blind belief in another.

—G. C. LICHTENBERG

Skeptics are never deceived.

—FRENCH PROVERB

I am ready to reject all belief and reasoning, and can look upon no opinion even as more probable or likely than another.

—HUME, *A Treatise on Human Nature*

Believe nothing and be on your guard against everything.
—LATIN PROVERB

Great intellects are skeptical.
—NIETZSCHE

Sky

And that inverted Bowl they call the Sky,
Whereunder crawling coop'd we live and die,
   Lift not your hands to it for help—for it
As impotently moves as you or I.
—OMAR KHAYYÁM,
Rubaiyat

Sometimes gentle, sometimes capricious, sometimes
awful, never the same for two moments together; almost
human in its passions, almost spiritual in its tenderness,
almost Divine in its infinity.
—RUSKIN, *The Sky*

Slander

A slander is like a hornet; if you cannot kill it dead the
first blow, better not strike at it.
—H. W. SHAW

I hate the man who builds his name
On ruins of another's fame.
—GAY, *The Poet and the
Rose*

If slander be a snake, it is a winged one—it flies as well as creeps.

—DOUGLAS JERROLD,
Slander

I am disgrac'd, impeach'd and baffled here,—
Pierc'd to the soul with slander's venom'd spear.

—SHAKESPEARE, *Richard II.*
Act I. Sc. 1

Slavery

If you put a chain around the neck of a slave, the other end fastens itself around your own.

—EMERSON, *Compensation*

The compact which exists between the North and the South is a covenant with death and an agreement with hell; involving both parties in atrocious criminality and should be immediately annulled.

—WILLIAM LLOYD
GARRISON

I believe this government cannot endure permanently half slave and half free.

—LINCOLN, Speech, 1858

Corrupted freemen are the worst slaves.

—DAVID GARRICK

The man who gives me employment, which I must have or suffer, that man is my master, let me call him what I will.

—HENRY GEORGE, *Social
Problems*

They are slaves who fear to speak
For the fallen and the weak;

• • •

They are slaves who dare not be
In the right with two or three.
> —LOWELL, *Stanzas on
> Freedom*

They (the blacks) had no right which the white man was
bound to respect.
> —ROGER B. TANEY, *The
> Dred Scott Case*

Englishmen never will be slaves; they are free to do whatever the Government and public opinion allow them to
do.

> —GEORGE BERNARD
> SHAW, *Man and
> Superman*

Sleep

Over my slumber your loving watch keep—
Rock me to sleep, mother; rock me to sleep.
> —ELIZABETH AKERS ALLEN

Fatigue is the best pillow.
> —FRANKLIN

Sleep is the best cure for waking troubles.
> —CERVANTES

The sleep of a labouring man is sweet.
> —ECCLESIASTES. V. 12

One hour's sleep before midnight is worth three after.
——GEORGE HERBERT

　　Soft closer of our eyes!
Low murmur of tender lullabies!
　　　　　——KEATS, *Sleep and Poetry*

Sleep, rest of nature, O sleep, most gentle of the divinities, peace of the soul, thou at whose presence care disappears, who soothest hearts wearied with daily employments, and makest them strong again for labour!
——OVID, *Metamorphoses*

I will both lay me down in peace, and sleep: for thou, Lord, only makest me dwell in safety.
——PSALMS. IV. 8

He giveth His beloved sleep.
——PSALMS. CXXVII. 2

I never sleep comfortably except when I am at sermon or when I pray to God.
——RABELAIS, *Gargantua*

To all, to each, a fair goodnight,
And pleasing dreams, and slumbers light.
——SCOTT, *Marmion*

She slept the sleep of the just.
——RACINE

To sleep! perchance to dream; ay, there's the rub;
For in that sleep of death what dreams may come,
When we have shuffled off this mortal coil,
Must give us pause.
　　　　　——SHAKESPEARE, *Hamlet.*
　　　　　　Act III. Sc. 1

O sleep, O gentle sleep,
Nature's soft nurse.

—SHAKESPEARE, *Henry IV.*
Pt. II. Act III. Sc. 1

Hush, my dear, lie still and slumber!
    Holy angels guard they bed!
Heavenly blessings without number
    Gently falling on thy head.

—ISAAC WATTS, *Cradle
Hymn*

Smile

Smiles form the channels of a future tear.

—BYRON, *Childe Harold*

'Tis easy enough to be pleasant,
    When life flows along like a song;
But the man worth while is the one who will smile
    When everything goes dead wrong.

—ELLA WHEELER WILCOX,
Worth While

What's the use of worrying?
    It never was worth while, so
Pack up your troubles in your old kit-bag,
    And smile, smile, smile.

—GEORGE ASAF, *Smile,
Smile, Smile*

The thing that goes the farthest towards making life worth
    while,
That costs the least, and does the most, is just a pleasant
    smile.

• • •

It's full of worth and goodness too, with manly kindness
    blent,
It's worth a million dollars and it doesn't cost a cent.
                —WILBUR D. NESBIT, *Let*
                Us Smile

Sneer

Who can refute a sneer?
                —WILLIAM PALEY

It is just as hard to do your duty when men are sneering
at you as when they are shooting at you.
                —WOODROW WILSON,
                Speech, 1914

Snow

Year of snow
Fruit will grow.
                —OLD ENGLISH RHYME

But where are the snows of yesteryear?
                —VILLON

Socialism

Socialism is that contemplated system of industrial society which proposes the abolition of private property in
the great material instruments of production, and the
substitution therefor of collective property; and advocates
the collective management of production, together with

the distribution of social income by society, and private
property in the larger proportion of this social income.

—RICHARD T. ELY,
Socialism and Social
Reform

These monstrous views, . . . these venomous teachings.

—POPE LEO XIII

All Socialism involves slavery.

—SPENCER, The Coming
Slavery

Society

These families, you know, are our upper crust, not upper
ten thousand.

—COOPER, The Ways of the
Hour

He might have proved a useful adjunct, if not an ornament to society.

—LAMB, Captain Starkey

Man is a social animal.

—SENECA

It is impossible, in our condition of Society, not to be
sometimes a Snob.

—THACKERARY, Book of
Snobs

To get into the best society nowadays, one has either to
feed people, amuse people, or shock people.

—WILDE, A Woman of No
Importance

Soldier

The king of France with twenty thousand men
Went up the hill, and then came down again:
The king of Spain with twenty thousand more
Climbed the same hill the French had climbed before.
　　　　　　　—ANONYMOUS

God and a soldier all people adore
In time of war, but not before;
And when war is over and all things are righted,
God is neglected and an old soldier slighted.
　　　　　　　—ANONYMOUS

Home they brought her warrior dead.
　　　　　　　—TENNYSON, *The Princess*

How sleep the brave, who sink to rest.
By all their country's wishes blest!
　　　　　　　—WILLIAM COLLINS, *Ode*

We are coming, Father Abraham, three hundred thousand more.
　　　　　　　—J. S. GIBBONS

Every citizen should be a soldier. This was the case with
the Greeks and Romans, and must be that of every free
state.
　　　　　　　—JEFFERSON, Letter, 1813

Let not him that girdeth on his harness boast himself as
he that putteth it off.
　　　　　　　—I KINGS. XX. 11

For it's Tommy this an' Tommy that, and "Chuck 'im
    out, the brute."
But it's "Savior of 'is country," when the guns begin to
    shoot.
                       —KIPLING, *Tommy*

It is not the guns or armament
    Or the money they can pay,
It's the close co-operation
    That makes them win the day.
It is not the individual
    Or the army as a whole,
But the everlastin' teamwork
    Of every bloomin' soul.
                       —J. MASON KNOX

A soldier is an anachronism of which we must get rid.
                       — GEORGE BERNARD
                       SHAW, *Devil's Disciple*

But in a larger sense we cannot dedicate, we cannot con-
secrate, we cannot hallow this ground. The brave men,
living and dead, who struggled here, have consecrated it
far above our poor power to add or detract.
                       —LINCOLN, *Gettysburg
                       Address*

The muffled drum's sad roll has beat
    The soldier's last tattoo;
No more on Life's parade shall meet
    The brave and fallen few.
On Fame's eternal camping-ground
    Their silent tents are spread,
And Glory guards, with solemn round
    The bivouac of the dead.
                       —THEODORE O'HARA, *The
                       Bivouac of the Dead*

I want to see you shoot the way you shout.
                              —THEODORE ROOSEVELT

Solitude

In solitude, when we are *least* alone.
                              —BYRON, *Childe Harold*

We enter the world alone, we leave it alone.
                              —FROUDE

Far from the madding crowd's ignoble strife.
                              — GRAY, *Elegy in a
                              Country Churchyard*

Alone, alone, all, all alone,
   Alone on a wide, wide sea.
                              —COLERIDGE, *Ancient
                              Mariner*

I praise the Frenchman; his remark was shrewd,—
"How sweet, how passing sweet is solitude."
But grant me still a friend in my retreat,
Whom I may whisper—Solitude is sweet.
                              —COWPER, *Retirement*

The strongest man is the one who stands most alone.
                              —IBSEN, *An Enemy of the
                              People*

Solitude is as needful to the imagination as society is
wholesome for the character.
                              —LOWELL, *Among My
                              Books*

The thoughtful Soul to Solitude retires.
>—OMAR KHAYYÁM,
>Rubaiyat

I never found the companion that was so companionable
as solitude.
>—THOREAU, *Solitude*

Song

Swans sing before they die—'twere no bad thing
Should certain persons die before they sing.
>—COLERIDGE, *On a Bad
>Singer*

A song will outlive all sermons in the memory.
>—HENRY GILES

The morning stars sang together, and all the sons of God
shouted for joy.
>—JOB. XXXVIII. 7

And so make life, death and that vast forever
One grand, sweet song.
>—KINGSLEY, *A Farewell*

God sent his Singers upon earth
With songs of sadness and of mirth,
That they might touch the hearts of men,
And bring them back to heaven again.
>—LONGFELLOW, *The
>Singers*

Our sweetest songs are those that tell of saddest thought.
>—SHELLEY, *To a Skylark*

Sorrow

The busy have no time for tears.
> —BYRON, *The Two Foscari*

I walked a mile with Sorrow
    And ne'er a word said she;
But, oh, the things I learned from her
    When Sorrow walked with me.
> —ROBERT BROWNING
> HAMILTON, *Along the
> Road*

Every noble crown is, and on earth will ever be, a crown
of thorns.
> —CARLYLE

All sorrows are bearable, if there is bread.
> —CERVANTES

Hang sorrow, care'll kill a cat.
> —BEN JONSON, *Every Man
> in His Humour*

To Sorrow
    I bade good-morrow,
And thought to leave her far away behind;
    But cheerly, cheerly,
    She loves me dearly:
She is so constant to me, and so kind.
> —KEATS, *Endymion*

Sorrows are like thunderclouds—in the distance they
look black, over our heads scarcely gray.
> —JEAN PAUL RICHTER,
> *Hesperus*

The deeper the sorrow, the less tongue hath it.
                                —THE TALMUD

Joy was a flame in me
    Too steady to destroy.
Lithe as a bending reed,
Loving the storm that sways her—
I found more joy in sorrow
    Than you could find in joy.
                                —SARA TEASDALE, *The
                                    Answer*

More in sorrow than in anger.
                                —SHAKESPEARE, *Hamlet*.
                                    Act. I. Sc. 2

There can be no rainbow without a cloud and a storm.
                                —J. H. VINCENT

Soul

John Brown's body lies a mould'ring in the grave,
His soul goes marching on.
                                —THOMAS BRIGHAM
                                    BISHOP, *John Brown's
                                    Body*

The one thing in the world, of value, is the active soul.
                                —EMERSON, *American
                                    Scholar*

It matters not how strait the gate,
    How charged with punishments the scroll,
I am the master of my fate:
    I am the captain of my soul.
                                —W. E. HENLEY, *Invictus*

Out of the night that covers me,
    Black as the Pit from pole to pole,
I thank whatever gods may be
    For my unconquerable soul.
              —W. E. HENLEY, *Invictus*

Soul, thou hast much goods laid up for many years; take
thine ease, eat, drink and be merry.
              —LUKE. XII. 19

What is a man profited, if he shall gain the whole world,
and lose his own soul?
              —MATTHEW. XVI. 26

I sent my Soul through the Invisible,
Some letter of that After-life to spell,
And by and by my Soul returned to me,
And answered "I Myself am Heav'n and Hell."
              —OMAR KHAYYÁM,
                Rubaiyat

The iron entered into his soul.
              —PSALMS. CV. 18

Self is the only prison that can ever bind the soul.
              —HENRY VAN DYKE, *The
                Prison and the Angel*

A charge to keep I have,
    A God to glorify:
A never-dying soul to save,
    And fit it for the sky.
              —CHARLES WESLEY,
                Hymns

I loafe and invite my soul,
I lean and loafe at my ease, observing a spear of summer
    grass.

—WALT WHITMAN, *Song of
Myself*

The windows of my soul I throw
Wide open to the sun.

—WHITTIER, *My Psalm*

Sound

The empty vessel makes the greatest sound.

—SHAKESPEARE, *Henry V.*
Act IV. Sc. 4

Hark! from the tombs a doleful sound.

—ISAAC WATTS, *Hymns
and Spiritual Songs*

Speech

Hear much; speak little.

—BIAS

That which is repeated too often becomes insipid and
tedious.

—BOILEAU

Let him now speak, or else hereafter for ever hold his
peace.

—BOOK OF COMMON
PRAYER

His speech was a fine sample, on the whole,
Of rhetoric, which the learn'd call *"rigmarole."*
> —BYRON, *Don Juan*

Speech is silvern, silence is golden.
> —CARLYLE, *A Swiss
> Inscription*

He mouths a sentence as curs mouth a bone.
> —CHARLES CHURCHILL,
> *The Rosciad*

Let your speech be alway with grace, seasoned with salt.
> —COLOSSIANS. IV. 6

Congress shall make no law . . . abridging the freedom of speech or of the press.
> —CONSTITUTION OF THE
> UNITED STATES.
> Amendment I

Seeing then that we have such hope, we use great plainness of speech.
> —II CORINTHIANS. III. 12

A sophistical rhetorician, inebriated with the exuberance of his own verbosity.
> —DISRAELI, Speech, 1878

I will sit down now, but the time will come when you will hear me.
> —DISRAELI, Maiden Speech
> in the House of
> Commons

The hare-brained chatter of irresponsible frivolity.
> —DISRAELI, Speech, 1878

Miss not the discourse of the elders.
> —ECCLESIASTES. VIII. 9

For that man is detested by me as the gates of hell, whose outward words conceal his inmost thoughts.
> —HOMER, *Iliad*

His speech flowed from his tongue sweeter than honey.
> —HOMER, *Iliad*

For God's sake, let us freely hear both sides!
> —JEFFERSON, Letter, 1814

Every man has a right to utter what he thinks truth, and every other man has a right to knock him down for it.
> —SAMUEL JOHNSON

Woe unto you, when all men shall speak well of you!
> —LUKE. VI. 26

They think that they shall be heard for their much speaking.
> —MATTHEW. VI. 7

Out of the abundance of the heart the mouth speaketh.
> —MATTHEW. XII. 34

If you your lips would keep from slips,
    Five things observe with care;
To whom you speak, of whom you speak,
    And how, and when, and where.
> —W. E. NORRIS, *Thirlby Hall*

Rhetoric is the art of ruling the minds of men.
> —PLATO

It is a tiresome way of speaking, when you should despatch the business, to beat about the bush.
—PLAUTUS

Let no one be willing to speak ill of the absent.
—PROPERTIUS

A soft answer turneth away wrath.
—PROVERBS. XV. 1

He replies nothing but monosyllables. I believe he would make three bites of a cherry.
—RABELAIS, *Pantagruel*

Speak after the manner of men.
—ROMANS. VI. 19

Speech is the index of the mind.
—SENECA

I disapprove of what you say, but I will defend to the death your right to say it.
—Attributed to VOLTAIRE

Spirit

Not of the letter, but of the spirit; for the letter killeth, but the spirit giveth life.
—II CORINTHIANS. III. 6

The spirit indeed is willing, but the flesh is weak.
—MATTHEW. XXVI. 41

He that is slow to anger is better than the mighty; and he that ruleth his spirit than he that taketh a city.
—PROVERBS. XVI. 32

Sport

I have never been able to understand why pigeon-shooting at Hurlingham should be refined and polite, while a rat-killing match in Whitechapel is low.
—T. H. HUXLEY

When I play with my cat, who knows whether I do not make her more sport, than she makes me?
—MONTAIGNE

If all the year were playing holidays,
To sport would be as tedious as to work.
—SHAKESPEARE, *Henry IV.*
Pt. I. Act I. Sc. 2

When a man wants to murder a tiger he calls it sport: when the tiger wants to murder him he calls it ferocity.
—GEORGE BERNARD
SHAW, *Maxims for
Revolutionists*

Spring

If there comes a little thaw,
Still the air is chill and raw,
Here and there a patch of snow,
Dirtier than the ground below,
Dribbles down a marshy flood;
Ankle-deep you stick in mud
In the meadows while you sing,
"This is Spring."
—C. P. CRANCH, A *Spring
Growl*

For, lo! The winter is past, the rain is over and gone; the flowers appear on the earth; the time of the singing of birds is come, and the voice of the turtle is heard in our land.

> —SONG OF SOLOMON. II.
> 11, 12

Came the Spring with all its splendor
All its birds and all its blossoms,
All its flowers, and leaves, and grasses.

> —LONGFELLOW, *Hiawatha*

Yet Ah, that Spring should vanish with the Rose.
That Youth's sweetscented manuscript should close!
The Nightingale that in the branches sang
Ah whence and whither flown again, who knows?

> — OMAR KHAYYÁM,
> *Rubiayat*

In the Spring a livelier iris changes on the burnish'd dove;
In the Spring a young man's fancy lightly turns to thoughts
  of love.

> —TENNYSON, *Locksley Hall*

Star

Hitch your wagon to a star.

> —EMERSON, *Society and
> Solitude*

The stars in their courses fought against Sisera.

> —JUDGES. V. 21

Silently, one by one, in the infinite meadows of heaven,
Blossomed the lovely stars, the forget-me-nots of the
  angels.

> —LONGFELLOW,
> *Evangeline*

The morning stars sang together, and all the sons of God shouted for joy.

—JOB. XXXVIII. 7

Stars are the daisies that begem
The blue fields of the sky.

—D. M. MOIR, *Dublin
University Magazine*

No star is ever lost we once have seen,
We always may be what we might have been.

—ADELAIDE A. PROCTOR,
Legend of Provence

Her blue eyes sought the west afar,
For lovers love the western star.

—SCOTT, *Lay of the Last
Minstrel*

These blessed candles of the night.

—SHAKESPEARE, *Merchant
of Venice.* Act V. Sc. 1

Twinkle, twinkle, little star!
How I wonder what you are,
Up above the world so high,
Like a diamond in the sky!

—ANNE TAYLOR, *Rhymes
for the Nursery*

State

A state is a perfect body of free men, united together to enjoy common rights and advantages.

—HUGO GROTIUS

A state from which religion is banished can never be well governed.

—POPE LEO XIII

I am the state.

—LOUIS XIV of France

States are as the men are; they grow out of human characters.

—PLATO, *The Republic*

Statesmanship

I have the courage of my opinions, but I have not the temerity to give a political blank cheque to Lord Salisbury.

—GOSCHEN, In
Parliament, 1884

Ambassadors are the eye and ear of states.

—GUICCIARDINI, *Storia
d'Italia*

Learn to think continentally.

—ALEXANDER HAMILTON

Peace, commerce, and honest friendship with all nations—entangling alliances with none.

—JEFFERSON, First
Inaugural Address

'Tis our true policy to steer clear of permanent alliances, with any portion of the foreign world—as far, I mean, as we are now at liberty to do it.

—WASHINGTON, Farewell
Address, 1796

You can always get the truth from an American statesman after he has turned seventy, or given up all hope of the Presidency.

—WENDELL PHILLIPS

An ambassador is an honest man sent to lie abroad for the commonwealth.

—SIR HENRY WOTTON

Storm

Rides in the whirlwind, and directs the storm.

—ADDISON, *The Campaign*

He used to raise a storm in a teapot.

—CICERO

For many years I was self-appointed inspector of snow-storms and rain-storms and did my duty faithfully.

—THOREAU, *Walden*

Story-Telling

An' all us other children, when the supper things is done,
We set around the kitchen fire an' has the mostest fun
A-list'nin' to the witch tales 'at Annie tells about
An' the gobble-uns 'at gits you
    Ef you
        Don't
            Watch
                Out!

—JAMES WHITCOMB RILEY,
Little Orphant Annie

A schoolboy's tale, the wonder of an hour!

—BYRON, *Childe Harold*

This story will never go down.
> —FIELDING, *Tumble-Down
> Dick*

And what so tedious as a twice-told tale.
> —HOMER, *Odyssey*

But that is another story.
> —KIPLING, *Plain Tales from
> the Hills*

I cannot tell how the truth may be;
I say the tale as 'twas said to me.
> —SCOTT, *Lay of the Last
> Minstrel*

And thereby hangs a tale.
> —SHAKESPEARE, *Taming of
> the Shrew.* Act IV.
> Sc. 1

For seldom shall she hear a tale
So sad, so tender, yet so true.
> —SHENSTONE, *Jenny
> Dawson*

Stranger

A stranger in a strange land.
> —EXODUS. II. 22

I was a stranger, and ye took me in.
> —MATTHEW. XXV. 35

A stranger's eyes see clearest.
> —READE, *The Cloister and
> the Hearth*

Strength

My strength is made perfect in weakness.
—II CORINTHIANS. XII. 9

As thy days, so shall thy strength be.
—DEUTERONOMY. XXXIII.
25

A threefold cord is not quickly broken.
—ECCLESIASTES. IV. 12

They go from strength to strength.
—PSALMS. LXXXIV. 7

I feel like a Bull Moose.

—THEODORE ROOSEVELT
on returning from the
Spanish War

O, it is excellent
To have a giant's strength, but it is tyrannous
To use it like a giant.
—SHAKESPEARE, *Measure
for Measure.* Act II.
Sc. 2

Three things give hardy strength: sleeping on hairy mat-
tresses, breathing cold air, and eating dry food.
—WELSH PROVERB

Study

Histories make men wise; poets, witty; the mathematics,
subtle; natural philosophy, deep; morals, grave; logic and
rhetoric, able to contend.
—BACON, *Of Studies*

There are more men ennobled by study than by nature.
— CICERO

Much study is a weariness of the flesh.
—ECCLESIASTES. XII. 12

The world's great men have not commonly been great scholars, nor its great scholars great men.
—HOLMES, *Autocrat of the Breakfast-Table*

As turning the logs will make a dull fire burn, so change of studies a dull brain.
—LONGFELLOW, *Drift-Wood*

You are in some brown study.
—LYLY, *Euphues*

Iron sharpens iron; scholar, the scholar.
—THE TALMUD

Stupidity

Peter was dull; he was at first
    Dull,—Oh, so dull—so very dull!
Whether he talked, wrote, or rehearsed—
    Still with this dulness was he cursed—
Dull—beyond all conception—dull.
—SHELLEY, *Peter Bell the Third*

We are growing serious, and, let me tell you, that's a very next step to being dull.
—ADDISON, *The Drummer*

The bookful blockhead, ignorantly read,
With loads of learned lumber in his head.
                    —POPE, *Essay on Criticism*

Against stupidity the very gods
Themselves contend in vain.
                    —SCHILLER, *Maid of
                              Orleans*

Style

One who uses many periods is a philosopher; many inter-
rogations, a student; many exclamations, a fanatic.
                    —J. L. BASFORD

Style is the dress of thoughts.
                    —CHESTERFIELD, Letter to
                              his son

Montesquieu had the style of a genius;
Buffon, the genius of style.
                    —BARON GRIMM

Neat, not gaudy.
                    —LAMB, Letter to
                          Wordsworth

Long sentences in a short composition are like large rooms
in a little house.
                    —SHENSTONE

Clearness ornaments profound thoughts.
                    —VAUVENARGUES

Success

Successful minds work like a gimlet,—to a single point.
—BOVEE

All you need in this life is ignorance and confidence, and
then Success is sure.

—S. L. CLEMENS (MARK
TWAIN), 1887

Success is counted sweetest
By those who ne'er succeed.

—EMILY DICKINSON,
Success

Nothing succeeds like success.
—DUMAS, *Ange Pitou*

The race is not to the swift, nor the battle to the strong.
—ECCLESIASTES. IX. 11

There are but two ways of rising in the world: either by
one's own industry or profiting by the foolishness of
others.

—LA BRUYÈRE

I have always observed that to succeed in the world one
should appear like a fool but be wise.
—MONTESQUIEU

Faith, mighty faith, the promise sees,
    And looks to that alone;
Laughs at impossibilities,
    And cries it shall be done.

—CHARLES WESLEY,
Hymns

Either do not attempt at all, or go through with it.
—OVID

> To climb steep hills
Requires slow pace at first.
>
> —SHAKESPEARE, *Henry*
> VII. Act I. Sc, 1

Somebodys said that it couldn't be done,
    But he with a chuckle replied
That "maybe it couldn't," but he would be one
    Who wouldn't say so till he'd tried.

So he buckled right in with the trace of a grin
    On his face. If he worried he hid it.
He started to sing as he tackled the thing
    That couldn't be done, and he did it.
> —EDGAR A. GUEST, *It*
> *Couldn't Be Done*

And he gave it for his opinion, that whoever could make
two ears of corn, or two blades of grass, to grow upon a
spot of ground where only one grew before, would deserve
better of mankind and do more essential service to his
country, than the whole race of politicians put together.
> —SWIFT, *Gulliver's Travels*

Suffering

I have trodden the winepress alone.
> —ISAIAH. LXIII. 3

It requires more courage to suffer than to die.
> —NAPOLEON

No pain, no palm; no thorns, no throne; no gall, no glory;
no cross, no crown.
> —WILLIAM PENN

We are healed of a suffering only by experiencing it to the full.

—MARCEL PROUST, *The Sweet Cheat Gone*

I reckon that the sufferings of this present time are not worthy to be compared with the glory which shall be revealed in us.

—ROMANS. VIII. 18

Suicide

I have a hundred times wished that one could resign life as an officer resigns a commission.

—ROBERT BURNS, Letter, 1788

It is cowardice to commit suicide.

—NAPOLEON, 1817

The relatives of a suicide always take it in bad part, that he did not remain alive out of consideration for the family dignity.

—NIETZSCHE, *Human All-too-Human*

There is no refuge from confession but suicide; and suicide is confession.

—DANIEL WEBSTER

Summer

One swallow alone does not make the summer.

—CERVANTES, *Don Quixote*

Oh, the summer night
Has a smile of light
And she sits on a sapphire throne.
>   —B. W. PROCTER, *The*
>   *Nights*

Sun

Make hay while the sun shines.
>   —CERVANTES, *Don*
>   *Quixote*

Truly the light is sweet, and a pleasant thing it is for the
eyes to behold the sun.
>   —ECCLESIASTES. XI. 7

Whence are thy beams, O sun! thy everlasting light?
Thou comest forth, in thy awful beauty; the stars hide
themselves in the sky; the moon, cold and pale, sinks in
the western wave. But thou, thyself, movest alone.
>   —MACPHERSON, *Ossian*

The sun shines even on the wicked.
>   —SENECA

Superiority

There are three marks of a superior man: being virtuous,
he is free from anxiety; being wise, he is free from per-
plexity; being brave, he is free from fear.
>   —CONFUCIUS

We can all perceive the difference between ourselves and
our inferiors, but when it comes to a question of the
difference between us and our superiors we fail to appre-
ciate merits of which we have no proper conceptions.
>   —COOPER, *The American*
>   *Democrat*

Superiority is always detested.
　　　　　　　　　　—BALTASAR GRACIÁN

Superstition

The general root of superstition is that men observe when
things hit, and not when they miss; and commit to memory the one, and forget and pass over the other.
　　　　　　　　　　—BACON

Superstition is the religion of feeble minds.
　　　　　　　　　　—BURKE

I die adoring God, loving my friends, not hating my
enemies, and detesting superstition.
　　　　　　　　　　—VOLTAIRE

Religion is not removed by removing superstition.
　　　　　　　　　　—CICERO

There is in superstition a senseless fear of God.
　　　　　　　　　　—CICERO

Suspicion

Suspicion is far more apt to be wrong than right; oftener
unjust than just. It is no friend to virtue, and always an
enemy to happiness.
　　　　　　　　　　—HOSEA BALLOU

As to Caesar, when he was called upon, he gave no tes-
timony against Clodius, nor did he affirm that he was
certain of any injury done to his bed. He only said, "He
had divorced Pompeia because the wife of Caesar ought
not only to be clear of such a crime, but of the very
suspicion of it."
　　　　　　　　　　—PLUTARCH, Life of Cicero

Suspicion always haunts the guilty mind;
The thief doth fear each bush an officer.
>—SHAKESPEARE, *Henry VI.*
>Pt. III. Act V. Sc. 6

The less we know the more we suspect.
>—H. W. SHAW

A woman of honor should not suspect another of things she would not do herself.

>—MARGUERITE DE VALCIS

Swans

All our geese are swans.
>—BURTON, *Anatomy of*
>*Melancholy*

You think that upon the score of fore-knowledge and divining I am infinitely inferior to the swans. When they perceive approaching death they sing more merrily than before, because of the joy they have in going to the God they serve.

>—SOCRATES

Sweetness

The pursuit of the perfect, then, is the pursuit of sweetness and light.
>—MATTHEW ARNOLD,
>*Culture and Anarchy*

Every sweet hath its sour, every evil its good.
>—EMERSON, *Compensation*

Sweet meat must have sour sauce.
>—BEN JONSON, *Poetaster*

Sweets to the sweet.

> —SHAKESPEARE, *Hamlet*.
> Act V. Sc. 1

Sympathy

Of a truth, men are mystically united: a mystic bond of brotherhood makes all men one.

> —CARLYLE, *Essays*

> The man who melts
> With social sympathy, though not allied,
> Is of more worth than a thousand kinsmen.

> —EURIPIDES

He watch'd and wept, he pray'd and felt for all.

> —GOLDSMITH, *The
> Deserted Village*

Never elated while one man's oppress'd;
Never dejected while another's bless'd.

> —POPE, *Essay on Man*

Rejoice with them that do rejoice, and weep with them that weep.

> —ROMANS. XII. 15

No one really understands the grief or joy of another.

> —FRANZ SCHUBERT

Tact

Women and foxes, being weak, are distinguished by superior tact.

> —BIERCE

Without tact you can learn nothing.
—DISRAELI, *Endymion*

To have the reputation of possessing the most perfect social tact, talk to every woman as if you loved her, and to every man as if he bored you.
—WILDE, *A Woman of No Importance*

Tale

Beware of him that telleth tales.
—ANONYMOUS

A schoolboy's tale, the wonder of an hour.
—BYRON, *Childe Harold*

Tush! These are trifles, and mere old wives' tales.
—MARLOWE, *Dr. Faustus*

What so tedious as a twice-told tale?
—POPE

I cannot tell how the truth may be;
I say the tale as 'twas said to me.
—SCOTT, *The Lay of the Last Minstrel*

A tale never loses in the telling.
—SCOTTISH PROVERB

I will a round unvarnish'd tale deliver.
—SHAKESPEARE, *Othello*.
Act I. Sc. 3

Talent

Concealed talent brings no reputation.
—ERASMUS

The world is always ready to receive talent with open arms.
—HOLMES

Every man hath his proper gift of God, one after this manner, and another after that.
—I CORINTHIANS. V. 7

Talk

"The time has come," the Walrus said,
    "To talk of many things;
Of shoes—and ships—and sealing-wax—
    Of cabbages—and kings—
And why the sea is boiling hot—
    And whether pigs have wings."
—LEWIS CARROLL, *Through the Looking Glass*

But far more numerous was the herd of such,
Who think too little, and who talk too much.
—DRYDEN, *Absalom and Achitophel*

Talk is cheap.
—ENGLISH PROVERB

In much of your talking, thinking is half murdered.
—KAHLIL GIBRAN, *The Prophet*

They never taste who always drink;
They always talk who never think.
>—PRIOR

Talkers are no good doers.
>—SHAKESPEARE, *Richard
III*. Act I. Sc. 3

In general those who nothing have to say
Contrive to spend the longest time in doing it.
>—LOWELL, *An Oriental
Apologue*

Those who have few things to attend to are great babblers; for the less men think, the more they talk.
>—MONTESQUIEU

He who talks too much commits a sin.
>—THE TALMUD

The secret of being tiresome is in telling everything.
>—VOLTAIRE

Taste

Taste is nothing but a delicate good sense.
>—M. J. DE CHENIER

Everyone to his taste.
>—FRENCH PROVERB

My tastes are aristocratic; my actions democratic.
>—VICTOR HUGO

A man's palate can, in time, become accustomed to anything.
>—NAPOLEON

Good taste is the flower of good sense.
—POINCELOT

The finer impulse of our nature.
—SCHILLER

Every man as he loveth, quoth the good man when he kissed the cow.
—JOHN HEYWOOD

Taxes

The art of taxation consists in so plucking the goose as to obtain the largest amount of feathers with the least possible amount of hissing.
—Attributed to
J. B. COLBERT

Death and taxes are inevitable.
—HALIBURTON

Teaching

You cannot teach old dogs new tricks.
—ANONYMOUS

A man should first direct himself in the way he should go. Only then should he instruct others.
—BUDDHA

You cannot teach a man anything; you can only help him to find it within himself.
—GALILEO

A teacher who is attempting to teach without inspiring the pupil with a desire to learn is hammering on cold iron.

—HORACE MANN

Speak to the earth, and it shall teach thee.
—JOB. XII. 8

Public instruction should be the first object of government.

—NAPOLEON

Everybody who is incapable of learning has taken to teaching.

—WILDE, *The Decay of Lying*

Tears

Tears are Summer showers to the soul.
—ALFRED AUSTIN, *Savonarola*

For Beauty's tears are lovelier than her smile.
—CAMPBELL, *Pleasures of Hope*

Words that weep and tears that speak.
—COWLEY, *The Prophet*

Never a tear bedims the eye
That time and patience will not dry.
—BRET HARTE, *Lost Galleon*

Oh! would I were dead now,
Or up in my bed now,
To cover my head now
And have a good cry!

—HOOD, *A Table of Errata*

Jesus wept.

—JOHN. XI. 35 (Shortest
verse in the Bible)

If the man who turnips cries,
Cry not when his father dies,
'Tis proof that he had rather
Have a turnip than his father.

—SAMUEL JOHNSON

There shall be weeping and gnashing of teeth.
—MATTHEW. VIII. 12

It is some relief to weep; grief is satisfied and carried off
by tears.

—OVID

If you have tears, prepare to shed them now.
—SHAKESPEARE, *Julius
Caesar.* Act III. Sc. 2

Tears are the silent language of grief.
—VOLTAIRE, *A
Philosophical
Dictionary*

Temperance

The first draught serveth for health, the second for pleasure, the third for shame, and the fourth for madness.
—ANACHARSIS

Temperate in all things.

—I CORINTHIANS. IX. 25

Every moderate drinker could abandon the intoxicating cup if he would; every inebriate would if he could.

—J. B. GOUGH

Drinking water neither makes a man sick, nor in debt, nor his wife a widow.

—JOHN NEALE

The smaller the drink, the clearer the head, and the cooler the blood.

—WILLIAM PENN

Temptation

Blessed is the man that endureth temptation; for when he is tried, he shall receive the crown of life.

—JAMES. I. 12

Honest bread is very well—it's the butter that makes the temptation.

—DOUGLAS JERROLD, *The Catspaw*

Get thee behind me, Satan.

—MATTHEW. XVI. 23

Never resist temptation: prove all things: hold fast that which is good.

—GEORGE BERNARD SHAW, *Maxims for Revolutionists*

I can resist everything except temptation.

—WILDE, *Lady Windermere's Fan*

Thankfulness

O give thanks unto the Lord, for he is good: for his mercy endureth forever.
—PSALMS. CVII. 1

Beggar that I am, I am even poor in thanks.
—SHAKESPEARE, *Hamlet*.
Act II. Sc. 2

How sharper than a serpent's tooth it is
To have a thankless child.
—SHAKESPEARE, *King Lear*.
Act I. Sc. 4

Thanksgiving Day

Heap high the board with plenteous cheer, and gather
to the feast,
And toast the sturdy Pilgrim band whose courage never
ceased.
Give praise to that All-Gracious One by whom their steps
were led,
And thanks unto the harvest's Lord who sends our "daily
bread."
—ALICE WILLIAMS
BROTHERTON, *The
First Thanksgiving
Day*

So once in every year we throng
Upon a day apart,
To praise the Lord with feast and song
In thankfulness of heart.
—ARTHUR GUITERMAN,
The First Thanksgiving

Thieving

Thou shalt not steal.

—EXODUS. XX. 15

There is honor among thieves.

—ENGLISH PROVERB

Set a thief to catch a thief.

—ENGLISH PROVERB

A plague upon it when thieves cannot be true one to another!

—SHAKESPEARE, *Henry IV.*
Pt. I. Act II. Sc. 2

When thieves fall out, honest men come by their own.

—ENGLISH PROVERB

Stolen waters are sweet, and bread eaten in secret is pleasant.

—PROVERBS, IX. 17

Thought

The power of Thought,—the magic of the Mind!

—BYRON, *Corsair*

My thoughts ran a wool-gathering.

—CERVANTES, *Don Quixote*

Any man may make a mistake; none but a fool will stick to it. Second thoughts are best as the proverb says.

—CICERO

Learning without thought is labor lost.

—CONFUCIUS

I think, therefore I am.
—DESCARTES

Thoughts that breathe and words that burn.
— GRAY, *Progress of Poesy*

Great thoughts reduced to practice become great acts.
—HAZLITT

The mind grows by what it feeds on.
—J. G. HOLLAND

A penny for your thought.
—LYLY

Which of you by taking thought can add one cubit unto his stature?
—MATTHEW. VI. 27

As he thinketh in his heart, so is he.
—PROVERBS. XXIII. 7

There is nothing either good or bad, but thinking makes it so.
—SHAKESPEARE, *Hamlet.*
Act II. Sc. 2

Yond Cassius has a lean and hungry look;
He thinks too much: such men are dangerous.
—SHAKESPEARE, *Julius Caesar.* Act I. Sc. 2

They are never alone that are accompanied with noble thoughts.
—SIR PHILIP SIDNEY,
Arcadia

Great thoughts come from the heart.
—VAUVENARGUES

Thrift

It's no use filling your pocket with money if you have got a hole in the corner.

—GEORGE ELIOT

A penny saved is a penny earned.

—ENGLISH PROVERB

It is better to have a hen tomorrow than an egg today.

—THOMAS FULLER

He that will not stoop for a pin will never be worth a pound.

—ENGLISH PROVERB

A man who both spends and saves money is the happiest man, because he has both enjoyments.

—SAMUEL JOHNSON

Thunder

The Lord thundered from heaven, and the Most High uttered his voice.

—II SAMUEL. XXII. 14

That great artillery of God Almighty.

—WILLIAM TEMPLE

Time

Backward, turn backward, O Time in your flight;
Make me a child again just for tonight.

—ELIZABETH AKERS
ALLEN, *Rock Me to
Sleep*

In time take time while time doth last, for time
Is no time when time is past.
> —ANONYMOUS

Time whereof the memory of man runneth not to the contrary.
> —BLACKSTONE,
> *Commentaries*

Time is money.
> —BULWER-LYTTON, *Money*

Time was made for slaves.
> —JOHN B. BUCKSTONE,
> *Billy Taylor*

I recommend you to take care of the minutes, for the hours will take care of themselves.
> —CHESTERFIELD

Know the true value of time; snatch, seize, and enjoy every moment of it. No idleness, no laziness, no procrastination: never put off till tomorrow what you can do today.
> —CHESTERFIELD, Letters to
> his son

O tempora! O mores!
O what times! what morals!
> —CICERO

Now is the accepted time.
> —II CORINTHIANS, VI. 2

See Time has touched me gently in his race,
And left no odious furrows in my face.
> —CRABBE, *Tales of the Hall*

To everything there is a season, and a time to every purpose under the heaven.

—ECCLESIASTES. III. 1

Time and tide wait for no man.

—ENGLISH PROVERB

Do not squander time for that is the stuff life is made of.

—FRANKLIN

A stitch in time saves nine.

—ENGLISH PROVERB

Gather ye rose-buds while ye may,
    Old Time is still aflying,
And this same flower that smiles today,
    Tomorrow will be dying.

—HERRICK, *To the Virgins, to Make Much of Time*

Enjoy the present day, trusting very little to the morrow.

—HORACE, *Carmina*

My days are swifter than a weaver's shuttle.

—JOB. VII. 6

My time has not yet come.

—JOHN. VII. 6

Better late than never.

—LIVY

The signs of the times.

—MATTHEW. XVI. 3

The bird of time has but a little way
To flutter—and the bird is on the wing.

—OMAR KHAYYÁM, *Rubaiyat*

Time is a great legalizer, even in the field of morals.
—H. L. MENCKEN, A Book
of Prefaces

These are the times that try men's souls.
—THOMAS PAINE, The
American Crisis

Time is the wisest counselor.
—PERICLES

Seize time by the forelock.
—PITTACUS OF MITYLENE

A thousand years in thy sight are but as yesterday when
it is past, and as a watch in the night.
—PSALMS. XC. 4

We spend our years as a tale that is told.
—PSALMS. XC. 9

An age builds up cities: an hour destroys them.
—SENECA

There's a time for all things.
—SHAKESPEARE, Comedy of
Errors. Act II. Sc. 2

The time is out of joint.
—SHAKESPEARE, Hamlet.
Act I. Sc. 5

O, call back yesterday, bid time return.
—SHAKESPEARE, Richard II.
Act III. Sc. 2

Make use of time, let not advantage slip.
—SHAKESPEARE, Venus and
Adonis

A wonderful stream is the River Time,
    As it runs through the realms of Tears,
With a faultless rhythm, and a musical rhyme,
    As it blends with the ocean of Years.
            —BENJAMIN F. TAYLOR,
                The Long Ago

Once in Persia reigned a king
Who upon his signet ring
Graved a maxim true and wise,
Which if held before the eyes
Gave him counsel at a glance
Fit for every change and chance.
Solemn words, and these are they:
"Even this shall pass away."
            —THEODORE TILTON, *The*
                King's Ring

Toasts

Some hae meat, and canna eat,
    And some wad eat that want it;
But we hae meat, and we can eat,
    And sae the Lord be thankit.
            —BURNS, *The Selkirk Grace*

Here's a sigh to those who love me
    And a smile to those who hate;
And whatever sky's above me,
    Here's a heart for every fate.
            —BYRON, Letter to Thomas
                Moore

Ho! Stand to your glasses steady!
    'Tis all we have left to prize.

A cup to the dead already,—
>Hurrah for the next that dies.
>>—BARTHOLOMEW
>>DOWLING, *Revelry in
>>India*

Drink to me only with thine eyes,
>And I will pledge with mine;
Or leave a kiss but in the cup,
>And I'll not look for wine.
>>—BEN JONSON, *To Celia*

Here's to your good health, and your family's good health,
and may you all live long and prosper.
>—IRVING, *Rip Van Winkle*

A glass is good, and a lass is good,
>And a pipe to smoke in cold weather;
The world is good and the people are good,
>And we're all good fellows together.
>>—JOHN O'KEEFE, *Sprigs of
>>Laurel*

Here's to you, as good as you are,
>And here's to me, as bad as I am,
But as good as you are, and as bad as I am,
>I am as good as you are, as bad as I am.
>>—OLD SCOTCH TOAST

May you live all the days of your life.
>—SWIFT, *Polite
>Conversation*

Here is a toast that I want to give
To a fellow I'll never know;
To the fellow who's going to take my place
When it's time for me to go.
>—LOUIS E. THAYER, *To My
>Successor*

May all your labors be in vein.

> —YORKSHIRE MINERS'
> TOAST

Tobacco

Little tube of mighty pow'r,
Charmer of an idle hour,
   Object of my warm desire.

> —ISAAC HAWKINS
>   BROWNE, A Pipe of
>   Tobacco

A woman is only a woman, but a good cigar is a smoke.

> —KIPLING, The Betrothed

For thy sake, tobacco, I
Would do anything but die.

> —LAMB, A Farewell to
>   Tobacco

What this country needs is a good five-cent cigar.

> —THOMAS R. MARSHALL

A cigarette is the perfect type of a perfect pleasure. It is exquisite, and it leaves one unsatisfied. What more can you want?

> —WILDE, Picture of Dorian
>   Gray

Today

We are here today and gone tomorrow.

> —ANONYMOUS

Out of Eternity
The new Day is born;
Into Eternity
At night will return.

> —CARLYLE, *Today*

Happy the man, and happy he alone,
He, who can call today his own:
He who, secure within, can say,
Tomorrow, do thy worst, for I have liv'd today.

> —DRYDEN, *Imitation of
> Horace*

One today is worth two tomorrows.

> —FRANKLIN

Tomorrow life is too late: live today.

> —MARTIAL

Toleration

Every man must get to heaven his own way.

> —FREDERICK THE GREAT

Tolerance is the only real test of civilization.

> —ARTHUR HELPS

Toleration is the best religion.

> —VICTOR HUGO

It is intolerance to speak of toleration. Away with the word from the dictionary!

> —MIRABEAU

Live and let live.

> —SCOTTISH PROVERB

Tomorrow

There is a budding tomorrow in midnight.
                              —KEATS

Never leave that till tomorrow which you can do today.
                              —FRANKLIN, *Poor Richard's
                                   Almanac*

Tomorrow!—Why, tomorrow I may be
Myself with yesterday's sev'n thousand years.
                              —OMAR KHAYYÁM,
                                   Rubaiyat

Tomorrow never yet
On any human being rose or set.
                              —WILLIAM MARSDEN,
                                   What Is Time?

Boast not thyself of tomorrow; for thou knowest not what
a day may bring forth.
                              —PROVERBS. XXVII. 1

Tomorrow, tomorrow, not today,
Hear the lazy people say.
                              —WEISSE

Tongue

Birds are entangled by their feet and men by their tongues.
                              —THOMAS FULLER

Keep thy tongue from evil, and thy lips from speaking
guile.
                              —PSALMS. XXXIV. 13

Many a man's tongue shakes out his master's undoing.
—SHAKESPEARE, *All's Well That Ends Well*. Act II. Sc. 4

The tongue can no man tame; it is an unruly evil.
—JAMES. III. 8

Traveling

Travel teaches toleration.
—DISRAELI

I have been a stranger in a strange land.
—EXODUS. II. 22

I am fevered with the sunset,
    I am fretful with the bay,
For the wander-thirst is on me
    And my soul is in Cathay.
—RICHARD HOVEY, *A Sea Gypsy*

A wise traveler never despises his own country.
—GOLDONI, *Pamela*

As the Spanish proverb says, "He who would bring home the wealth of the Indies must carry the wealth of the Indies with him." So it is in traveling: a man must carry knowledge with him, if he would bring home knowledge.
—SAMUEL JOHNSON, *Boswell's Life of Johnson*

Down to Gehenna or up to the throne,
    He travels the fastest who travels alone.
—KIPLING, *The Winners*

The more I see of other countries the more I love my own.

—MME. DE STAËL

The little Road says, Go;
The little House says, Stay;
And oh, it's bonny here at home,
But I must go away.

—JOSEPHINE P. PEABODY,
*The House and the
Road*

Good company in a journey makes the way to seem the shorter.

—IZAAK WALTON, *The
Compleat Angler*

Treachery

There is treachery, O Ahaziah.

—II KINGS. IX. 23

Treachery, though at first very cautious, in the end betrays itself.

—LIVY

Et tu Brute! (You too, Brutus!)

—SHAKESPEARE, *Julius
Caesar.* Act III.
Sc. 1

Tree

I think that I shall never scan
A tree as lovely as a man.

• • •

A tree depicts divinest plan,
But God himself lives in a man.
                    —ANONYMOUS

This is the forest primeval.
                    —LONGFELLOW,
                        Evangeline

Tall oaks from little acorns grow.
                    —DAVID EVERETT

The tree of knowledge of good and evil.
                    —GENESIS. II. 9

I think that I shall never see
A poem lovely as a tree.

• • •

Poems are made by fools like me,
But only God can make a tree.
                    —JOYCE KILMER, *Trees*

The tree is known by his fruit.
                    —MATTHEW. XII. 33

Woodman, spare that tree!
        Touch not a single bough!
In youth it sheltered me,
        And I'll protect it now.
                    —GEORGE P. MORRIS,
                        *Woodman, Spare That
                        Tree*

Trial

'Tis a lesson you should heed,
    Try, try, try again
If at first you don't succeed,
    Try, try, try again.

—W. E. HICKSON, *Try and Try Again*

There are no crown-bearers in heaven who were not cross-bearers here below.

—SPURGEON, *Gleaning among the Sheaves*

Trifle

Little deeds of kindness, little words of love,
Help to make earth happy, like the heaven above.

—JULIA F. CARNEY, *Little Things*

For precept must be upon precept, precept upon precept; line upon line, line upon line; here a little, and there a little.

—ISAIAH. XXVIII. 10

A little one shall become a thousand, and a small one a strong nation.

—ISAIAH. IX. 22

Events of great consequence often spring from trifling circumstances.

—LIVY

Trifles make perfection—and perfection is no trifle.

—Attributed to MICHELANGELO

For the maintenance of peace, nations should avoid the
pin-pricks which forerun cannon-shots.
—NAPOLEON to the Czar
Alexander

Trouble

The true way to soften one's troubles is to solace those
of others.
—MME. DE MAINTENON

Never trouble trouble till trouble troubles you.
—AMERICAN PROVERB

He that seeks trouble always finds it.
—ENGLISH PROVERB

Troubles, like babies, grow larger by nursing.
—LADY HOLLAND

Man is born unto trouble, as the sparks fly upward.
—JOB. V. 7

To take arms against a sea of troubles.
—SHAKESPEARE, Hamlet.
Act III. Sc. 1

Though life is made up of mere bubbles,
    'Tis better than many aver,
For while we've a whole lot of troubles,
    The most of them never occur.
—NIXON WATERMAN, Why
Worry?

Trust

Government is a trust, and the officers of the government are trustees; and both the trust and the trustees are created for the benefit of the people.
—HENRY CLAY, Speech

Trust in God, and keep your powder dry.
—CROMWELL

Thou trustest in the staff of this broken reed.
—ISAIAH. XXXVI. 6

When a man assumes a public trust, he should consider himself as public property.
—JEFFERSON

Public office is a public trust.
—DAN S. LAMONT

To be trusted is a greater compliment than to be loved.
— GEORGE MacDONALD,
The Marquis of Lossie

In God have I put my trust: I will not be afraid what man can do unto me.
—PSALMS. LVI. 11

Truth

Truth is mighty and will prevail.
—THOMAS BROOKS, 1662

If it is not true it is very well invented.
—GIORDANO BRUNO

Truth crushed to earth shall rise again.
>—BRYANT, *The Battle Field*

'Tis strange—but true; for truth is always strange,
Stranger than fiction.
>—BYRON, *Don Juan*

Truth ever lovely—since the world began,
The foe of tyrants, and the friend of man.
>—CAMPBELL

"It was as true," said Mr. Barkis, . . . "as taxes is. And
nothing's truer than them."
>—DICKENS, *David
>Copperfield*

Time is precious, but truth is more precious than time.
>—DISRAELI

For truth has such a face and such a mien,
As to be lov'd needs only to be seen.
>—DRYDEN, *The Hind and
>the Panther*

Truth is immortal; error is mortal.
>—MARY BAKER EDDY,
>*Science and Health*

The greater the truth the greater the libel.
>—LORD ELLENBOROUGH

Great is truth, and mighty above all things.
>—I ESDRAS. IV. 41

And ye shall know the truth, and the truth shall make
you free.
>—JOHN. VIII. 32

There is no truth in him.
> —JOHN. VIII. 44

The truth, the whole truth, and nothing but the truth.
> —LEGAL OATH

'Tis true, 'tis pity;
And pity 'tis 'tis true.
> —SHAKESPEARE, *Hamlet.*
> Act II. Sc. 2

Truth forever on the scaffold. Wrong forever on the throne.
> —LOWELL, *The Present*
> *Crisis*

To thine own self be true,
And it must follow, as the night the day,
Thou canst not then be false to any man.
> —SHAKESPEARE—HAMLET.
> Act I. Sc. 3

My man's as true as steel.
> —SHAKESPEARE, *Romeo*
> *and Juliet*. Act II. Sc.
> 4

All great truths began as blasphemies.
> —GEORGE BERNARD
> SHAW, *Annajanska*

My way of joking is to tell the truth.
It's the funniest joke in the world.
> —GEORGE BERNARD
> SHAW, *John Bull's*
> *Other Island*

It takes two to speak the truth—one to speak, and another to hear.

> —THOREAU

Twilight

How lovely are the portals of the night,
  When stars come out to watch the daylight die.

> —THOMAS COLE, *Twilight*

The west is broken into bars
    Of orange, gold, and gray,
Gone is the sun, come are the stars,
    And night infolds the day.

> —GEORGE MACDONALD,
> *Songs of the Summer*

Twilight and evening bell
And after that the dark.

> —TENNYSON, *Crossing the
> Bar*

Tyranny

Bad laws are the worst sort of tyranny.

> —BURKE

Unlimited power corrupts the possessor; and this I know, that, where law ends, there tyranny begins.

> —LORD CHATHAM

He who strikes terror into others is himself in continual fear.

> —CLAUDIAN

Tyrants have not yet discovered any chains that can fetter the mind.

—COLTON

Resistance to tyrants is obedience to God.
—JEFFERSON

Arbitrary power is most easily established on the ruins of liberty abused to licentiousness.
—WASHINGTON

'Tis time to fear when tyrants seem to kiss.
—SHAKESPEARE, *Pericles*.
Act I. Sc. 2

Ugliness

Better an ugly face than an ugly mind.
—JAMES ELLIS

Absolute and entire ugliness is rare.
—RUSKIN

Nobody's sweetheart is ugly.

—J. J. VADÉ

Union

Then join in hand, brave Americans all!
By uniting we stand, by dividing we fall.
—JOHN DICKINSON, *Liberty Song*, 1768

All for one; one for all.

—DUMAS, *The Three Musketeers*

We must all hang together or assuredly we shall hang separately.

—FRANKLIN

Behold how good and how pleasant it is for brethren to dwell together in unity.

—PSALMS. CXXXIII. 1

By union the smallest states thrive, by discord the greatest are destroyed.

—SALLUST

The union of lakes—the union of lands—
    The union of States none can sever—
The union of hearts—the union of hands—
    And the flag of our union for ever!

—GEORGE P. MORRIS, *The Flag of Our Union*

United we stand; divided we fall.

—Motto of Kentucky

Liberty and Union, now and forever, one and inseparable.

—DANIEL WEBSTER, 1830

Valor

Discretion, the best part of valor.

—BEAUMONT and FLETCHER

The mean of true valor lies between the extremes of cowardice and rashness.

—CERVANTES

Vanity

Oh, wad some power the giftie gie us
To see oursel's as ithers see us!
It wad frae monie a blunder free us,
    And foolish notion.

—BURNS, *To a Louse*

Vanity of vanities; all is vanity.

—ECCLESIASTES. I. 2

All is vanity and vexation of spirit.

—ECCLESIASTES. I. 14

Variety

Variety's the very spice of life,
That gives it all its flavour.

—COWPER, *The Task*

It takes all sorts to make a world.

—ENGLISH PROVERB

Age cannot wither her, nor custom stale
Her infinite variety.

—SHAKESPEARE, *Antony
    and Cleopatra*. Act II.
    Sc. 2

Vice

What's vice today may be virtue tomorrow.

—FIELDING

What maintains one vice would bring up two children.
                              —FRANKLIN, *Poor Richard's*
                              Almanac

When our vices leave us we flatter ourselves with the
idea that we have left them.
                              —LA ROCHEFOUCAULD

Human nature is not of itself vicious.
                              —THOMAS PAINE

Victory

How beautiful is victory, but how dear!
                              —BOUFFLERS

Victories that are cheap are cheap. Those only are worth
having which come as the result of hard fighting.
                              —HENRY WARD BEECHER

The race is not to the swift, nor the battle to the strong.
                              —ECCLESIASTES. IX. 11

To the victors belong the spoils.
                              —ANDREW JACKSON

                    Who overcomes
By force, hath overcome but half his foe.
                              —MILTON, *Paradise Lost*

There are some defeats more triumphant than victories.
                              —MONTAIGNE

We have met the enemy and they are ours.
                              —OLIVER HAZARD PERRY

Hannibal knew how to gain a victory, but not how to use it.

—PLUTARCH

But if
We have such another victory, we are undone.
—Attributed to PYRRHUS by
BACON, *Apothegms*

There is nothing so dreadful as a great victory—except a great defeat.

—Attributed to
WELLINGTON

Virtue

One's outlook is a part of his virtue.
—ALCOTT, *Concord Days*

Virtue is like a rich stone, best plain set.
—BACON, *Essays*

Recommend to your children virtue; that alone can make them happy, not gold.

—BEETHOVEN

Honor is the reward of virtue.
—CICERO

I believe that Virtue shows quite as well in rags and patches as she does in purple and fine linen.
—DICKENS

There are those who have nothing chaste but their ears, and nothing virtuous but their tongues.
—DE FINOD

The only reward of virtue is virtue.
—EMERSON, *Essays*

Most men admire
Virtue, who follow not her lore.
—MILTON, *Paradise
Regained*

Our virtues are most frequently but vices disguised.
—LA ROCHEFOUCAULD

Virtue is an angel, but she is a blind one, and must ask of Knowledge to show her the pathway that leads to her goal.
—HORACE MANN

I prefer an accommodation vice to an obstinate virtue.
—MOLIÈRE

Virtue is health, vice is sickness.
—PETRARCH

Virtue consists, not in abstaining from vice, but in not desiring it.
—GEORGE BERNARD SHAW

Virtue often trips and falls on the sharp-edged rock of poverty.
—EUGÈNE SUE

Vision

Abou Ben Adhem (may his tribe increase!)
Awoke one night from a deep dream of peace,
And saw, within the moonlight in his room,
Making it rich, and like a lily in bloom,
An angel, writing in a book of gold;
Exceeding peace had made Ben Adhem bold,
And to the presence in the room he said—
"What writest thou?" The Vision raised its head,
And, with a look made all of sweet accord,
Answered, "The names of those who love the Lord."
—LEIGH HUNT, *Abou Ben*
Adhem and the Angel.

Where there is no vision, the people perish.
—PROVERBS. XXIX. 18

And it shall come to pass afterward, that I will pour out
my Spirit upon all flesh; and your sons and your daughters shall prophesy, your old men shall dream dreams,
your young men shall see visions.
—JOEL. II. 28

My thoughts by night are often filled
  With visions false as fair:
For in the past alone, I build
  My castles in the air.

—THOMAS LOVE PEACOCK,
Castles in the Air

Voice

The voice of the people is the voice of God.
—HESIOD

A still, small voice.
                    —I KINGS. XIX. 12

The voice of one crying in the wilderness.
                    —MATTHEW. III. 3

                    Her voice was ever soft,
Gentle and low, an excellent thing in woman.
                    —SHAKESPEARE, *King Lear.*
                    Act V. Sc. 3

Wages

A fair day's wages for a fair day's work: it is as just a demand as governed men ever made of government.
                    —CARLYLE, *Past and
                    Present*

It is but a truism that labor is most productive where its wages are largest. Poorly paid labor is inefficient labor, the world over.

                    —HENRY GEORGE, *Progress
                    and Poverty*

The laborer is worthy of his hire.
                    —LUKE. X. 7

Be content with your wages.
                    —MARK. III. 14

If a business be unprofitable on account of bad management, want of enterprise, or out-worn methods, that is not a just reason for reducing the wages of its workers.
                    —POPE PIUS XI

The iron law of wages.

                    —A. R. J. TURGOT

Want

Man wants but little here below,
Nor wants that little long.
— GOLDSMITH, *The Hermit*

Constantly choose rather to want less, than to have more.
—THOMAS À KEMPIS

The stoical scheme of supplying our wants by lopping off our desires is like cutting off our feet when we want shoes.

—SWIFT

How few our real wants, and how vast our imaginary ones!

—LAVATER

War

War is the science of destruction.
—JOHN S. C. ABBOTT

War cannot be put on a certain allowance.
—ARCHIDAMUS III

The inevitableness, the idealism, and the blessing of war, as an indispensable and stimulating law of development, must be repeatedly emphasized.

—BERNHARDI, *Germany
and the Next War*

Just for a word—"neutrality," a word which in wartime had so often been disregarded—just for a scrap of paper,

Great Britain was going to make war on a kindred nation who desired nothing better than to be friends with her.
—BETHMANN-HOLLWEG,
German Chancellor,
1914

Better pointed bullets than pointed speeches.
—BISMARCK, Speech, 1850

War never leaves, where it found a nation.
—BURKE

Veni, vidi, vici. (I came, I saw, I conquered.)
—JULIUS CAESAR

(The great questions of the day) are not decided by speeches and majority votes, but by blood and iron.
—BISMARCK, To the
Prussian House of
Delegates.

What millions died—that Caesar might be great!
—CAMPBELL

What distinguishes war is, not that man is slain, but that he is slain, spoiled, crushed by the cruelty, the injustice, the treachery, the murderous hand of man.
—WILLIAM ELLERY
CHANNING

General Taylor never surrenders.
—THOMAS L.
CRITTENDEN, Reply
to Gen. Santa Ana

We give up the fort when there's not a man left to defend it.
—GENERAL CROGHAN at
Fort Stevenson, 1812

War, he sung, is toil and trouble;
Honour but an empty bubble.

> —DRYDEN, *Alexander's
> Feast*

I ... propose to fight it out on this line if it takes all summer.

> —U. S. GRANT, Despatch
> from Spotsylvania

By the rude bridge that arched the flood,
    Their flag to April's breeze unfurl'd;
Here once the embattl'd farmers stood,
    And fired the shot heard round the world.

> —EMERSON, Hymn sung at
> the completion of the
> Concord Monument

The essence of war is violence. Moderation in war is imbecility.

> —Attributed to LORD
> FISHER

My right has been rolled up.
My left has been driven back.
My center has been smashed.
I have ordered an advance from all directions.

> —Attributed to GENERAL
> FOCH, World War I

There never was a good war or a bad peace.

> —FRANKLIN, Letter to
> Quincy

Hang yourself, brave Crillon. We fought at Arques, and you were not there.

> —HENRY IV, to Crillon
> after a great victory.

It is not right to exult over slain men.
> —HOMER, *Odyssey*

War is as much a punishment to the punisher as to the sufferer.
> —JEFFERSON, Letter, 1794

Mine eyes have seen the glory of the coming of the Lord:
He is trampling out the vintage where the grapes of wrath
    are stored:
He hath loosed the fateful lightning of his terrible swift
    sword:
His truth is marching on.
> —JULIA WARD HOWE,
> *Battle Hymn of the*
> *Republic*

We don't want to fight, but by jingo if we do,
We've got the ships, we've got the men, we've got the
    money too.
We've fought the Bear before and while we're Britons
    true,
    The Russians shall not have Constantinople.
> —G. W. HUNT

I have prayed in her fields of poppies,
    I have laughed with the men who died—
But in all my ways and through all my days
    Like a friend He walked beside.
I have seen a sight under Heaven
    That only God understands,
In the battle's glare I have seen Christ there
    With the Sword of God in His hand.
> —GORDON JOHNSTONE,
> *On Fields of Flanders*

Modern warfare is an intricate business about which no
one knows everything and few know very much.
—FRANK KNOX, Speech,
1942

There is no such thing as an inevitable war. If war comes
it will be from failure of human wisdom.
—BONAR LAW, Speech
before World War I

O God assist our side: at least, avoid assisting the enemy
and leave the rest to me.
—PRINCE LEOPOLD of
Anhalt-Dessau

The ballot is stronger than the bullet.
—LINCOLN, 1856

To arms! to arms! ye brave!
The avenging sword unsheathe,
March on! march on! all hearts resolved
On victory or death!
—ROUGET DE LISLE, *The
Marseillaise*

Ez for war, I call it murder,—
There you hev it plain and flat;
I don't want to go no furder
Than my Testyment for that.
—LOWELL, *The Biglow
Papers*

Providence is always on the side of the last reserve.
—Attributed to NAPOLEON

War is the greatest plague that can afflict humanity; it
destroys religion, it destroys states, it destroys families.
Any scourge is preferable to it.
—MARTIN LUTHER

I beg that the small steamers ... be spared if possible, or else sunk without a trace being left. (Spurlos versenkt.)

—Count Karl von
Luxburg, Chargé
d'Affaires at Buenos
Aires to his Berlin
Foreign Office, 1917

The warpipes are pealing.
"The Campbells are coming."
They are charging and cheering,
O dinna ye hear it?

—Alexander MacLagan,
Jennie's Dream

Take up our quarrel with the foe!
To you from failing hands we throw
The torch; be yours to hold it high.
If ye break faith with us who die
We shall not sleep, though poppies grow
In Flanders' fields.

—John McCrae, *In
Flanders' Fields*

War hath no fury like a noncombatant.

—C. E. Montague,
Disenchantment

Wars and rumours of wars.

—Mathew. XXIV. 6

And this I hate—not men, nor flag nor race,
But only War with its wild, grinning face.

—Joseph Dana Miller,
The Hymn of Hate

When after many battles past,
Both tir'd with blows, make peace at last,
What is it, after all, the people get?
Why! taxes, widows, wooden legs, and debt.
> —FRANCIS MOORE,
> *Almanack*

These are the times that try men's souls. The Summer
soldier and the sunshine patriot will, in this crisis, shrink
from the service of their country, but he that stands it
now deserves the love and thanks of man and woman.
Tyranny, like Hell, is not easily conquered; yet we have
this consolation with us, that the harder the conflict the
more glorious the triumph. What we obtain too cheaply
we esteem too lightly; it is dearness only that gives everything its value. Heaven knows how to put a proper price
upon its goods; and it would be strange indeed if so
celestial an article as *freedom* should not be highly rated.
> —THOMAS PAINE, *The*
> *Crisis*

The brazen throat of war.
> —MILTON, *Paradise Lost*

England expects every officer and man to do his duty
this day.
> —NELSON before the battle
> of Trafalgar

God how the dead men
    Grin by the wall,
Watching the fun
    Of the Victory Ball.
> —ALFRED NOYES, *The*
> *Highwayman*

Hell, Heaven or Hoboken by Christmas.
>   —Attributed to GENERAL
>   JOHN JOSEPH
>   PERSHING, 1918

War its thousands slays,
Peace its ten thousands.

>   —PORTEUS, *Death*

O war! thou son of Hell!

>   —SHAKESPEARE, *Henry VI.*
>   Pt. II. Act V. Sc. 2

A bad peace is even worse than war.
>   —TACITUS

As long as war is regarded as wicked, it will always have
its fascination. When it is looked upon as vulgar, it will
cease to be popular.

>   —WILDE

Washington

The father of his country.

>   —FRANCIS BAILEY

Every countenance seeked to say, "Long live George
Washington, the Father of the People."

>   —*Pennsylvania Packet,*
>   April 21, 1789

Wealth

I have mental joys and mental health,
Mental friends and mental wealth,
I've a wife that I love and that loves me;
I've all but riches bodily.
> —WILLIAM BLAKE,
> *Mammon*

Surplus wealth is a sacred trust which its possessor is
bound to administer in his life-time for the good of the
community.
> —ANDREW CARNEGIE,
> *Gospel of Wealth*

If you would be wealthy, think of saving as well as of
getting.
> —FRANKLIN

The ideal social state is not that in which each gets an
equal amount of wealth, but in which each gets in proportion to his contribution to the general stock.
> —HENRY GEORGE, *Social
> Problems*

Rich in good works.
> —I TIMOTHY. VI. 18

Ill fares the land, to hastening ills a prey,
Where wealth accumulates, and men decay;
Princes and Lords may flourish, or may fade—
A breath can make them, as a breath has made—
But a bold peasantry, their country's pride,
When once destroy'd can never be supplied.
> —GOLDSMITH, *Deserted
> Village*

Riches either serve or govern the possessor.
> —HORACE

The wealth of nations is men, not silk and cotton and gold.

—RICHARD HOVEY, *Peace*

Life is short. The sooner that a man begins to enjoy his wealth the better.

—SAMUEL JOHNSON

Our Lord commonly giveth Riches to such gross asses, to whom he affordeth nothing else that is good.

—LUTHER, *Colloquies*

It is easier for a camel to go through the eye of a needle, than for a rich man to enter into the kingdom of God.

—MATTHEW. XIX. 24

I am rich beyond the dreams of avarice.

—EDWARD MOORE, *The Gamester*

All wealth is the product of labor

—LOCKE

Get place and wealth, if possible, with grace;
If not, by any means get wealth and place.

—POPE, *Epistles of Horace*

Riches certainly make themselves wings.

—PROVERBS. XXIII. 5

He that maketh haste to be rich shall not be innocent.

—PROVERBS. XXVIII. 20

He heapeth up riches, and knoweth not who shall gather them.

—PSALMS. XXXIX. 6

No good man ever became suddenly rich.

—SYRUS

Weather

As a rule man is a fool,
When it's hot he wants it cool,
When it's cool he wants it hot,
Always wanting what is not.
—ANONYMOUS

Everybody talks about the weather but nobody does anything about it.
—Attributed to
S. L. CLEMENS
(MARK TWAIN)

Change of weather is the discourse of fools.
—THOMAS FULLER

I was born with a chronic anxiety about the weather.
—JOHN BURROUGHS, *Is It
Going to Rain?*

Fair weather cometh out of the north.
—JOB. XXXVII. 22

Oh, what a blamed uncertain thing
This pesky weather is;
It blew and snew and then it thew,
And now, by jing, it's friz.
—PHILANDER JOHNSON

When two Englishmen meet, their first talk is of the weather.
—SAMUEL JOHNSON

Welcome

'Tis sweet to hear the watchdog's honest bark
    Bay deep-mouth'd welcome as we draw near home.
        —BYRON, *Don Juan*

Come in the evening, come in the morning,
Come when expected, come without warning;
Thousands of welcomes you'll find here before you,
And the oftener you come, the more we'll adore you.
        —IRISH RHYME

Welcome as the flowers in May.
        —SCOTT, *Rob Roy*

West

Westward the course of empire takes its way.
        —BISHOP BERKELEY

Out where the handclasp's a little stronger,
Out where the smile dwells a little longer,
   That's where the West begins.
        —ARTHUR CHAPMAN

Go West, young man, and grow up with the country.
        —HORACE GREELEY

Westward, Ho!

        —GEORGE PEELE

Wickedness

God bears with the wicked, but not forever.
        —CERVANTES, *Don*
          Quixote

No man ever became very wicked all at once.
—JUVENAL

The world loves a spice of wickedness.
—LONGFELLOW, *Hyperion*

Wickedness is weakness.

—MILTON, *Samson
Agonistes*

The wicked flee when no man pursueth; but the righteous
are bold as a lion.
—PROVERBS. XXVIII. 1

The sun also shines on the wicked.
—SENECA

As saith the proverb of the Ancients,
  Wickedness proceedeth from the wicked.
—I SAMUEL. XXIV. 13

'Cause I's wicked,—I is. I's mighty wicked, anyhow, I
can't help it.

—HARRIET BEECHER
STOWE, *Uncle Tom's
Cabin*

Wife

Wives are young men's mistresses; companions for mid-
dle age; and old men's nurses.
—BACON, *Of Marriage and
Single Life*

She is a winsome wee thing,
She is a handsome wee thing,
She is a bonny wee thing,
 This sweet wee wife o' mine.
     —BURNS, *My Wife's a*
        Winsome Wee Thing

Think you, if Laura had been Petrarch's wife,
He would have written sonnets all his life?
     —BYRON, *Don Juan*

The wife of thy bosom.
     —DEUTERONOMY. XIII. 6

In every mess I find a friend,
In every port a wife.
     —CHARLES DIBDIN, *Jack in*
        His Element

An undutiful Daughter will prove an unmanageable Wife.
     —FRANKLIN, *Poor Richard*

He knows little who will tell his wife all he knows.
     —THOMAS FULLER, *Holy*
        and Profane State

A miss for pleasure, and a wife for breed.
     —JOHN GAY, *The Toilette*

Alas! another instance of the triumph of hope over experience.
     —SAMUEL JOHNSON,
       referring to the second
       marriage of a friend

All other goods by fortune's hand are given:
A wife is the peculiar gift of Heav'n.
     —POPE

She looketh well to the ways of her household, and eateth not the bread of idleness.
—PROVERBS. XXXI. 27

It is a woman's business to get married as soon as possible, and a man's to keep unmarried as long as he can.
—GEORGE BERNARD
SHAW, *Man and
Superman*

My dear, my better half.
—PHILIP SIDNEY, *Arcadia*

Will

Where there's a will there's a way.
—ENGLISH PROVERB

There is nothing good or evil save in the will.
—EPICTETUS

He who is firm in will molds the world to himself.
—GOETHE

Not my will, but thine, be done.
—LUKE. XXII. 42

Wind

An ill wind that bloweth no man good—
The blower of which blast is she.
—JOHN HEYWOOD, *Idleness*

Who walketh upon the wings of the wind.
—PSALMS. CIV. 3

Blow, wind, and crack your cheeks. Rage! Blow!
>—SHAKESPEARE, *King Lear.*
>Act III. Sc. 1

>O wind,
If Winter comes, can Spring be far behind?
>—SHELLEY, *Ode to the West Wind*

Sweet and low, sweet and low,
>Wind of the western sea,
Low, low, breathe and blow,
>Wind of the western sea!
>>—TENNYSON, *The Princess*

Wine and Spirits

Few things surpass old wine; and they may preach
Who please, the more because they preach in vain,—
Let us have wine and women, mirth and laughter,
Sermons and soda-water the day after.
>—BYRON, *Don Juan*

No nation is drunken where wine is cheap; and none
sober where the dearness of wine substitutes ardent spirits as the common beverage. It is, in truth, the only
antidote to the bane of whiskey.
>—JEFFERSON, 1818

Claret is the liquor for boys; port for men; but he who
aspires to be a hero must drink brandy.
>—SAMUEL JOHNSON

There is a devil in every berry of the grape.
>—THE KORAN

Wine is the most healthful and most hygienic of beverages.

—LOUIS PASTEUR

Look not thou upon the wine when it is red, when it giveth his colour in the cup; ... at the last it biteth like a serpent, and stingeth like an adder.

—PROVERBS. XXIII. 31

Wine that maketh glad the heart of man.

—PSALMS. CIV. 15

Drink no longer water, but use a little wine for thy stomach's sake.

—I TIMOTHY. V. 23

Winter

Oh, the long and dreary Winter!
Oh, the cold and cruel Winter!

—LONGFELLOW, *Hiawatha*

If Winter comes, can Spring be far behind?

—SHELLEY, *Ode to the West Wind*

Wisdom

The wisdom of our ancestors.

—BURKE

Wise men learn more from fools than fools from the wise.

—CATO THE CENSOR

In much wisdom is much grief.

—ECCLESIASTES. I. 18

The words of the wise are as goads.
—ECCLESIASTES. XII. 11

It is easy to be wise after the event.
—ENGLISH PROVERB

No one could be so wise as Thurlow looked.
—CHARLES JAMES FOX

Some are weather-wise, some are otherwise.
—FRANKLIN, *Poor Richard*

Wisdom is only found in truth.
—GOETHE

The heart is wiser than the intellect.
—J. G. HOLLAND, *Katrina*

Days should speak, and multitude of years should teach wisdom.
—JOB. XXXII. 7

In youth and beauty wisdom is but rare!
—HOMER, *Odyssey*

The price of wisdom is above rubies.
—JOB. XXVII. 18

Great men are not always wise.
—JOB. XXXII. 7

It is easier to be wise for others than for ourselves.
—LA ROCHEFOUCAULD

Be ye therefore wise as serpents, and harmless as doves.
—MATTHEW. X. 16

Wisdom crieth without; she uttereth her voice in the street.

—PROVERBS. I. 20

Go to the ant, thou sluggard; consider her ways, and be wise.

—PROVERBS. VI. 6

Wisdom is the principal thing; therefore get wisdom; and with all thy getting get understanding.

—PROVERBS. VIII. 11

The fear of the Lord is the beginning of wisdom.

—PSALMS. CXI. 10

Nine-tenths of wisdom consists in being wise in time.

—THEODORE ROOSEVELT,
Speech, 1917

As for me, all I know is that I know nothing.

—SOCRATES

The doorstep to the temple of wisdom is a knowledge of our own ignorance.

—SPURGEON, Gleanings
among the Sheaves

The children of this world are in their generation wiser than the children of light.

—I TIMOTHY. XVI. 8

Wisdom is the gray hair unto men, and an unspotted life is old age.

—WISDOM OF SOLOMON.
IV. 8

Wish

If wishes were horses, beggars might ride.
>—ENGLISH PROVERB

If a man could half his wishes he would double his Troubles.
>—FRANKLIN, *Poor Richard*

I wish I knew the good of wishing.
>—HENRY S. LEIGH,
>*Wishing*

Thy wish was father to that thought.
>—SHAKESPEARE, *Henry IV.*
>Pt. II. Act IV. Sc. 5

As you cannot do what you wish, you should wish what you can do.
>—TERENCE

Wit

At their wits' end.
>—PSALMS. CVII. 27

Sharp wits, like sharp knives, do often cut their owner's fingers.
>—ARROWSMITH

Wit is the salt of conversation, not the food.
>—HAZLITT

Avoid witticisms at the expense of others.
>—HORACE MANN

True wit is nature to advantage dress'd
What oft was thought, but ne'er so well expressed.
                    —POPE, *Essay on Criticism*

Great men may jest with saints; 'tis wit in them;
But, in the less foul profanation.
                    —SHAKESPEARE, *Measure
                        for Measure*. Act. II.
                        Sc. 2

Women

Oh, the shrewdness of their shrewdness when they're
    shrewd.
And the rudeness of their rudeness when they're rude;
But the shrewdness of their shrewdness and the rudeness
    of their rudeness,
Are nothing to their goodness when they're good.
                    —ANONYMOUS

Women always have some mental reservation.
                    —DESTOUCHES

You see, dear, it is not true that woman was made from
man's rib; she was really made from his funny bone.
                    —BARRIE, *What Every
                        Woman Knows*

In her first passion woman loves her lover;
In all the others, all she loves is love.
                    —BYRON, *Don Juan*

Suffer women once to arrive at an equality with you,
and they will from that moment become your superiors.
                    —CATO THE CENSOR

A woman is like your shadow; follow her, she flies; fly from her, she follows.
> —CHAMFORT

Heaven has no rage like love to hatred turned,
Nor hell a fury like a woman scorned.
> —CONGREVE, *The*
> *Mourning Bride*

But what is woman? Only one of nature's agreeable blunders.
> —COWLEY

Men *say* of women what pleases them! women *do* with men what pleases them.
> —DE SEGUR

Cherchez la femme. (Find the woman.)
> —DUMAS, *Les Mohicans de*
> *Paris*

There is no worse evil than a bad woman; and nothing has ever been produced better than a good one.
> —EURIPIDES

Where is the man who has the power and skill
To stem the torrent of a woman's will?
For if she will, she will, you may depend on't;
And if she won't, she won't; so there's an end on't.
> —From the Pillar Erected in
> Dane John Field,
> Canterbury

The society of women is the foundation of good manners.
> —GOETHE

Most men who run down women are running down one woman only.
> —REMY DE GOURMONT

Women forgive injuries, but never forget slights.
—HALIBURTON

The crown of creation.

—HERDEB

Man has his will,—but woman has her way.
—HOLMES, *Autocrat of the
Breakfast Table*

It is God who makes woman beautiful, it is the devil
who makes her pretty.

—VICTOR HUGO

The weaker vessel.
—I PETER. III. 7

A woman's guess is much more accurate than a man's
certainty.

—KIPLING, *Plain Tales*

An' I learned about women from 'er.
—KIPLING, *The Ladies*

The colonel's lady and Judy O'Grady
Are sisters under their skins.
—KIPLING, *The Ladies*

For the female of the species is more deadly than the
male.

—KIPLING, *The Female of
the Species*

A rag and a bone and a hank of hair.
—KIPLING, *The Vampire*

There are no ugly women; there are only women who
do not know how to look pretty.
—LA BRUYÈRE

Earth's noblest thing, a Woman perfected.
—LOWELL, *Irene*

The great fault in women is to desire to be like men.
—DE MAISTRE

Too fair to worship, too divine to love.
—MILMAN, *Apollo Belvedere*

Grace was in all her steps, heaven in her eye,
In every gesture dignity and love.
—MILTON, *Paradise Lost*

Offend her, and she knows not to forgive;
Oblige her, and she'll hate you while you live.
—POPE, *Moral Essays*

Woman's at best a contradiction still.
—POPE, *Moral Essays*

It is better to dwell in a corner of the housetop than with
a brawling woman in a wide house.
—PROVERBS. XXI. 9

O wild, dark flower of woman,
    Deep rose of my desire,
An Eastern wizard made you
    Of earth and stars and fire.
—C. G. D. ROBERTS, *The
    Rose of My Desire*

It is easier for a woman to defend her virtue against men
than her reputation against women.
—ROCHEBRUNE

Men who flatter women do not know them; men who
abuse them know them still less.
—MME. DE SALM

Such, Polly, are your sex—part truth, part fiction;
Some thought, much whim, and all contradiction.

—RICHARD SAVAGE, *To a
Young Lady*

Honor women! they entwine and weave heavenly roses
in our earthly life.

—SCHILLER

The weakness of their reasoning faculty also explains why
women show more sympathy for the unfortunate than
men; . . . and why, on the contrary, they are inferior to
men as regards justice, and less honourable and conscientious.

—SCHOPENHAUER, *On
Women*

O Woman! in our hours of ease,
Uncertain coy, and hard to please,
And variable as the shade
By the light quivering aspen made;
When pain and anguish wring the brow,
A ministering angel thou!

—SCOTT, *Marmion*

Age cannot wither her, nor custom stale
Her infinite variety.

—SHAKESPEARE, *Antony
and Cleopatra.* Act II.
Sc. 2

Fraily, thy name is woman!

—SHAKESPEARE, *Antony
and Cleopatra.* Act. I
Sc. 2

You are pictures out of doors,
Bells in your parlours, wildcats in your kitchens,
Saints in your injuries, devils being offended,

Players in your housewifery, and housewives in your beds.

—SHAKESPEARE, *Othello*.
Act II. Sc. 1

In the beginning, said a Persian poet—Allah took a rose, a lily, a dove, a serpent, a little honey, a Dead Sea apple, and a handful of clay. When he looked at the amalgram— it was a woman.

—WILLIAM SHARP

The fickleness of the woman I love is only equalled by the infernal constancy of the women who love me.

—GEORGE BERNARD
SHAW, *Philanderer*

Woman's dearest delight is to wound Man's self-conceit, though Man's dearest delight is to gratify hers.

—GEORGE BERNARD
SHAW, *Unsocial
Socialist*

A man may brave opinion; a woman must submit to it.

—MME. DE STAËL

A woman either loves or hates: she knows no medium.

—SYRUS

Regard the society of women as a necessary unpleasant- ness of social life, and avoid it as much as possible.

—TOLSTOY, *Diary*

There is no such thing as romance in our day, women have become too brilliant; nothing spoils a romance so much as a sense of humor in the woman.

—WILDE, *A Woman of No
Importance*

I am glad that I am not a man, for then I should have to marry a women.
—MME. DE STAËL

She was a Phantom of delight
When first she gleamed upon my sight;
A lovely Apparition, sent
To be a moment's ornament.
—WORDSWORTH, *She Was a Phantom of Delight*

Wonder

A schoolboy's tale, the wonder of an hour!
—BYRON, *Childe Harold*

Wonder is the basis of worship.
—CARLYLE

Men love to wonder and that is the seed of our science.
—EMERSON, *Works and Days*

No wonder can last more than three days.
—ITALIAN PROVERB

Wooing

Come live in my heart and pay no rent.
—SAMUEL LOVER

There is a tide in the affairs of women
Which, taken at the flood, leads—God knows where.
—BYRON, *Don Juan*

"Yes," I answered you last night;
    "No," this morning, sir, I say:
Colors seen by candle-light
    Will not look the same by day.
                        —E. B. BROWNING, *The
                            Lady's "Yes"*

And let us mind, faint heart ne'er wan
A lady fair.
                        —BURNS to Dr. Blacklock

                'Tis enough—
Who listens once will listen twice;
    Her heart be sure is not of ice,
And one refusal no rebuff.
                        —BYRON, *Mazeppa*

Never wedding, ever wooing,
Still a lovelorn heart pursuing,
Read you not the wrong you're doing
    In my cheek's pale hue?
All my life with sorrow strewing;
    Wed or cease to woo.
                        —CAMPBELL, *The Maid's
                            Remonstrance*

Ye shall know my breach of promise.
                        —NUMBERS. XIV. 34

If I am not worth the wooing, I surely am not worth the
winning.
                        —LONGFELLOW, *Courtship
                            of Miles Standish*

Thrice happy's the wooing that's not long a-doing,
So much time is saved in the billing and cooing.
                        —R. H. BARHAM, *Sir
                            Rupert the Fearless*

Why don't you speak for yourself, John?
> —LONGFELLOW, *Courtship
> of Miles Standish*

Perhaps if you address the lady
> Most politely, most politely,
Flatter and impress the lady
> Most politely, most politely,
Humbly beg and humbly sue,
> She may deign to look on you.
> > —W. S. GILBERT, *Princess
> > Ida*

The time I've lost in wooing,
In watching and pursuing
> The light that lies
In woman's eyes,
Has been my heart's undoing.
> > —MOORE, *The Time I've
> > Lost in Wooing*

They dream in courtship, but in wedlock wake.
> —POPE, *Wife of Bath*

Sigh no more, ladies, sigh no more,
> Men were deceivers ever,
One foot in sea and one on shore;
> To one thing constant never.
> > —SHAKESPEARE, *Much Ado
> > About Nothing*. Act II.
> > Sc. 3

A fool there was and he made his prayer
> (Even as you and I!)
To a rag and a bone and a hank of hair
> (We called her the woman who did not care)
But the fool he called her his lady fair—
> (Even as you or I!)
> > —KIPLING, *The Vampire*

Men are April when they woo, December when they
wed.

> —SHAKESPEARE, *As You
> Like It*. Act IV. Sc. 1

The way of an eagle in the air; the way of a serpent upon
a rock; the way of a ship in the midst of the sea; and the
way of a man with a maid.

> —PROVERBS. XXX. 19

She's beautiful and therefore to be woo'd:
She is a woman, therefore to be won.

> —SHAKESPEARE, *Henry* VI.
> Pt. I. Act V. Sc. 3

    O gentle Romeo,
If thou dost love, pronounce it faithfully.
Or if thou think'st I am too quickly won,
I'll frown and be perverse and say thee nay,
So thou wilt woo: but else, not for the world.

> —SHAKESPEARE, *Romeo
> and Juliet*. Act II. Sc.
> 2

Word

Words of truth and soberness.

> —ACTS. XXVI. 25

Words of affection, howsoe'er expressed,
The latest spoken still are deem'd the best.

> —JOANNA BAILLIE

A very great part of the mischiefs that vex this world
arises from words.

> —BURKE

Words writ in waters.

> —GEORGE CHAPMAN,
> *Revenge for Honour*

Fair words butter no parsnips.

> —JOHN CLARKE,
> *Paraemiologia*

Mum is the word.

> —MIGUEL DE CERVANTES,
> *Don Quixote*. Pt. II.
> Bk. IV

Words that weep, and tears that speak.

> —COWLEY, *The Prophet*

But words once spoke can never be recall'd.

> —WENTWORTH DILLON

Let thy words be few.

> —ECCLESIASTES. V. 2

Our words have wings, but fly not where we would.

> —GEORGE ELIOT, *The
> Spanish Gypsy*

How forcible are right words!

> —JOB. VI. 25

Let no man deceive you with vain words.

> —EPHESIANS. V. 6

Words are feminine; deeds are masculine.

> —BALTASAR GRACIÁN

Who is this that darkeneth counsel by words without knowledge?

> —JOB. XXXVIII. 2

In the beginning was the Word, and the Word was with God, and the Word was God.
—JOHN. I. 1

I am not yet so lost in lexicography, as to forget that words are the daughters of earth, and that things are the sons of heaven.
—SAMUEL JOHNSON,
Preface to His
Dictionary

Words are the most powerful drug used by mankind.
—KIPLING, Speech, 1923

We should have a great many fewer disputes in the world if words were taken for what they are, the signs of our ideas only, and not for things themselves.
—LOCKE, *Essay on the
Human Understanding*

Speaking words of endearment where words of comfort availed not.
—LONGFELLOW,
Evangeline

Sticks and stones may break my bones,
But words can never harm me.
—OLD ENGLISH RHYME

Words will build no walls.
—PLUTARCH

A word spoken in good season, how good it is!
—PROVERBS. XV. 23

A word fitly spoken is like apples of gold in pictures of silver.
—PROVERBS. XXV. 11

The words of his mouth were smoother than butter, but war was in his heart; his words were softer than oil, yet were they drawn swords.

> —PSALMS. LV. 21

One of our defects as a nation is a tendency to use what have been called "weasel words." When a weasel sucks eggs the meat is sucked out of the egg. If you use a "weasel word" after another there is nothing left of the other.

> —THEODORE ROOSEVELT,
> Speech, 1916

My word fly up, my thoughts remain below:
Words without thoughts never to heaven go.

> —SHAKESPEARE, *Hamlet*.
> Act III. Sc. 3

A word to the wise is sufficient.

> —TERENCE

Man does not live by words alone, despite the fact that sometimes he has to eat them.

> —ADLAI STEVENSON,
> Speech, September 5,
> 1952

But yesterday the word of Caesar might
Have stood against the world; now lies he there,
And none so poor to do him reverence.

> —SHAKESPEARE, *Julius
> Caesar*. Act III. Sc. 2

Taffeta phrases, silken terms precise,
Three-piled hyperboles, spruce affectation,
Figures pedantical.

> —SHAKESPEARE, *Love's
> Labour's Lost*. Act V.
> Sc. 2

I sometimes hold it half a sin
    To put in words the grief I feel;
    For words, like Nature, half reveal
And half conceal the Soul within.
        —TENNYSON, *In Memoriam*

He utters empty words, he utters sound without mind.
        —VERGIL, *Aeneid*

You (Pindar) who possessed the talent of speaking much
without saying anything.
        —VOLTAIRE

For of all sad words of tongue or pen,
The saddest are these: "It might have been!"
        —WHITTIER, *Maud Muller*

Hold fast the form of sound words.
        —II TIMOTHY. I. 13

Work

When Adam dolve, and Eve span,
Who was then the gentleman?
        —JOHN BALL, *Wat Tyler's
          Rebellion*

All Nature seems at work, slugs leave their lair—
    The bees are stirring—birds are on the wing—
And Winter, slumbering in the open air,
    Wears on his smiling face a dream of Spring!
And I the while, the sole unbusy thing,
    Nor honey make, nor pair, nor build, nor sing.
        —COLERIDGE, *Work
          Without Hope*

Every man's work shall be made manifest.
        —I CORINTHIANS. III. 13

Better to wear out than to rust out.
                              —BISHOP CUMBERLAND

The workers are the saviors of society, the redeemers of the race.
                              —EUGENE V. DEBS,
                                   Speech, 1905

Handle your tools without mittens.
                              —FRANKLIN, *Poor Richard*

Tools were made and born were hands,
Every farmer understands.
                              —WILLIAM BLAKE, *Proverbs*

All things are full of labour; man cannot utter it: the eye is not satisfied with seeing, nor the ear filled with hearing.
                              —ECCLESIASTES. I. 8

I never did anything worth doing by accident, nor did any of my inventions come by accident; they came by work.

                              —EDISON

It's all in the day's work.
                              —ENGLISH SAYING

A ploughman on his legs is higher than a gentleman on his knees.
                              —FRANKLIN, *Poor Richard*

In every rank, or great or small,
'Tis industry supports us all.
                              —GAY, *Man, Cat, Dog,
                                   and Fly*

In the sweat of thy face shalt thou eat bread.
                              —GENESIS. III. 19

All work and no play makes Jack a dull boy.
—JAMES HOWELL

I like work; it fascinates me. I can sit and look at it for hours. I love to keep it by me: the idea of getting rid of it nearly breaks my heart.
—JEROME K. JEROME,
Three Men in a Boat

And only the Master shall praise us, and only the Master
    shall blame;
And no one shall work for money, and no one shall work
    for fame;
But each for the joy of the working, and each, in his
    separate star,
Shall draw the Thing as he sees It, for the God of things
    as They Are!
—KIPLING, *L'Envoi.* In
Seven Seas

No man is born into the world whose work
Is not born with him; there is always work,
And tools to work withal, for those who will;
And blessed are the horny hands of toil!
—LOWELL, A *Glance
Behind the Curtain*

The laborer is worthy of his hire.
—LUKE. X. 7

How many a rustic Milton has passed by,
Stifling the speechless longings of his heart,
In unremitting drudgery and care!
How many a vulgar Cato has compelled
His energies, no longer tameless then,
To mould a pin, or fabricate a nail!
—SHELLEY, *Queen Mab*

Many hands make light work.

—WILLIAM PATTEN, 1547

Heaven is blessed with perfect rest but the blessing of earth is toil.

—HENRY VAN DYKE,
Toiling of Felix

World

This is the best world, that we live in,
To lend and to spend and to give in:
But to borrow, or beg, or to get a man's own,
It is the worst world that ever was known.

—ANONYMOUS

This world's a bubble.

—BACON

Believe everything you hear said of the world; nothing is too impossibly bad.

—BALZAC

The world is like a board with holes in it, and the square men have got into the round holes, and the round into the square.

—BISHOP BERKELEY

The pomps and vanity of this wicked world.

—BOOK OF COMMON
PRAYER

But in this world nothing is sure but death and taxes.

—FRANKLIN, Letter to M.
Leroy, 1789

The year's at the Spring
　And day's at the morn;
　　Morning's at seven;
　　　The hillside's dew-pearled;
The lark's on the wing;
　The snail's on the thorn:
　　God's in his Heaven—
　　　All's right with the world!
　　　　　　　　　—BROWNING, *Pippa Passes*

I have not loved the world, nor the world me;
I have not flatter'd its rank breath, nor bow'd
To its idolatries a patient knee.
　　　　　　　　—BYRON, *Childe Harold*

Socrates, indeed, when he was asked of what country he
called himself, said, "Of the world"; for he considered
himself an inhabitant and a citizen of the whole world.
　　　　　　　　—CICERO

Such stuff the world is made of.
　　　　　　　　—COWPER, *Hope*

Come, follow me, and leave the world to its babblings.
　　　　　　　　—DANTE

Good-bye, proud world! I'm going home;
Thou are not my friend; I am not thine.
　　　　　　　　—EMERSON, *Good-bye,*
　　　　　　　　　　Proud World!

But it does move.

　　　　　　　　—GALILEO before the
　　　　　　　　　　Inquisition

The world is a beautiful book, but of little use to him
who cannot read it.
　　　　　　　　—GOLDONI, *Pamela*

The nations are as a drop of a bucket.
—ISAIAH. XL. 15

World without end.
—ISAIAH. XLV. 17

It takes all sorts of people to make a world.
—DOUGLAS JERROLD, *Story
of a Feather*

If there is one beast in all the loathsome fauna of civilization I hate and despise it is a man of the world.
—HENRY ARTHUR JONES,
The Liars

The world is God's world, after all.
—KINGSLEY

The world goes up and the world goes down,
And the sunshine follows the rain;
And yesterday's sneer and yesterday's frown
Can never come over again,
Sweet wife.
No, never come over again.
—KINGSLEY, *Dolcino to
Margaret*

You'll never have a quiet world till you knock the patriotism out of the human race.
—GEORGE BERNARD
SHAW,
O'Flaherty, V. C.

If all the world must see the world
As the world the world hath seen,
Then it were better for the world
That the world had never been.
—LELAND, *The World and
the World*

The world is full of beauty, as other worlds above,
And if we did our duty, it might be as full of love.
>   —GERALD MASSEY, *This
>   World*

This world is all a fleeting show,
>   For man's illusion given;
The smiles of joy, the tears of woe,
>   Deceitful shine, deceitful flow,—
>   There's nothing true but Heaven.
>   —MOORE, *This World is All
>   a Fleeting Show*

Half the world does not know how the other half lives.
>   —RABELAIS, *Pantagruel*

All nations and kindreds and people and tongues.
>   —REVELATION. VII. 9

All the world's a stage,
And all the men and women merely players.
>   —SHAKESPEARE, *As You
>   Like It*. Act II. Sc. 7

Why, then, the world's mine oyster,
Which I with sword will open.
>   —SHAKESPEARE, *Merry
>   Wives of Windsor*. Act
>   II. Sc. 2

This world surely is wide enough to hold both thee and
me.
>   —LAURENCE STERNE,
>   *Tristram Shandy*

There was all the world and his wife.
>   —SWIFT, *Polite
>   Conversation*

A mad world, my masters.

> —JOHN TAYLOR, *Western Voyage*

So many worlds, so much to do,
So little done, such things to be.

> —TENNYSON, *In Memoriam*

Everything is for the best in this best of all possible worlds.

> —VOLTAIRE, *Candide*

This world is a comedy to those who think, a tragedy to those who feel.

> —HORACE WALPOLE, Letter to Sir Horace Mann

Worship

It is only when men begin to worship that they begin to grow.

> —CALVIN COOLIDGE, Speech, 1922

And what greater calamity can fall upon a nation than the loss of worship.

> —EMERSON

Ay, call it holy ground,
   The soil where first they trod.
They have left unstained, what there they found—
   Freedom to worship God.

> —FELICIA D. HEMANS, *The Landing of the Pilgrim Fathers*

Yet, if he would, man cannot live all to this world. If not religious, he will be superstitious. If he worship not the true God, he will have his idols.

—THEODORE PARKER

Worth

This was the penn'worth of his thought.
—BUTLER, *Hudibras*

Nothing common can seem worthy of you.
—CICERO to Caesar

We are valued either too highly or not high enough; we are never taken at our real worth.
—MARIE EBNER-
ESCHENBACH

Worth makes the man, and want of it the fellow;
The rest is all but leather and prunello.
—POPE, *Essay on Man*

The game is not worth the candle.
—FRENCH PROVERB

Of whom the world was not worthy.
—HEBREWS. XI. 38

Wound

What deep wounds ever closed without a scar?
The hearts bleed longest, and but heal to wear
That which disfigures it.
—BYRON, *Childe Harold*

A certain Samaritan . . . bound up his wounds, pouring
in oil and wine.
—LUKE. X. 33–34

I was wounded in the house of my friends.
—ZECHARIAH. XIII. 6

Writing

The reason why so few good books are written is that so
few people who can write know anything.
—WALTER BAGEHOT

Whatever we conceive well we express clearly.
—BOILEAU

Talent alone cannot make a writer. There must be a man
behind the book.
—EMERSON, *Representative
Men*

If you wish to be a writer, write.
—EPICTETUS

Writers seldom write the things they think. They simply
write the things they think other folks think they think.
—ELBERT HUBBARD

Think much, speak little, and write less.
—ITALIAN PROVERB

Bad writers are those who try to express their own feeble
ideas in the language of good ones.
—G. C. LICHTENBERG

A man may write himself out of reputation when nobody else can do it.

> —THOMAS PAINE, *The Rights of Man*

Wrong

The multitude is always in the wrong.

> —WENTWORTH DILLON

Two wrongs do not make a right.

> —ENGLISH PROVERB

Brother, brother; we are both in the wrong.

> —GAY, *Beggar's Opera*

It is better to suffer wrong than to do it, and happier to be sometimes cheated than not to trust.

> —SAMUEL JOHNSON

Truth forever on the scaffold, wrong forever on the throne.

> —LOWELL

The remedy for wrongs is to forget them.

> —SYRUS

Youth

In the lexicon of youth, which fate reserves
For a bright manhood, there is no such word
As *fail*.

> —BULWER-LYTTON, *Richelieu*

Ah! happy years! once more who would not be a boy!

> —BYRON, *Childe Harold*

As I approve of a youth that has something of the old man in him, so I am no less pleased with an old man that has something of the youth. He that follows this rule may be old in body, but can never be so in mind.
—CICERO

I remember my youth and the feeling that will never come back any more—the feeling that I could last forever, outlast the sea, the earth, and all men.
—JOSEPH CONRAD, *Youth*

Reckless youth makes rueful age.
—FRANKLIN

In youth we learn; in age we understand.
—MARIE EBNER-
ESCHENBACH

Youth will be served.
—ENGLISH PROVERB

Forty is the old age of youth; fifty is the youth of old age.
—FRENCH PROVERB

Yes, you may depend upon it he has the ability! He is the younger generation that stands ready to knock at my door—to make an end of Halvard Solness.
—IBSEN, *The Master
Builder*

Youth! youth! how buoyant are thy hopes; they turn,
Like marigolds, toward the sunny side.
—JEAN INGELOW, *The Four
Bridges*

All the world's a mass of folly,
Youth is gay, age melancholy:
Youth is spending, age is thrifty,
Mad at twenty, cold at fifty;
Man is nought but folly's slave,
From the cradle to the grave.

—W. H. IRELAND, *Modern
Ship of Fools*

Your old men shall dream dreams; your young men shall
see visions.

—JOEL. II. 28

Youth comes but once in a lifetime.

—LONGFELLOW, *Hyperion*

How beautiful is youth! how bright it gleams
With its illusions, aspirations, dreams!
Book of Beginnings, Story without End,
Each maid a heroine, and each man a friend!

—LONGFELLOW, *Morituri
Salutamus*

The atrocious crime of being a young man.

—WILLIAM PITT to Walpole

We think our fathers fools, so wise we grow;
Our wiser sons, no doubt, will think us so.

—POPE, *Essay on Criticism*

If youth but knew, and age were able,
Then poverty would be a fable.

—PROVERB

Keep true to the dreams of thy youth.

—SCHILLER

All sorts of allowances are made for the illusions of youth;
and none, or almost none, for the disenchantments of
age.

> —STEVENSON, *Virginibus
> Puerisque*

Crabbed age and youth cannot live together;
    Youth is full of pleasure, age is full of care;
Youth like summer morn, age like winter weather;
    Youth like summer brave, age like winter bare.
Youth is full sport, age's breath is short;
    Youth is nimble, age is lame;
Youth is hot and bold, age is weak and cold;
    Youth is wild, age is tame.
Age, I do abhor thee; youth, I do adore thee.

> —SHAKESPEARE, *The
> Passionate Pilgrim*

For God's sake give me the young man who has brains
enough to make a fool of himself.

> —STEVENSON, *Crabbed Age*

Live as long as you may, the first twenty years are the
longest half of your life.

> —SOUTHEY

She bid me take love easy, as the leaves grow on the tree;
But I, being young and foolish, with her would not agree.

> —WILLIAM BUTLER YEATS,
> *Down by the Salley
> Gardens*

Yukon

There's a land where the mountains are nameless
    And the rivers all run God knows where;
There are lives that are erring and aimless
    And deaths that just hang by a hair;

There are hardships that nobody reckons;
    There are valleys unpeopled and still;
There's a land—oh, it beckons and beckons,
    And I want to go back—and I will.
              —ROBERT W. SERVICE,
                Spell of th Yukon

Zeal

It is good to be zealously affected always in a good thing.
              —GALATIANS. IV. 18

Zeal is very blind, or badly regulated, when it encroaches
upon the rights of others.
              —PASQUIER QUESNEL

Blind zeal can only do harm.
              —MAGNUS GOTTFRIED
              LICHTWER

My zeal hath consumed me.
              —PSALMS. CXIX. 139

To be furious in religion is to be irreligiously religious.
              —WIILIAM PENN

Index

27 million Americans can't read a bedtime story to a child.

It's because 27 million adults in this country simply can't read.

Functional illiteracy has reached one out of five Americans. It robs them of even the simplest of human pleasures, like reading a fairy tale to a child.

You can change all this by joining the fight against illiteracy.

Call the Coalition for Literacy at toll-free **1-800-228-8813** and volunteer.

**Volunteer
Against Illiteracy.
The only degree you need
is a degree of caring.**

Ad Council Coalition for Literacy

LV-3